# THE FRENCH PREFECTORAL CORPS
## 1814–1830

*FOR THE AGEDS*

# THE FRENCH
# PREFECTORAL CORPS
## 1814-1830

BY

NICHOLAS RICHARDSON

*Fellow of Trinity Hall, Cambridge*

CAMBRIDGE
AT THE UNIVERSITY PRESS
1966

CAMBRIDGE UNIVERSITY PRESS
Cambridge, New York, Melbourne, Madrid, Cape Town, Singapore, São Paulo, Delhi

Cambridge University Press
The Edinburgh Building, Cambridge CB2 8RU, UK

Published in the United States of America by Cambridge University Press, New York

www.cambridge.org
Information on this title: www.cambridge.org/9780521060806

First published 1966
This digitally printed version 2008

*A catalogue record for this publication is available from the British Library*

ISBN 978-0-521-06080-6 hardback
ISBN 978-0-521-08905-0 paperback

# CONTENTS

v

# CONTENTS

## APPENDICES

# PREFACE

This book is a study of the Prefectoral Corps during the Restoration. Constructed in terms of the personnel of the Corps, it is not concerned with their day-to-day duties, but with their recruitment, careers, and with the organization of the prefectoral system. A large number of the Corps belonged to families already noble before 1789: my final chapter is designed to explore the extent and nature of the nobility's participation in this branch of government service. Although the study of a single administration can provide no more than a modest springboard for further generalization, I have tried, in the introduction, both to put the Restoration Corps in its historical context as an instrument of local government, and to suggest the issues which the social background of its personnel evokes.

I began work on the Corps in Paris in 1960. I owe my thanks to the Master and Fellows of Peterhouse for grants which made an initial two and a half years in Paris possible, and to the Master and Fellows of Trinity Hall for a Research, later an Official, Fellowship, which has enabled me to continue work on the subject, as for their stoic suspension of disbelief at seeing their initiative rewarded. I should also like to thank all those in France and England who have given me advice and encouragement over the last five years, and in particular Professors Sir Denis Brogan and Bertier de Sauvigny.

That this book should resemble a thesis may be the less surprising since it began life as one. For this as for its other imperfections I should like to take full responsibility.

N. J. M. R.

*Cambridge*
*1966*

# ABBREVIATIONS

| | |
|---|---|
| AAG | Archives Administratives de la Guerre, Château de Vincennes. |
| AAG, CG | Classement Général of Officers, military dossiers 1791–1847. |
| AAG, Emigrés | Reports of commission examining the claims of émigré officers (519, 1–22). |
| *ADLN* | *Annuaire de la noblesse.* |
| AN | Archives nationales. |
| AN doss. | Personal dossiers of members of the prefectoral corps, series [F1bI], 155(1)–180. |
| AP | Archives parlementaires. |
| *BL* | *Bulletin des Lois.* |
| Chaix | Chaix d'Est-Ange, *Dictionnaire des familles françaises.* |
| *DBF* | *Dictionnaire de biographie française.* |
| *GA* | *Grand armorial de France.* |
| R + C | Robert and Cougny, *Dictionnaire des parlementaires françaises.* |
| Révérend, *Armorial* | Révérend, *Armorial du premier Empire.* |
| Révérend, *Restauration* | Révérend, *Les familles titrées et anoblies au XIX^e siècle. . .la Restauration.* |
| Woelmont | Woelmont de Brumagne, *Notices généalogiques.* |

# INTRODUCTION

'Que la centralisation administrative est une institution de l'ancien régime, et non pas l'œuvre de la Révolution ni de l'Empire, comme on le dit.' Tocqueville's thesis has needed substantial modification since its first appearance over one hundred years ago. Certainly the administrative system created by Napoleon in 1800 had similarities to that of the Ancien Régime.[1] The intendant may be seen as the prototype of the Napoleonic prefect; the sub-delegate, of the sub-prefect. But if they were centralizing agents, there was no overall system of centralization. The intendant's power depended to a considerable extent on his own personality, and on the support his superiors would, or could, give him. As Mégret d'Etigny found in his struggle with the Parlement of Bordeaux, such support was not always forthcoming.[2] More important, the intendant was surrounded by a congeries of competing authorities, the provincial Estates, Parlement, and Governor, any or all of whom might act as counterbalancing influences to centralization. The first prerequisite for fully centralized government was therefore the suppression of any rival influence in the provinces. This was achieved by the abolition of privileges, territorial and corporate as well as personal, after the night of the Fourth August, and by the subsequent division of France into departments, areas of a more or less uniform size, uniformly administered. By eliminating the administrative anomalies of the Ancien Régime the Assembly made a centralized system of government possible. It was left to Napoleon to make it a reality. The decree of 28 Pluviôse An VIII (25 March 1800) removed the last obstacle to centralization, the elected councils which had previously administered the departments. These councils did not disappear entirely, but they

---

[1] Local government from 1789 to 1800 is well covered in J. Godechot, *Les institutions de la France sous la Révolution et l'Empire* (1951). There is a brief summary, in English, of local government since 1800 in B. Chapman, *The Prefects and Provincial France* (1955).

[2] M. Bordes, 'Les intendants de Louis XV', *Revue historique*, CCXXIII (1960), 60–1.

INTRODUCTION

were now co-opted, not elected, and their role was reduced to that of deliberation, not administration. As a spokesman for the new régime put it, '... administrer doit être le fait d'un seul homme; et juger le fait de plusieurs'.[1] The new system was streamlined and rigidly hierarchic. A sub-prefect administered each *arrondissement* (the new administrative sub-unit), a prefect each department, the latter being directly subordinate to the Ministry of the Interior. It was a system wonderfully pleasing to the rationalist eye: 'le préfet, essentiellement occupé de l'exécution, transmet les ordres au sous-préfet; celui-ci aux maires des villes, bourgs, et villages; de manière que la chaîne d'exécution descend sans interruption du ministre à l'administré, et transmet la loi et les ordres du gouvernement jusqu'aux dernières ramifications de l'ordre social avec la rapidité du fluide électrique'.[2] Authoritarian and highly centralized, the prefectoral corps was a typically Napoleonic innovation: indeed, if government was to mean not only Paris but the provinces, it was *the* essential innovation. Understandably, therefore, it appealed little to the royalists in the early years of the Restoration. There was talk of doing away with the Corps, of bringing back the intendants. It remained talk. The Bourbons might temporarily revive the cumbrous councils of the Ancien Régime in place of the imperial Council of State, the prefectoral system remained unscathed. But though the Bourbons left the machine intact, they greatly modified its working. As the mechanics of parliamentary government evolved in the years after 1815, so the prefects came to play a crucial political role. They and their subordinates, as readers of *Lucien Leuwen* will remember, were indispensable electoral agents. This in turn affected the career. It was only to be expected that a change of régime would mean a change of administrative personnel; but since no ministry could risk hostile administrators, change became endemic. It became customary for a new ministry to dismiss or transfer those members of the Corps it distrusted, in the 'massacres' and

---

[1] Roederer to the C[orps] L[égislatif] 18 Pluviôse An VIII (7 Feb. 1800) (AP, 2nd ser., I, 169).
[2] Chaptal to the CL, 28 Pluviôse An VIII (17 Feb. 1800) (AP, 2nd ser., I, 230).

'waltzes' which characterized the nineteenth-century administration. Decazes established the precedent in 1819, with what an opponent called a Saint Bartholomew's Day of prefects and sub-prefects.[1] The practice reached a climax in the early years of the Third Republic, before and immediately after the Sixteenth May (as Paul Cambon's prefectoral career shows), but the last massacre was that carried out by the Cartel des Gauches as recently as 1924 'toutes les places et tout de suite'.

The prefectoral system was inevitably a target for criticism. It lay at the heart of the perennial French discussion of the evils of excessive centralization, the target in particular for counter-revolutionary theorists: in Bonald's world of the enlarged commune, or Maurras' of the semi-autonomous province, the Corps could play no part. It was nevertheless too valuable an instrument for any government to destroy it. This had become obvious as early as the Restoration, when critics of the system like Villèle or La Bourdonnaye forgot their distrust once they controlled the mechanism. As Vaublanc naïvely put it, the prefectoral administration was one of the most monarchical institutions ever conceived.[2] The only attempt to suppress the Corps was made by Ledru-Rollin in February 1848, when he replaced the prefects by *commissaires*. The experiment was short-lived. The prefects returned: and the twenty-three-year-old Emile Ollivier, briefly *commissaire* at Marseilles, found himself translated to the modest prefecture of the Haute-Marne.[3] The administration emerged from the nineteenth century almost unchanged in organization, if perhaps more limited in its powers. It was to remain unchanged until the 1920s, arguably until Vichy's Regional Prefects or M. Jules Moch's creation of the *Igames* in 1948.

The study of the social background of the Corps has a wider relevance. The ruling class of the Restoration remains something of an enigma, a premissed amalgam of *noblesse de race* and *gens*

[1] Crignon d'Ouzouer's printed but unspoken speech, addenda to debate of 23 March 1819 (AP, 2nd ser., XXIII, 362).
[2] Comte Viennot de Vaublanc, *Mémoires sur la Révolution de France...* (4 vols., 1833), III, 85.
[3] P. Saint-Marc, *Emile Ollivier, 1825–1913* (Paris, 1950), pp. 15–53.

*nantis* which had not yet hardened into a self-conscious corps of *notables*. Contemporaries themselves seem to have been unclear, disputing the desirability, composition and even existence of an aristocracy. One reason for confusion lay in the word aristocracy. It had an uncomfortable historical resonance, and during the Restoration the Left used it with something of the same pejorative purpose it had possessed during the early years of the Revolution. 'What is this aristocracy?', a deputy interrupted during one of General Foy's speeches. The reply was impressively brutal. 'Je vais vous dire: l'aristocratie au XIXe siècle, c'est la ligue, c'est la coalition de ceux qui veulent consommer sans produire, vivre sans travailler, tout savoir sans rien avoir appris, envahir tous les honneurs sans les avoir mérités, occuper tous les emplois sans être en état de les remplir; voilà l'aristocratie...'[1] The Left might grudgingly recognize a political aristocracy, the Chamber of Peers. They admitted no legitimate aristocracy outside the Peers. Their view had a pleasing simplicity. On the one side were those who wanted equality, and not merely paper guarantees, on the other a faction fighting to recover its lost privileges, the legions of the counter-revolution. The antinomy between the old and the new doctrines stemmed from the antipathy between the men of the Ancien Régime and those who owed their rise to the Revolution and Empire, whose rights were enshrined in the Charter. With political divisions the product of social differences, politics were omnipresent: Saint-Chamans found that the division in his regiment between so-called *gentilshommes* and *vilains* persisted even in Church, the *gentilshommes* sitting on the right, the *vilains* on the left.[2] It was a view that Balzac and Stendhal dramatized, and that Tocqueville was to endorse: 'Notre histoire, de 1789 à 1830, vue de loin et dans son ensemble, ne doit apparaître que comme le tableau d'une lutte acharnée entre l'ancien régime, ses traditions, ses souvenirs, ses espérances et ses hommes représentés par l'aristocratie, et la France nouvelle conduite par la classe moyenne.'[3]

[1] Sitting of 20 March 1821 (AP, 2nd ser., XXX, 407).
[2] *Mémoires du général comte de Saint-Chamans...* (Paris, 1896), pp. 354–5.
[3] *Souvenirs*, ed. L. Monnier (Paris, 1942), p. 26.

The Right disagreed in detail as in principle. Constitutional theorists might revel in recondite analyses of checks and balances, might discover in the Chamber of Peers an admirable constitutional artifice on the analogy of the English House of Lords.[1] Reality lay elsewhere. Even social reality—'il n'y a de bourgeois ici que quelques pairs'. The Peers were economically emasculated and politically powerless. There was no stable aristocracy which could form a barrier between the throne and the people, only a series of disputed and ephemeral groups. Some spokesmen preached the virtues of an aristocracy which would be the equivalent of the English gentry, Molé, less vaguely, the claims of the 90,000 citizens who had the vote, a group whom he saw, prophetically, as a 'corps de notables'. They alone could form an aristocracy, he argued, since in the political and social situation of post-revolutionary France property was the sole possible criterion.[2] But this was merely to push the question a stage further, for the social background of the 90,000 electors was itself disputed. This supplementary controversy turned on the role of the nobility: that is (and it is in this sense alone that the terms noble and nobility have been used throughout this book), members of families already noble in 1789.

The Right saw the nobility as scattered and powerless, the débris of a few families whose power had been waning even in 1789, whose only possessions were their memories: 's'effrayer de cette aristocratie, c'est avoir peur des morts: les résurrections sont des miracles trop rares pour que les plus craintifs s'inquiètent de celui-là'.[3] With a wealth of corroborative detail, the Right displayed the decline of a nobility whose economic and political position had been threatened before the Revolution, and whose ruin had been consummated by emigration, confiscations, and the abolition of the *droit d'aînesse*. The Left remained sceptical. The nobility played a major part in political life, they alleged; far from being a minority in the electoral colleges, they and their auxiliaries were the most powerful elements, for aristocratic

---

[1] An analogy which shrewd outsiders like Charles Greville thought to be false.
[2] Molé to Chamber of Peers, 25 Jan. 1817 (AP, 2nd ser., XVIII, 286).
[3] Duc de Doudeauville to Chamber of Peers, 24 June 1820 (AP, 2nd ser., XXVIII, 693).

wealth had not been destroyed by the Revolution, but merely dispersed. In so far as the Revolution had adversely affected the nobility, it had led them to look for state employment:

> encombrant les hôtels
> Des ministres, — rampante, avide et dégradée. . .

And here the Restoration had fully indemnified them, employing a mass of untrained and incompetent nobles in posts to which they had no right.

The prefectoral personnel provide some means of checking the truth of these allegations. The task of establishing the social background of this personnel meets certain difficulties: the complexity of the regulations governing ennoblement under the Ancien Régime, the application of these criteria to genealogies not always remarkable for their rigour. But this is nothing compared to the subsequent step, that of estimating the political, social and economic position of the noble families concerned. No evaluation of an aristocracy goes unchallenged. There is a pervasive feeling that interest in an aristocracy is merely the exterior manifestation of a desire to belong to it (a prejudice presumably absent in the case of those describing *classes laborieuses et dangereuses*). Should the interest survive, then there is the allegation that no outsider can ever really pierce the arcana that surround aristocracy. Balzac's beloved Faubourg, his 'tolerably befingered pack of cards', hardly survives Madame de Villeparisis' scrutiny: 'D'abord il n'y était pas allé, on ne le recevait pas, qu'est-ce-qu'il pouvait en savoir?' And Proust's own picture is alternately seen as the product of a naïvely snobbish admiration, or as vitiated by a corroding and unhistorical irony. A foreign historian is in a position of added delicacy. Alice in an aristocratic Wonderland, he may contrive to avoid the grosser solecisms, at the risk of trampling over nuances of social difference, of producing an unlovely blend of the dogmatic and jejune. Yet, in an age when private initiative in nomenclature found its sanction in official complaisance, when plain Le Roy could burgeon forth as Le Roy de Saint-Arnaud, or Delattre be distended into de Lattre de Tassigny, some criterion of

nobility more rigorous than that of the possession of a euphoni-
ous name or a particule is imperative; and with it, an evaluation
of a family's social standing based on more satisfactory grounds
than its alleged antiquity.[1]

Viel, a labourer's son, became a sub-prefect during the Restoration. Locard, whose father was a haberdasher, André d'Arbelle,
whose father had been a baker at Montluel before the Revolution,
became prefects.[2] They were exceptions. The Restoration Corps
included few men of humble origin. The majority of its members
came from families of well-established bourgeoisie, the Hardy
from Laval or Sèze from Bordeaux, the Bovis from Provence or
Rendu from the Bresse.[3] At the top of the scale were members
of families who had been in the process of acquiring nobility
in 1789, whether by legal means, like the Clock or Le Noir de
Cantelou, or by the scarcely less reputable procedure of usurping
it, like the Balahu de Noiron.[4] A second group owed their rise
to the Revolution and Empire. These are the families who have
found their historian—or judge—in M. Beau de Loménie, the
bourgeois dynasties who rode every nineteenth-century change
of régime. The Cornudet, for example, were a family of notaries
and procureurs from the Marche. Etienne-Emile, the Restoration
sub-prefect, was the grandson of a notary, the son of a deputy
to the Legislative Assembly and the Five Hundred, who rallied
to Napoleon, became a senator and count of the Empire, rallied to
the Bourbons in 1814 and was made a peer, rallied to Napoleon
in March 1815 and was made a Hundred Days peer. A progress
Monsieur Dambreuse would have appreciated. Etienne-Emile
was deputy for the Creuse from 1831 to 1846, when he in turn

[1] Saint-Arnaud: P. Chalmin, *L'officier français de 1815 à 1870* (Paris, 1957),
p. 93. Delattre: Ph. Du Puy de Clinchamps, *La noblesse* (Collection Que
sais-je?), p. 109.
[2] AN doss. Viel, 176(11). Locard, 166(34). André d'Arbelle, 155(6); Révérend,
*Restauration*, I, 37.
[3] Hardy: Angot, *Dictionnaire...de la Mayenne* (4 vols., 1900), II, 403–4. Sèze:
*ADLN* (1894), pp. 512–14. Bovis: Chaix, VI, 300–2. Rendu: Révérend,
*Restauration*, VI, 61–2.
[4] Clock: Chaix, XI, 112–13. Le Noir de Cantelou: Révérend, *Restauration*, IV,
305. Balahu de Noiron: R. de Lurion, *Nobiliaire de Franche-Comté* (1890),
p. 47.

became a peer; his son was deputy for the same department during the Second Empire; one grandson sat for the Seine-et-Oise, another for the Creuse.[1]

Thus far the social composition of the Restoration Corps hardly differs from that of its imperial predecessor. Where it did differ was in the number of nobles given posts. At the end of the Empire 21 per cent of the personnel in office in France were of noble extraction, in July 1830 nearly 45 per cent.[2] The allegation that the nobility flocked into state service had, therefore, some justification. But the rise in the proportion of nobles serving in the Corps does not necessarily indicate that nobility was either a relevant criterion for office, or a major advantage. Indeed, the juridical concept of nobility may seem altogether irrelevant in an age when its possession no longer entailed special privileges. Differences in social status may seem less important than the very marked division between the two levels of the administration, in terms of official standing, salary, and above all private income. If some one-fifth of the prefects the Bourbons appointed could be regarded as very rich in their own right, the same was true of only some one-hundredth of the subordinate personnel.[3] In this sense, to adapt Robert de Jouvenel, a prefect who was a noble may have had less in common with another noble who was a sub-prefect than with a prefect of bourgeois background. The ruling class might therefore be defined, in M. Reinhard's phrase, as an *élite de fonction*, the criterion for membership of the ruling class being the post occupied rather than the juridical status enjoyed.[4] Such a definition is misleading. It was true, in contrast to the Ancien Régime, that birth was no longer an indispensable qualification for the majority of important posts, that the *noblesse de race* no longer occupied such posts as of right. But it was also true, in so far as the prefectoral corps is representative, that for this *de jure*

[1] AN doss. Cornudet, 157(32); Révérend, *Restauration*, II, 201–2; Raoul de Warren, *Les pairs de France...*, I (no page numbers).
[2] See below, Appendix III.
[3] See below, pp. 175–6.
[4] See M. Reinhard, 'Elite et noblesse dans la deuxième moitié du XVIIIᵉ siècle', *Revue d'histoire moderne et contemporaine*, III (1956), 5–37.

possession the nobility, during the Restoration, substituted one *de facto*. Forty per cent of the subordinate personnel named by the Bourbons were noble: 70 per cent of the prefects. The Restoration ruling class may have rested on a different theoretical justification to that of the Ancien Régime, but its composition hardly reflected the extent of the change.

The preponderant part played by the nobility is one characteristic of the Restoration Corps. There are two further senses in which it might seem to have been a reflexion of the 'old' France, rather than the new. The first is simply a matter of its members' age.[1] In April 1814, just over a quarter of those serving in France had been over fifty years old and their average age was forty-three and a half. In July 1830 the average age was fifty, and just under half of the Corps were older. Two in every five functionaries had been under forty in 1814: the figure for 1830 was two in every twenty-nine. Since forty was thought to be the threshold of old age in early nineteenth-century France—in 1826 only one-third of the population was aged forty or more—the contrast between the country and its rulers, the *pays réel* and the *pays légal*, already strongly enough marked in terms of numbers and wealth, was sufficiently dramatic in terms of age as well. Fazy's denunciation of the gerontocracy has its echo in Falloux's disabused comment on Villèle's ministry, that it too much resembled an old husband married to a young wife.[2] The younger generation found a world in which the great issues had disappeared, and with them the great opportunities. Here had lain the real attraction of Revolution and Empire, less their political aspect than the possibility they had promised of rapid advancement, 'des représentants du peuple et des généraux de vingt ans'. That possibility barely existed after 1814. In place of Michel Ney, son of an artisan, volunteer in 1787 and Marshal of France in 1804 at the age of thirty-six, the Restoration could offer only

[1] See below, Appendix IV. The question of generations is treated briefly by G. de Bertier de Sauvigny, *La Restauration* (1st ed., 1955), pp. 319–23, and at greater length by L. Mazoyer, 'Catégories d'âge et groupes sociaux. Les jeunes générations françaises de 1830', *Annales...*, x (Sept. 1938), 385–423.
[2] J. Fazy, *De la gérontocratie...* (Paris, 1828); Comte de Falloux, *Mémoires d'un royaliste* (2 vols., Paris, 1888), I, 27.

the prince de Hohenlohe, Marshal in 1827 at the age of sixty-two, whose lineage was impeccable but whose military service was exiguous and, worse, irrelevant, since it had been gained during the emigration as general-major in Austrian service.[1] There were administrators enough who might have echoed Alfred de Vigny's complaint

> J'ai servi seize ans la Restauration
> Moi, dont elle a laissé vieiller l'ambition
> Dans les honneurs obscurs de quelque légion.

From *Le Rouge et le Noir* to *Les Déracinés*, the dichotomy between generations was one of the major themes of French literature, crystallizing in the person of the *arriviste* hero, the young man with no defined place in a society which, while paying lip-service to the doctrine of equality of opportunity, contrived to block most means of entry to the governing class. An education for which the kindest term would be non-vocational produced the *fonctionomanie* contemporaries already deplored during the Restoration: an overcrowding in certain professions was doubled by a physical overcrowding in the capital, the result of the Parisian vortex, which in turn further reduced a young man's chances of employment. The result was the formation of a *prolétariat de bacheliers*, young men denied the opportunities equivalent to their aspirations. Julien Sorel had wondered what would happen to people like himself, with a good education but insufficient funds to stake a career, now that Napoleon had gone. Vautrin gave one answer, when he outlined for Rastignac's benefit the probable course of the latter's legal career: Rubempré or Racadot's career gave another.

Allowance should be made for literary exaggeration, the tragi-comedy of lost illusions inherent in the theme of a young provincial arriving in Paris, the conscious exploitation of a myth of the capital dating back to Restif de la Bretonne and forward to Fantomas. But the tension between generations, exemplified in the frustration of a younger generation of superfluous men whose way to the top was blocked by their elders, had solid roots in

[1] Warren, *Les pairs de France*, II.

nineteenth-century French history. At first sight this may seem surprising, given the numerous changes of régime which characterized the period, but if a change of régime meant a change of personnel, this personnel was often new only in name. Along with other serving officers, Castellane noted sourly that 1830 was 1815 all over again, with the difference that to the *voltigeurs de Louis XIV* had succeeded the *voltigeurs de Napoléon*.[1] The same phenomenon can be seen in the prefectoral corps. Bondy, Rolland de Villarceaux and Sainte-Suzanne were all recalled after the July Revolution. None had administered a department since 1815: all were aged sixty or more.[2] The disaffected youth of the July Monarchy, Deslauriers and his friends, Z. Marcas, even Jérôme Paturot, had their forebears during the Restoration: Stendhal's Julien Sorel or Octave de Malivert, the officers in *Servitudes et grandeurs*, the long list of young Balzacian noblemen. This division between generations was accentuated by the events of the Revolution and Empire. Boissy d'Anglas remarked in 1795 that the previous six years had been more like six centuries.[3] For an *enfant du siècle* an administrator like Dalmas, pensioned for his gallantry at Yorktown, or Saporta, former chamberlain in a dukedom now as remote as the castle of Thunder ten-Tronckh, must have seemed bizarre survivals indeed.[4] It was not simply their age, but the quality of their experience. In particular, the Restoration Corps included a high proportion of émigrés, one in five of the prefects appointed by the Bourbons, one in six of the new sub-prefects and secretaries-general. Along with the impenitent survival from the Ancien Régime is the related literary stereotype, the intransigent émigré. The powdered and bewigged representative of 'la génération des poupées qui ont fait la Révolution de 1788', the vidame de Pamiers or commandeur de Soubirane, has his complement in the former émigré or Chouan, unable or unwilling to understand

---

[1] And that the latter had worse manners (*Journal du Maréchal de Castellane 1804–1862*, 5 vols., Paris, 1895–7, II, 364–5, 384).

[2] AN doss. Bondy, 156(31); Rolland de Villarceaux, 172(15); Sainte-Suzanne, 156(48), 173(6).

[3] Quoted in Mazoyer, 'Catégories d'âge...', p. 404.

[4] AN doss. F.-J. Dalmas, 158(1); Saporta, 173(8).

the new France. It was a favourite Balzacian theme, the marquis d'Esgrignon fearing that his son's escapades would elicit a *lettre de cachet* and sending him to Paris in the belief that he had only to appear at the Court to be given a post commensurate with his quarterings, the baron du Guénic accounting for the failure of the duchesse de Berry's rising with the single phrase, 'tous les barons n'ont pas fait leur devoir'. Both figures remain obstinately locked the wrong side of 1789: neither has any truck with the Empire, both emerge as Ultras during the Restoration. Inevitably, these stereotypes are oversimplified. Emigration was a complex phenomenon; by no means a blanket brevet of incompetence, inexperience and intransigence. For many, like the comte de Mortsauf, it meant Coblentz and the army of Condé, the loss of an education but the affirmation of a set of obsolete prejudices: but for Goyon it meant several years in commerce at Hamburg, for Jahan a post as librarian to the landgrave of Hesse-Rheinsfald, for Emmanuel de Thuisy an apprenticeship with Turnbull, Forbes and Company, then with MacDonnell and Bushell, before becoming director of his own banking-house in London.[1] Emigration, followed by a life of retirement during the Empire, did not necessarily produce an Ultra after the Restoration, as Saint-Aignan or Lestrade's career shows.[2] The son of an officer made *maréchal-de-camp* at Edinburgh in 1797, Lestrade was brought up in England and later served throughout the Peninsular War, only returning to France at the Restoration. Far from making him an Ultra, this background led Lestrade to appreciate 'la bonté du gouvernement représentatif et de la véritable force qu'il donne à la Royauté'. Nor was the converse uniformly true. Imperial service was no notorious breeding-ground of liberals. There were genuine Republicans among the emperor's subjects, as Private Wheeler discovered to his surprise, and as the career of a former naval person like Tristan Corbière's father proved during the Restoration; there were also proscribed or hard-core

[1] AN doss. Goyon, 161(16); BB¹ 86 plaque 2. Jahan, 164(1); F⁷ 5168. Thuisy, 174(7).
[2] AN doss. Saint-Aignan, 173(1); AAG, Emigrés, 519(3); Raoul de Warren, *Les pairs de France*, II. Lestrade, 166(31), 169(1); AAG, Emigrés, 519(8).

Bonapartists who affected a tactical liberalism in the years after
1815: but several found in the Extreme Right a more congenial
successor to the authoritarian Empire. 'Monarchiste solide comme
l'était alors tout homme qui avait servi sous l'Empire sans être
un Jacobin', Frénilly noted of an acquaintance in 1819—and in
Frénilly's eyes only an Ultra *pur et dur* could qualify for such an
encomium.[1] It was a progress followed by several members of
the Corps with Napoleonic training. The premiss that imperial
service meant an appreciation of the new France, a realism that
would in turn produce a Moderate after 1814 (on the model of
the comte de Fontaine in the *Bal de Sceaux*) ignores the variety
of motives that might lead men to serve the emperor. Just as
there were inflexible royalists like La Villegontier who could
boast at the Restoration of their unblemished loyalty to the
Bourbons only because they had been refused the posts they had
demanded during the Empire, so there were men who had served
the Usurper simply because they had been given no choice:
Nays-Candau, for example, who was conscripted as *garde
d'honneur*, involved in a conspiracy against the régime, and
imprisoned in the Château d'If.[2] The least unsatisfactory ground
for generalization may, once again, be that of age. The younger
generation lacked the almost umbilical attachment to the Bourbons their fathers often had. Whatever the limits to their enthusiasm for the emperor, the Empire was the only régime the
majority of them knew or could envisage serving. They had fewer
scruples and greater opportunities than their elders, which naturally
enough led to tension. When the young Gondreville joined the
army during the Consulate, it was in the face of disapproval
from his uncles, former émigrés: Philippe de Tournon's father was
displeased when his son became an imperial chamberlain: Terray's
uncle forbade him to follow his friends into the auditoriat.[3]

[1] *Souvenirs du baron de Frénilly pair de France 1768–1828* (new ed. 1909), p. 425.
[2] AN doss. La Villegontier, 166(17). In his petition 27 Apr. 1814 he states that
he had been unwilling to serve Napoleon: but AF IV 1334, his demand for a
place as auditor, 1813. Nays-Candau, 168(1).
[3] *Souvenirs militaires du colonel de Gondreville* (Paris, 1875), p. 3; Abbé J. Moulard, *Le comte Camille de Tournon... 1778–1833* (3 vols., 1927–32), I, 51–2. For
Terray, *Souvenirs du baron de Barante* (8 vols., 1890–1901), I, 145–6.

The same division was obvious in 1814. The middle-aged
Frénilly wept with joy when he read of the Restoration. The
ten-year-old La Motte Rouge, for all his family background of
Breton nobility, emigration and Chouannerie, wept also—at
the abdication.[1] An exaggerated contrast, no doubt: but whatever
their family antecedents the younger generation might hesitate
before transferring their allegiance. Camille de Tournon's is an
instructive example. He acknowledged the new régime, certainly,
but he found it necessary to rationalize his recognition and to
take the advice of his friends. Loyalty to a dynasty he could
barely remember was bound to be a matter of reflexion rather
than instinct.[2] The division recurred, in a more acute form,
during the Hundred Days. Canrobert's father was a former
émigré and Vendéen whose loyalty to the Bourbons was absolute,
but the Marshal's elder brother had joined the army in 1813 and,
in spite of his father's objurgations, rejoined during the Hundred
Days. Canrobert's father neither forgot nor forgave. Although
his son was killed at Ligny, he referred to him simply as 'disparu
en juin 1815 sans qu'on ait jamais pu savoir ce qu'il est devenu'.[3]

However inaccurate the stereotypes, myth may have been
more important than truth. The prefectoral corps may not have
been the exclusive preserve of senile *hobereaux* nostalgic for the
abuses of the Ancien Régime, but it did include a high proportion
of nobles, émigrés, and men well advanced in age. Neither
separately nor taken together do these qualifications prove the
Corps' incapacity or obsolescence, but they did provide the raw
material for an image which pleasingly enhanced orthodox
Left-wing propaganda. Any attempt to provide a less hackneyed
picture of the Corps is hampered by the disparity in the age,
experience and social background of its members. At one
extreme was Busquet, sub-prefect in 1814 at the age of eighty,
who had joined the army the year after Rossbach; at the other
Bridieu, secretary-general of Calvados in 1830, who was born

[1] Frénilly, *Souvenirs*, p. 19; Général de la Motte Rouge, *Souvenirs et campagnes 1804–1883* (3 vols., Paris, 1888–9), I, 51.
[2] Moulard, *Le comte Camille de Tournon préfet de la Gironde 1815–1822* (1914), p. 537.
[3] G. Bapst, *Le Maréchal Canrobert...* (2nd ed., 6 vols., Paris, 1898–1913), I, 5–6.

the year before Ulm and lived to take his seat as a Monarchist
deputy the year after Sedan.[1] The Corps contained Chouans
like Bejarry and *bleus* like Giraud des Echerolles, veterans of the
Revolution like Cossonier and former royalist conspirators like
the comte de Scey.[2] The contrast might be dramatic: in November
1815 Dalmas, who had defended Louis XVI in the Convention,
took over the prefecture of the Charente-Inférieure from Richard
—a regicide.[3] It might verge on caricature. Sers replaced Castéja
as prefect of Haut-Rhin in January 1819. Sers was solid and
conscientious, the bureaucratic product of a bourgeois dynasty.
Castéja could prove his nobility back to the fifteenth century.
An aristocrat before he was an administrator, he was a noted
gambler and gourmet: in the phrase he used of an acquaintance,
'un homme qui s'écoute manger'. Sers disapproved discreetly.
Others were less inhibited: '[Il] ne passe son temps qu'à table,
au jeu, ou au lit. Jamais il ne se lève qu'à midi et souvent plus
tard.'[4]

For a great number of the Corps it was their second profession.
There were former officers, magistrates, diplomats, members of
the police and *Ponts-et-Chaussées*, former priests, even Pied-
montese like Stendhal's friend Mareste or Swiss like the secret
agent Wildermeth.[5] This heterogeneity was in part due to the
upheavals of the years 1789 to 1814, but it also stemmed from
the informal nature of the career. There were no formal regulations covering recruitment or promotion, no administrative
equivalent to the *loi Gouvion-Saint-Cyr*. With political patronage
all-important, technical qualifications were inessential. Croze
might have a degree, be an accomplished Latinist, speak Turkish,

[1] AN doss. Busquet, 156(50), 158(6, 30); AAG, YB 636. Bridieu, 156(45);
R+C, I, 488.
[2] AN doss. Bejarry, 156(13). Giraud des Echerolles, 158(18), 159(1); AAG,
CG 1610. Cossonier, 157(32). Scey, 173(11).
[3] AN doss. J.-B. Dalmas, 158(1); R+C, II, 244. Richard, 172(9); R+C, v, 138.
[4] AN doss. J.-A. Sers, 173(15); *Souvenirs d'un préfet de la Monarchie. Mémoires
du baron Sers 1786–1862* (1906), p. 175. Castéja, 157(9); J.-F. Bluche, *Les
honneurs de la cour* (2 vols., 1957), I, no page numbers; Comte de Puymaigre,
*Souvenirs sur l'émigration, l'Empire et la Restauration* (1884), pp. 219–20.
[5] AN doss. Mareste, 167(6); H. Martineau, *Petit Dictionnaire Stendhalien* (1948),
pp. 316–22. Wildermeth, 156(24), 177(2).

Italian, and a little English and German, all this was by the way. What mattered was Croze's sponsors, the ducs de Rivière, Polignac, Maillé, and Fitz-James, who saw to it that their protégé was given a prefecture in April 1830.[1] Informality was accompanied by more than a hint of leisure. This might in part be accounted for by slow communications, which gave the prefects a practical independence they were in theory denied, but it also reflected the nature of their duties. Entertainment, for instance, was an integral part of an administrator's life.[2] It was also a sphere in which business was somewhat difficult to distinguish from pleasure. But routine administration does not seem to have been a full-time occupation. Molé may have been indulging his characteristic affectation when he complained of boredom at Dijon, because his work was over by mid-day, but Barante found time to write several articles and edit Madame de la Rochejaquelin's Memoirs while administering the Vendée: 'l'administration me laissait beaucoup de temps libre'.[3] These examples belong to the Empire, but it is doubtful whether things changed much after 1814. Indeed, the elaboration of the parliamentary régime had one curious effect. To be a *maître-des-requêtes* or *conseiller d'état, en service extraordinaire*, was no more than an agreeable sinecure with minimal ceremonial obligations. But prefects or sub-prefects who were either peers or deputies found it possible to leave their departments for the length of the parliamentary session, while continuing in theory to administer them. It was a practice the opposition piously denounced, perhaps not entirely for its administrative ill effects. And several members of the Corps found time for activities other than administration. 'Fait des romans et des vers ridicules' his superior noted of Lamothe-Langon in 1811.[4] No Restoration

---

[1] AN doss. Croze, 157(37); AF IV 1335.
[2] Which may account for the excellence of prefectoral cellars. Rambuteau was celebrated for his magnificent Burgundies (he came from Mâcon), while Haussmann, a Bordelais by marriage, showed a proper preference for the *grands crus* of his adopted home and former prefecture, the '48s, an Yquem '46 or '52, a Laffite '47 or '51 (G.-N. Lameyre, *Haussmann*, 'préfet de Paris', Paris, 1958, p. 274).
[3] Molé: Frénilly, *Souvenirs*, p. 319. Barante, *Souvenirs*, I, 269–71, 322.
[4] AN doss. Lamothe-Langon, 166(9).

administrator rivalled Lamothe-Langon's output, but literature, as a glance at their dossiers shows, came easily to the Corps. Indeed it was almost an occupational disease. It might be purely apologetics, the brochures Arbaud-Jouques published to explain his conduct as prefect of Gard during the White Terror, or the distressing palinodes produced by administrators whose scansion was as uncertain as their loyalty.[1] Several members of the Corps wrote local history, Chaix on Briançon and the Briançonnais, Joulieton on the *pays de Combrailles*, Dufeugray on Toulon. Aubert de Vitry produced a refutation of Malthus, Bonnet a translation of Sheridan, Gavoty an Essay on Nature approved by the Institute.[2] Creuzé de Lesser's literary career antedates the Restoration, but Le Brun de Charmettes found time, as sub-prefect and prefect, to produce two edifying if hermetic epics devoted to Joan of Arc, praised by critics as discerning as Bonald and the comte d'Artois, in addition to an ingenious scheme for providing a scissors-and-paste anthology of Royalist sentiments and Republican misdeeds.[3] It is difficult to do justice to the personality of a Corps which contained individuals so diverse: Maurice Barrès' great-uncle, Moreau's brother, Hippolyte Taine's grandfather, Alexis de Tocqueville's father and the Président de Brosses' son.[4] At best there are vignettes; Joseph de Villeneuve-Bargemon practising on the violin while officially at work in the prefectoral offices at Draguignan: the future Pio Nono waltzing at Camille de Tournon's receptions at the prefecture of Rome—'E dire ch'io ho ballato a casa del padre', as he recalled when meeting Tournon's son: Stendhal's flat-mate Bellisle, prefect under the Restoration, with his distinction,

[1] AN doss. Arbaud-Jouques, 155(6): *DBF*, III, cols. 251–3. For a good example of an administrative versifier, Faure, 160(3).

[2] AN doss. Chaix, 157(13); *DBF*, VIII, col. 186. Joulieton, 164(6). Dufeugray, 158(32); G. Mancel, *Biographie de M. Du Feugray* (1861), p. 99. Aubert de Vitry, 155(9); *DBF*, IV, col. 79. Bonnet, 156(33). Gavoty, 161(6).

[3] AN doss. Creuzé, 157(36); R+C, II, 221. Le Brun de Charmettes, 166(19).

[4] AN doss. Barrès, 156(6); J.-B. Barrès, *Souvenirs d'un officier de la Grande Armée* (Paris, 1923), intro. pp. xvii–xviii. Moreau, 167(30); Révérend, *Restauration*, V, 185–7. Taine's grandfather; Bezanson, 156(22); H. *Taine, sa vie et sa correspondance* (2nd ed., 4 vols., Paris, 1902–7), I, 7–8. Tocqueville, 174(8); R+C, V, 425–6. Brosses, 156(46); Chaix, VII, 203–4.

melancholy, and the avarice that drove him quite unnecessarily
to shave every day, in case his putative beard should damage his
stock: or Basset de Chateaubourg, maintained at Niort by the
Bourbons, whose sole merit in Stendhal's eyes was the bayonet
thrust he had received at the Théâtre-Français, as a young man,
when the military were called in to quell a pitched battle between
the supporters of rival actresses.[1] And for the years after 1814
there is Plancy entertaining the comte d'Artois at Fontainebleau
during the First Restoration to the accompaniment of a running
commentary from the Bonapartist concierge: Fouché maliciously
assuming that the sincerely pious Arbaud-Jouques was a free-
thinker, and congratulating him on his appointment to the
fiercely Catholic Gard in July 1815: Castéja declaiming Racine
and Corneille with Mademoiselle Georges over dinner at the
prefecture in Colmar: Bluget de Valdenuit blasting a passage
through the wall which separated the prefecture at Angoulême
from the church, to avoid the inconvenience of using the street.[2]
These are no more than cameos, but the overall impression, at
least of the higher ranks of the administration, is of a body of
men more patrician than professional, whose training was in no
sense technical, whose experience was as wide-ranging as their
interests. Culture did not inhibit conscientiousness. Nor did
quarterings. Alban de Villeneuve-Bargemon, precursor of Social
Catholicism, was a philanthropic administrator in the same sense
as Adrien de Lezay-Marnésia or 'Papa' Rambuteau, both of
whom briefly served the Bourbons, Camille de Tournon a
similar figure with an almost Haussmann-like enthusiasm for
building.[3] There were no great prefects if this means two-fisted

[1] Comte Joseph de Villeneuve-Bargemon, *Souvenirs de soixante ans* (1854),
p. 23. Moulard, *Camille de Tournon...*, II, 132. For Bellisle and Basset: Stendhal, *Journal*, and *Vie de Henry Brulard*, in *Œuvres intimes*, ed. H. Martineau
(Bib. de la Pléiade), pp. 288, 955, 1043; and H. Martineau, *Petit Dictionnaire
Stendhalien*, pp. 46-8.
[2] *Souvenirs du comte de Plancy 1798–1816* (2nd ed., 1904), pp. 293–6. Arbaud-
Jouques: Villeneuve-Bargemon, *Souvenirs*, p. 66. Castéja: Puymaigre, *Souvenirs*, p. 220. AN doss. Bluget de V, 176(1).
[3] AN doss. Alban de Villeneuve-Bargemon, 176(13): J.-B. Duroselle, *Les débuts
du catholicisme social en France (1822–1870)* (Paris, 1951), pp. 59–70. Rambuteau, 172(2). Adrien de Lezay-Marnésia, 166(32). Tournon, 174(11).

prefects in the tradition of Jeanbon or Janvier de la Motte. Perhaps this was not altogether unfortunate. Amateurism had its virtues. Administrative incapacity might be no handicap (Lepère administered six *arrondissements* for a total of sixteen years only for his prefect to discover that 'sa capacité est médiocre et ses connaissances en administration *nulles*');[1] political chicanery might be more easily accepted than sexual immorality: but politics apart, the administration was characterized by a high level of honesty. The Restoration Corps may have lacked administrative training and expertise. It lacked neither distinction nor dignity. They were qualities whose loss was to be regretted.

[1] AN doss. Lepère, 166(27).

# PART I

## THE PREFECTS

# CHAPTER I

# PREFECTS, SUB-PREFECTS, SECRETARIES-GENERAL

The law of 28 Pluviôse An VIII (19 March 1800) reorganized the whole system of French local government.[1] Retaining the department as the largest administrative unit, the law replaced the canton as its subdivision by the *arrondissement*, the number varying from three to five according to the size of the department. Named by the head of state, the prefect was directly subordinate to the Minister of the Interior, and acted as the delegate of the government in his department. He was responsible for transmitting the government's laws and regulations, and for ensuring that they were obeyed; for the construction, supervision and development of essential services whether hospitals, prisons or roads; for the maintenance of public order; and, most important of all his functions under the Empire, the prefect was responsible for providing the quota of conscripts fixed for his department. In matters of finance he was aided and, in theory at least, to a certain extent controlled, by the *conseil général* of his department. This met once a year to apportion the amount of direct taxation which had to be paid by each *arrondissement*, to vote the *centimes additionnels* which were to be raised and spent by the department, and to consider the prefect's account of how those allotted in the previous budget had been spent.

The prefect's staff was his own concern. Paid from the allowance for expenses each prefecture was given, it would vary in number according to the importance of the department and the way in which the prefect chose to organize his work. At the head of this staff was the secretary-general, nominated and paid by the government. The secretary-general was also in charge

---

[1] *BL*, 3rd ser., vol. 1, bulletin 17. The sketch of the administrative system that follows is based on Godechot, *Les institutions*, pp. 508–16, and A. Aulard, 'La centralisation napoléonienne. Les préfets', in *Etudes et leçons sur la Révolution française*, 7th ser. (1913), pp. 113–95.

of the archives of the prefecture, and took over the prefect's functions in his absence, but not in the event of his death. They were then assumed by the senior *conseiller de préfecture*, member of an administrative tribunal which each department possessed and which dealt with the claims of private persons against the administration.

The prefect administered the department; the sub-prefect, also appointed and paid by the government, administered the *arrondissement*. His duties were mainly those of acting as executive agent for the prefect, to whom he was directly subordinate, and of ensuring that the prefect's instructions were known and carried out in the various communes of the *arrondissement*. As in the prefect's case, the sub-prefect's financial responsibility was limited by a deliberative council, the *conseil d'arrondissement*, whose functions were modelled on those the *conseil général* carried out in the department.

Such changes as were made in the administrative system during the Restoration stemmed in great part from the defeats of 1814 and 1815. By the first Treaty of Paris France was reduced, with minor differences, to its frontiers of 1792. The number of prefectures, 98 in 1800, 130 at the height of the Empire in December 1810, was reduced to a mere 87. With the collapse of the Empire and the subsequent treaty, a large number of Frenchmen who had been in the administration of the departments now surrendered lost their posts. To those who had served in the prefectoral administration properly speaking should be added those who had held similar posts in the satellite or occupied states. Among future members of the Corps, Petiet had been an intendant in Tuscany, Heim secretary-general to the government of the Illyrian provinces, Lesseps the imperial commissioner in the Ionian Islands, Le Gras de Bercagny an administrator in Germany.[1] Had there been peace without a change of régime, the government would have found itself in an awkward enough situation. Napoleonic practice was to nominate young men to prefectures—at the start of April 1814, the prefects who held office in France itself were on average younger than their

[1] AN doss. Petiet, 170(11); Heim, 162(4); Lesseps, 166(30); Bercagny, 156(17).

24

subordinates—and the rapid expansion of the Empire had accentuated this tendency. As it was, the government of the First Restoration found itself with a surplus of trained administrators at a time when the partisans of the new régime, whatever administrative qualifications they possessed or lacked, naturally regarded themselves as having a prescriptive right to posts in the prefectoral corps as in all others.

The Hundred Days, the second Treaty of Paris and the indemnity France had to pay the allies necessitated economies which meant, for the prefectoral administration, a further reduction of the posts available. In December 1815 the sub-prefectures of the *arrondissement chef-lieu* were abolished.[1] Their value to the administration had been limited. In the majority of departments the sub-prefect of this *arrondissement* was doing work that the secretary-general or a *conseiller de préfecture* could have done, and which the prefect had himself done without difficulty before 1809, when the posts had been created. Their utility had lain in the opportunity they gave young men starting their career of holding a position sufficiently close to the prefect for them to get a wider view of the administration than would otherwise have been possible. However admirable in theory, such a scheme was a luxury for a government in the financial position of the Bourbons in 1815.

The abolition of the sub-prefectures of the *arrondissement chef-lieu* had been widely approved. A second government measure, the suppression of the secretaries-general in April 1817, met with less success.[2] A secretary-general's functions had been restricted: as one prefect put it, 'fonctionnaires sans gêne, salariés onéreux, [ils] sont à l'ordre administratif ce que ces Prélats joyeusement chantés étaient, disait-on, à l'ordre Ecclésiastique'.[3] Their duties as archivists were often so neglected that the same prefect believed there to be no archives worse kept than those of prefectures. He may well have been right. In 1814 the

---

[1] Ordinance of 20 Dec. 1815 (*BL*, 7th ser., vol. I, bulletin 53).
[2] Ordinance of 9 Apr. 1817 (*BL*, 7th ser., vol. IV, bulletin 151). See also AN, F1bI 290, particularly the 'Notes rapides...' concerning the ordinance.
[3] Roussy, pr. of the Vendée, to Min.Int. 9 Dec. 1815 (AN, F1bII Vendée (3)).

secretary-general of the Allier was denounced for giving the prefectoral archives to his mistresses 'pour en faire leur salon et leur cave'. Such aggressive insouciance would seem to have been rare, but in the Haute-Saône the archives were stored in an old damp church, in Corsica in a building infested by rats—who ate them.[1] Nevertheless, and particularly in the larger departments where the volume of administrative correspondence was considerable, like the Gironde, their functions had been useful. In addition, the career of a secretary-general being more stable than that of a prefect, they had provided a certain continuity of tradition and personnel in the administration. The secretaries-general were restored in 1820 by an ordinance which also empowered the prefects to delegate to them the administration of the *arrondissement chef-lieu*.[2] Even so, with 86 prefects, the same number of secretaries-general, and 277 sub-prefects, the administration was smaller in July 1830 than it had been when the law of 28 Pluviôse An VIII came into force thirty years before.

The logic of a chain of command which ran from minister to prefect, prefect to sub-prefect, and sub-prefect to mayor, which appointed a single administrator for each department and *arrondissement* as the delegate of the government, balanced by a deliberative council representing the governed, was not reflected in the organization of the prefectoral corps itself. The Corps included the prefects, sub-prefects and secretaries-general, but not, anomalously, the mayors or municipal officers. Inside the Corps there was no formal hierarchy and no organized pattern of promotion. The government had—it still has—complete freedom of choice to nominate whomsoever it wished to any post in the administration. It was a right the Bourbons exercised to the full. Of the 164 men made prefects between April 1814 and July 1830, only 82 were former sub-prefects or secretaries-general.

The figures need qualification. Lack of previous service in the

---

[1] Pr. Allier to Min.Int. 15 Sept. 1814 (AN doss. Gengoult-Knÿls, 161(8)); Pr. Haute-Saône to Min.Int. 18 May 1819 (F1bI 87(1) Haute-Saône); Pr. Corsica to Min.Int. 23 June 1817 (AN doss. Vittini, 176(16)).

[2] Ordinance of 1 Aug. 1820 (*BL*, 7th ser., vol. XI, bulletin 399).

prefectoral administration did not necessarily indicate either incapacity or total administrative inexperience. Several prefects had previously served in the Council of State. Others had been mayors of important towns, Fadate de Saint-Georges of Troyes, Vendeuvre of Caen, La Valette of Grenoble.[1] Saint-Genest, prefect of Corsica at the Second Restoration, was a polytechnician who had entered the diplomatic service in 1802 and had held various posts in Germany, Russia and the Netherlands before his nomination. Eymard had served eighteen years in the police, rising to Inspector General of Police at Marseille in 1818, when Decazes made him prefect. It is difficult to believe that this would not have supplied a more thorough administrative training than Dalon's ten months' noviciate as sub-prefect before becoming prefect of Cher in November 1823 at the age of twenty-eight.[2] But among other newcomers to the Corps there are some whose qualifications might seem less impressive or less relevant. Montagut had been an infantry officer before his emigration in 1791. He returned under the Consulate, did not serve the Empire, and in July 1814 was made prefect of Gers. Frondeville also emigrated in 1791. A former *président à mortier* in the Parlement of Normandy, and Right-wing deputy to the States General, he became prefect of the Allier at the First Restoration, after a period of over twenty years without functions.[3]

There is the same variety of experience among those promoted from inside the administration. The two parts of their career were not always directly consecutive. Creuzé de Lesser was sub-prefect of Autun from 1802 to 1804, and then left the administration until made prefect of the Charente at the Second Restoration. Frotier de Bagneux was made sub-prefect of Bourbon-Vendée in August 1815. When the sub-prefectures of the *arrondissement chef-lieu* were suppressed four months later, he spent some seven

[1] AN doss. Fadate de Saint-Georges, 160(1); Vendeuvre, 176(7); La Valette, 170(17).
[2] AN doss. Saint-Genest, 157(34), 173(3). Eymard, 159(3), F⁷ 9780. Dalon, 155(3), 158(1).
[3] AN doss. Montagut, 167(26) defective; F⁷* 105; Woelmont, I, 390. Frondeville, 160(15), defective; Henri de Frondeville, *Notice biographique sur le président de Frondeville 1757–1816* (1926), *passim*.

years out of the administration before becoming prefect of the Côtes-du-Nord.[1] If half of the eighty-two men promoted from inside the Corps had been sub-prefects for under five years, and nine for less than one year, at the other extreme eleven had spent ten years or more in subordinate office, the opposite experience to that of Dalon being the eighteen years Carrière spent in three different sub-prefectures before being made prefect of the Ardèche in 1829. In five of the nine cases rapid promotion can be explained by the upheavals of the First and Second Restorations, which displaced a large number of prefects and left the road open to men like Nugent, sub-prefect of Rambouillet in July 1814, replaced during the Hundred Days, and prefect of the Hautes-Alpes at the Second Restoration.[2] Nevertheless, it is impossible to formalize the discrepancies that appear. Even in the case of the promoted sub-prefects, administrative experience was only one criterion among many. While the nomination of men from outside the Corps suggests the variety of motives that governed the choice of prefects, the comparatively small number of sub-prefects promoted—they can be regarded only as the group of functionaries most favoured for the recruitment of prefects—served to reinforce the division between the two levels of the administration that was in any case strongly enough marked.

To a certain extent this division was inevitable; the ratio of sub-prefectures to prefectures being 4:1 before December 1815 and 3:1 after, there was little enough hope of a prefecture for the majority of sub-prefects. One result of this block in promotion was the emphasis on the sub-prefect as a local figure, locally recruited. Precisely because he had so small a chance of promotion and would in all likelihood spend his administrative life as sub-prefect, it was thought that a local post would be some compensation since it would involve less change of habits and less expense.[3] The sub-prefect, Rigny pointed out, was less an administrator

[1] AN doss. Creuzé, 157(36); Frotier, 156(1), 160(15).
[2] AN doss. Carrière, 157(8); Nugent, 168(4).
[3] Pasquier's circular to the prefects, 6 Sept. 1815 (*Recueil des lettres, circulaires, discours et autres actes publics émanés du ministre de l'Intérieur*, 20 vols., An V–1820, xv, 185).

than an agent of the administration. Placed between prefect and mayor less to communicate the prefect's orders than to ensure that they were carried out, he had much to gain from being a local figure. Rigny went on, more contestably, to draw the contrast between the sub-prefect in his home *arrondissement*, with no ambition other than that of keeping his post and enjoying the esteem of his fellow citizens, and the sub-prefect stranger to the *arrondissement*, less concerned with local interests and welfare than with attracting the government's attention, spurred on by an ambition which, at its healthiest, was purely financial.[1] The picture is overdrawn (Rigny had never been a sub-prefect himself) but it shows the tendency of Restoration administrators and prefects to make a virtue of what was at best an awkward necessity; and at the sub-prefect's expense. Finally, the very existence of these local roots tended to disqualify the sub-prefect from becoming prefect, as the administration of an *arrondissement* for several years would not teach the wider view of administration, and the understanding of politics, necessary to a prefect. Looking back on his nomination as prefect of Haut-Rhin, Jean-André Sers summed up the difficulties facing the promoted sub-prefect:

L'on suppose assez généralement que les sous-préfectures sont une bonne école pour devenir préfet. Elles apprennent, il est vrai, l'administration communale; mais elles permettent bien peu de voir l'administration départementale, et restent complètement étrangères à la comptabilité; elles participent fort peu aussi à la véritable action du gouvernement. L'horizon s'étend bien loin pour un petit sous-préfet transporté à la tête d'un département...[2]

The position of secretary-general, which gave its occupant a view of the administration which was wider than that of the average sub-prefect, might have offered some of the advantages —besides sharing the disadvantages—that the sub-prefecture of the *arrondissement chef-lieu* had possessed. As it was, and no doubt because of the comparative unimportance of their functions,

[1] Rigny, pr. of Puy-de-Dôme, to Min.Int. 29 July 1817 (AN doss. Bruand, 156(47)).
[2] *Souvenirs*, p. 172

the secretaries-general were regarded as inferior to the sub-prefects. For a secretary-general to become sub-prefect was rare, the converse rarer still under the Empire, and as a result their personnel had been more stable than that of the sub-prefects. At the start of the First Restoration, over 40 per cent of the secretaries-general in the eighty-seven departments of France had been in office from the creation of the prefectoral organization in 1800, and some 60 per cent had over ten years' experience.

From 1814 there was more interchange between the sub-prefects and secretaries-general, partly perhaps the result of the pressure for administrative places. The suppression of 1817 accentuated this movement, as the government attempted to find sub-prefectures for the secretaries-general who had lost their posts. Thirty-one of the eighty-five secretaries-general in office in April 1817 returned to the administration as sub-prefects. The movement continued after the re-establishment of the secretaries-general in 1820. Although there was still a tendency for the office of secretary-general to be a career apart, the government began to consider the post as one suitable for young men entering the administration. Far from being treated as an intermediate stage between sub-prefecture and prefecture, it was considered rather as the lowest post in the administration, from which the next step (if there was to be one) would be a sub-prefecture.

# CHAPTER 2

## THE CHOICE OF PREFECTS

The prefects were nominated by the king, on the suggestion of the Minister of the Interior. These nominations might be preceded by a discussion in the Council of Ministers, or at least be subject to other ministers' approval. In July 1815 Pasquier's list of prefects was accepted by the Council without discussion— or interest. Vaublanc also informed the Council of his proposed nominations, until his altercation with Richelieu, over the dismissal of Delaitre, prefect of the Seine-et-Oise. Subsequently he worked alone with the king. Under Lainé the nominations were once again discussed in the Council, but from the start of the Decazes ministry in 1818, until July 1830, there is almost no evidence that the Council were committed to prefectoral movements.[1]

Ministerial independence may account for some of the more bewildering choices. Also for what would appear to be a number of unprovoked nominations, and for a certain brusquerie in the ministerial manner of both appointing and dismissing prefects. 'Quant à moi, je bénis le ciel de ne plus être préfet'—Malartic's statement may be poor evidence, produced as it was immediately after his dismissal.[2] But at the Second Restoration Rémusat first learnt of his nomination to the Haute-Garonne from a local official; Albert de Lezay-Marnésia discovered that he was prefect of Lot from the pages of the *Gazette de Lausanne*; and Joseph de Villeneuve-Bargemon, interrupting Pasquier's morning shave in order to demand his own promotion in the judicature, found to his surprise that he had been given the prefecture of the Haute-Saône instead.[3] Dismissals could be equally abrupt. It was through

[1] Pasquier: *Mémoires et relations politiques du baron de Vitrolles* (3 vols., 1884), III, 140–1. Vaublanc: *Mémoires*, III, 307–13. Lainé: *Le comte Molé 1781–1855. Sa vie—ses mémoires* (6 vols., 1922–30), II, 274.
[2] Letter of 9 Sept. 1830 to Min.Int. AN doss. 167(2).
[3] Mme de Rémusat to Mme de X***, 17 July 1815 (*Correspondance de M. de Rémusat...*, 6 vols., 1883–6, I, 77); Albert de Lezay-Marnésia, *Mes souvenirs—A mes enfants* (1851), p. 96; Joseph de Villeneuve-Bargemon, *Souvenirs*, pp. 64–5.

the *Moniteur* that La Vieuville found he had been replaced in 1816, as Girardin had found in July 1818 and was again to find in 1820. This method, Girardin observed tartly, was in no sense new—but it recalled a régime he had imagined the royal government might prefer to forget.[1]

Since the king did not have the initiative, it is difficult to seek cases where the nomination might have been his, rather than that of the minister. The distinction becomes otiose when the king had a minister or ministry with whom he was as completely in agreement as Louis XVIII with Decazes or Charles X with Villèle or Polignac. Yet this does not preclude the possibility that on certain occasions the king might have decided between two or more candidates. In May 1816 he was presented with a list of eleven candidates for the prefecture of the Somme. He marked two names, those of La Vieuville and La Villegontier. The former was made prefect of the Somme the same day (15 May).[2] In the case of the princes, a distinction should be made between the times when they had special powers, the comte d'Artois as Lieutenant-General in 1814, the duc d'Angoulême in the south-west in 1814 and in the Midi at the start of the Second Restoration, and those when they could do no more than recommend their protégés to the Minister of the Interior at the time. In 1814 the position of both princes was sufficiently powerful for their nominations, provisional in theory, to be ratified automatically. At the Second Restoration the duc d'Angoulême acted independently of the Talleyrand–Pasquier ministry, and there was a considerable confusion of authorities. The hiatus between prince and ministry barely concealed their mutual hostility, Angoulême's nominees being almost immediately replaced—on paper at least—by ministerially appointed prefects. During the remainder of the Restoration, the success of the princes' recommendations was governed in their case as in others by the political bias of the ministry of the day. The comte d'Artois' political sympathies were not such as to endear his protégés to the majority of ministries during his brother's reign.

[1] La Vieuville to Min.Int. 25 July 1820 (AN doss. 166(17)); Girardin to Min.Int. 7 Apr. 1820 (AN doss. 161(11)).　　　[2] AN, F1bII Somme (5).

The duc d'Angoulême seems to have been more successful than his father, perhaps because he was less identified with the Extreme Right. Though his choice of provisional prefects in the Midi at the start of the Second Restoration had included two notable Ultras, Calvière and Limairac, in later years the duc d'Angoulême conformed, with however little enthusiasm, to Louis XVIII's views.[1] Nevertheless, his two protégés who became prefects between 1815 and 1824 were nominated by Right-wing ministries. Ferdinand de Bertier, previously on Angoulême's staff, was given the prefecture for which the prince recommended him by Vaublanc in November 1815. Giresse la Beyrie, who had been attached to Angoulême's staff during the Hundred Days and had followed him to Spain, became his secretary in 1817. In 1823 Villèle made him prefect of the Eure.[2] In both these cases the protégé had been attached to the prince or his household. There were other and more frequent cases where the petitioner would not be known personally to the prince, but would ask for his recommendation on the ground of the petitioner's previous services (often in emigration) or those of his family. Puymaigre had emigrated and fought in Condé's army. In 1815 he petitioned the prince de Condé for a place in the administration, and the latter recommended him in vain. Puymaigre was to describe the inefficacy of such recommendations in his *Souvenirs*:

... à moins d'une volonté déterminée, assez rare chez nos princes, il n'y a pas de protection plus stérile; mieux vaut celle d'un commis de ministère. S'ils ont pour vous une bienveillance réelle, ils vous recommandent à un ministre; celui-ci promet et ne fait rien. Il faut de nouveau importuner ses augustes patrons; s'ils reviennent à la charge, autre protestation de ministre que son plus grand désir est de se conformer à des intentions aussi expresses; avec de pareilles protestations, le ministre gagne du temps, les princes ne pensent plus à vous, ou s'ils ont cette persévérance, le ministre finit par se retrancher derrière une impossibilité notoire.[3]

---

[1] AN doss. Calvière, 157(3); R+C, I, 556–7. Limairac, 166(33); R+C, IV, 160–1.

[2] AN doss. Bertier, 156(19); G. de Bertier de Sauvigny, 'Ferdinand de Bertier, préfet du Calvados', *Bulletin...de Normandie*, LIV (1957–8), 195–6. Giresse, 161(12); AAG, CG 1642.　　　　[3] *Souvenirs*, p. 175.

With the initiative in nomination lying in the hands of the Minister of the Interior, those best placed to acquire a post were naturally the relatives or friends of the minister or of one of his colleagues. A prefecture might be given as a piece of personal patronage. This in turn had political overtones: a minister's protégé was by definition a prefect who could be relied upon to follow the ministerial line. The most striking example during the Restoration is the nomination of Dalon to the prefecture of Cher immediately after his father-in-law Peyronnet had become Garde des Sceaux in the Villèle ministry. It was a gesture Peyronnet may have regretted four years later, when his son-in-law failed to have him re-elected in the department he administered.[1] Similar nominations were those of Pasquier's brother and Talleyrand's cousin in 1814, of Decazes' brother and baron Louis' nephew, Rigny, in July 1815.[2] Nor are the examples limited to the period 1814–15. Hippolyte Jordan served as secretary to his relative Chabrol-Crousol when the latter was intendant-general in Illyria, and became *conseiller de préfecture* at Lyon when Chabrol was prefect. The insurrection of June 1817 at Lyon led to Marmont's mission, Chabrol's ambiguous promotion and Jordan's dismissal. He returned to the administration as secretary-general of Doubs in 1820, and sub-prefect of Bayonne in 1823, but nothing indicated that his career would differ from that of any other sub-prefect. Then Chabrol became Minister of Marine in August 1824. On 1 September Jordan was made prefect of Haut-Rhin. Five years later he was promoted to the Ille-et-Vilaine. It was August 1829 and Chabrol had just become Minister of Finance in the Polignac Cabinet.[3] The Minister of Public Works in the same Cabinet was Capelle. His son-in-law Vernhette, secretary-general and sub-prefect since 1821, was

---

[1] See S. Charléty, *La Restauration* (1921; vol. IV of *L'histoire de France contemporaine*, ed. Lavisse), p. 262.

[2] AN doss. Pasquier, 170(4); Talleyrand, 174(1); Decazes, 157(12), 158(6); Rigny, 172(10).

[3] AN doss. Jordan, 164(6). See P. Leuilliot, 'Le dernier préfet du Haut-Rhin sous la Restauration: le baron Locard', *Revue d'histoire moderne*, IV (1929), 418, for the relationship. Leuilliot confuses Jordan's early career with that of Jordan Duplessis—as he does in *L'Alsace au début du XIXᵉ siècle* (3 vols., 1959–60), I, 447, n. 1.

given the prefecture of the Vosges. A less obvious example is Feutrier's career. Auditor, and then intendant in Spain for two years before returning to France where he carried out various missions, Feutrier did not enter the administration until, in February 1819, Decazes made him prefect of the Saône-et-Loire. Replaced by Siméon in 1820, he served as *maître-des-requêtes* on the Council of State. His elder brother, François-Hyacinthe, became bishop of Beauvais in 1825, and in 1828 was made Minister of Ecclesiastical Affairs in the Martignac ministry. In November of the same year Feutrier returned to the administration as prefect of Lot-et-Garonne.[1]

Most ministers during the Restoration had a relative or friend to place: Decazes had a clan. Perhaps because he was something of an outsider himself, without family or friends already established, certainly as a conscious policy, he set himself to build up a clientèle.[2] In doing so he was singularly aided by the strength of his position, even as early as 1816. He had played a leading part in the elections of that year, and his role was more important still in those of 1817. He changed the administrative personnel freely, meeting the Minister of the Interior's complaints at this usurpation of his functions by telling the king that he could not answer for the elections in the department concerned unless the prefect was changed.[3] The basis of Decazes' power was his favour with the king. This was sufficient, the nominations being discussed by the Council in the king's presence, for him to prevent one candidate, suggested three times by the Minister of the Interior (Lainé), from being nominated.[4] The power seconded an exceptional tenacity in the service of his friends. Molé wrote acidly of Pasquier that 'lorsqu'il ne s'agissait que de sacrifier ses amis au bien public, Pasquier ne connaissait pas de borne à son dévouement', but although he despised and disliked Decazes, Molé recognized that his friends could have nothing but praise

[1] AN doss. Vernhette, 176(8); Feutrier, 160(6).
[2] Molé, *Mémoires*, I, 286–7, II, 17; *Histoire de mon temps. Mémoires du chancelier Pasquier* (5th ed., 1894–5), IV, 300.
[3] Molé, *Mémoires*, III, 109.
[4] See Lally-Tollendal's letter to Siméon 18 Apr. 1820 (AN doss. Bonnechose— the unfortunate candidate—156(32)).

3-2

for him.[1] Of Decazes' clientèle both his brother and Argout were made prefects at the Second Restoration. Germain, former chamberlain and aide-de-camp to Napoleon, had already been given a prefecture in 1814. Another friend, La Villegontier, was made sub-prefect of Versailles, after constant recommendation by Decazes, in August 1815. He became prefect of Allier in May 1816 and of the Ille-et-Vilaine in October 1817: an extremely rapid rise. Four months after La Villegontier, in September 1816, Germiny became prefect of Lot. If Molé is to be believed, Germiny had acted as Decazes' agent in the *Chambre Introuvable*, and was given a prefecture as compensation for the loss of his place as deputy owing to the new electoral law. A year later a member of Decazes' own administration, Bastard, commissioner-general of police in the Isère, quarrelled with the prefect, who demanded that Bastard be replaced. He was: but only to become prefect of the Haute-Loire in July 1817.[2] In two further cases, those of Sers and Angellier, Decazes recommended sub-prefects who had served during the Hundred Days. Decazes had known Sers' father, and recommended the son in July 1815 when he might well have risked dismissal. Angellier was a former school-fellow, who had entered the prefectoral administration in 1804, and had become sub-prefect of Saintes in 1809. During the Hundred Days he was dismissed by the Napoleonic *commissaire extraordinaire* in his department, only—so Vaublanc wrote Decazes in a note of March 1816—to travel to Paris and intrigue for another sub-prefecture. In this he succeeded, but no proof existed that he had ever taken up his new post, and at the Second Restoration he was once again sent to Saintes. Six months later Vaublanc dismissed him, not only for his equivocal behaviour during the Hundred Days, but for a wide variety of reasons, ranging from the unsuitable candidates he proposed for mayors

---

[1] Molé, *Mémoires*, II, 23, III, 244.
[2] AN doss. Decazes, 166(17). Argout, 155(6). Germain, 161(10). La Ville-gontier, 166(17). Germiny, 161(10); Molé, *Mémoires*, II, 122, 274 (the ordinance of 5 Sept. 1816 had fixed the minimum age of deputies at forty; Germiny was thirty-eight). Bastard, 156(8), F 9780; G. de Bertier de Sauvigny, *Le comte Ferdinand de Bertier (1782–1864) et l'énigme de la Congrégation* (1948), pp. 262–4, 267.

in his *arrondissement*, to his—alleged and untrue—relationship to the regicide Eschasseriaux, and the fact of his fortune consisting of *biens nationaux*. Decazes protested without effect, but when Vaublanc was replaced by Lainé as Minister of the Interior, Angellier returned to the administration. Five months later (September 1817) he was transferred to Decazes' own *arrondissement*, Libourne. In 1819, along with Sers, he was made prefect.[1] By April of that year, of Decazes' eight protégés, Bastard still held the same post, Sers and Angellier had recently been made prefects, baron Decazes had been transferred to one of the most important departments in France, Bas-Rhin, and Argout, Germain, Germiny and La Villegontier had been made peers, the latter three still remaining in office as prefects. No other minister of the Restoration had so impressive a record.

The extension of this personal patronage was one that was purely political. The Bourbons made 164 prefects. Nearly a quarter sat in the Chamber of Deputies during the Restoration. Excluding the small number of prefects, like Boula de Colombiers,[2] whose administrative career was over before they became deputies, the remainder fall into two fairly evenly divided classes: the prefects who were subsequently made deputies while still continuing their careers in the administration, and the deputies who were simultaneously or subsequently given prefectures. In both cases the political justification is clear. A prefect elected as deputy meant a vote the minister could justifiably regard as automatic, the prefecture acting as pledge. The deputy made prefect had often given his guarantee already, and the prefecture was a reward conditional on his continued fidelity. That a prefect subsequently became deputy may be important in any study of his career, but is irrelevant in determining the motives for his nomination as prefect, which might, as with Vaulchier or Emmanuel de Villeneuve-Bargemon, precede his election as deputy by five years or more.[3] The case of a deputy subsequently becoming prefect is, on the other hand, political patronage in

[1] AN doss. J.-A. Sers, 173 (15); Angellier, 155 (5).
[2] AN doss. 156(37); R+C, I, 420–1.
[3] AN doss. Vaulchier, 176(6); R+C, v, 493. E.-F. de Villeneuve-Bargemon, 176(13); R+C, v, 529.

its simplest form. Auberjon, after an uneventful career in local administration, ending in membership of the *conseil général* of his department, was elected deputy of the Aude in 1820 as a Constitutional Royalist. Once in Paris, he made his salon the centre of the group hostile to Villèle. His convictions were to change. Re-elected in 1824 he voted with the Ultras, and in September of the same year was made prefect of the Pyrénées-Orientales. Unsurprisingly he was replaced by Martignac in November 1828.[1] The risk of dismissal when the ministry that had named him changed was one to which the deputy made prefect was particularly exposed, the overtly political motives for his nomination also being those for his dismissal. Poyferré de Cère was elected deputy for the Landes in August 1815, sat with the ministerial minority in the *Chambre Introuvable*, and subsequently with the Centre. Prefect of Deux-Sèvres in June 1817, he was replaced by Villèle in 1822. La Valette, mayor of Grenoble and a Right-wing deputy from 1815, was given the prefecture of Gard in 1824, only to lose it when Martignac succeeded Villèle.[2]

These examples have all been of deputies made prefect without any previous experience in the prefectoral administration. There are only four cases of sub-prefects or secretaries-general becoming, first, deputies and then, subsequently, prefects. Limairac's career was exceptional, since he had lost his sub-prefecture at the Hundred Days, had been made provisional prefect of the Tarn-et-Garonne by the duc d'Angoulême in July 1815, and when replaced as prefect found that he had also been given a successor as sub-prefect of Toulouse. He sat as a deputy on the Right from 1815 to 1824, and was given the prefecture of Tarn-et-Garonne in 1822. There was a similar interval in Mortarieu's career, but two of the sub-prefects sat as deputies while continuing to hold their administrative posts. Fussy and Panat were both made sub-prefects by Villèle and prefects by Martignac. Fussy had become a deputy immediately after his nomination as sub-

---

[1] AN doss. 155 (9); M.-A. Lagarde, *Nouvelle biographie pittoresque des députés de la Chambre septennale* (1826), pp. 5-6.

[2] AN doss. Poyferré, 170(24); R + C, v, 38. La Valette, 170(7); R + C, III, 639.

prefect in 1824, Panat was elected in 1827 when he had already been a sub-prefect for three years, and given a prefecture within six months.[1]

Outside this personal and political patronage, it is far more difficult to ascribe the motives behind a nomination. The evidence may be lacking: it may be contradictory or impossible to evaluate. The conditions in which Restoration prefects were named make this inevitable. The Minister of the Interior was responsible for the nominations, but there is no indication of the part that the permanent officials of the ministry may have played. These officials should not be confused with the secretary, or director-general, certain ministries employed, since these latter were not members of the permanent staff: Guizot under Montesquiou in 1814 and under Decazes in 1819-20, Barante under Pasquier at the Second Restoration. Both played an important part in the nominations.[2] It would have been natural for the permanent officials to sift the applications and draw up a list of candidates. For the Empire, such lists, together with miscellaneous information of all kinds about the prefects, can be found in the Archives Nationales.[3] They cannot be found for the Restoration. The reason might be the suppression of the imperial Secretariat of State, so that information about Council meetings and the consequent nominations is scanty. Yet there are lists of candidates for the sub-prefectures scattered throughout the dossiers. If the permanent officials in the ministry drew up similar lists for the prefectures, they have left no trace.

The lack of written evidence is less serious a handicap than the need to rely on such evidence, in dealing with a period and profession in which personal and social contacts were of such importance. The dossiers contain written petitions and recommendations, but a candidate for any administrative post would rarely be contented with a written application. 'Je suis peut-être ... le seul sous-préfet nommé trois fois', Lastic de Saint-Jal wrote

[1] AN doss. Limairac, 166(33). Mortarieu, 167(31), 176(10); R+C, v, 512. Fussy, 160(15), 161(5); R+C, iii, 83. Panat, 170(2); R+C, iv, 540-1.
[2] Guizot: Ch. Pouthas, *Guizot pendant la Restauration* (1923), pp. 56-8, 203-4. Barante: his *Souvenirs*, ii, 177-8.
[3] AN series AF IV (Secretariat of State) and F1bI 150-154(2).

in his petition for a prefecture in 1822, 'sans être jamais allé à Paris.'[1] Candidates came to Paris because they could hope for an audience with the minister, because they could mobilize their friends or relatives on their behalf more easily, and because the world of Parisian society offered them the possibility of a chance meeting with the minister or one of his colleagues. That all these were—and are—important factors for a candidate's success is evident from the few accounts that exist, and the occasional comments that find their way into the dossiers. It was, for example, the hazard of meeting Lainé at Mézy's that led to Barthélemy's return to the administration in 1817.[2] Predictably, there is no mention of this meeting in Barthélemy's dossier. Nor can any indication be found in the Archives of the motives behind two of the most remarkable nominations of the Restoration, that of the comte de Kersaint as prefect of the Meurthe in 1815, and that of his son as prefect of the Orne fifteen years later. The comte de Kersaint, like his more famous brother the Conventionnel, had been a naval officer before the Revolution. He did not emigrate, and was made maritime prefect of Antwerp by Napoleon. Although a man of proved incapacity—Sers, who served under him as sub-prefect in the Meurthe, wrote: 'jamais homme n'a été plus étranger à l'administration et plus incapable de la comprendre'—he was the uncle of a mademoiselle de Kersaint whom the duc de Duras had married in the emigration. In August 1815 she found her uncle a prefecture, and having no illusions about his ability or intelligence, thoughtfully provided him with a former member of the Ministry of Marine as secretary and general factotum.[3] The comte de Kersaint nevertheless lasted only a year in office. Even so, he was more fortunate than his son. Armand-Guy-Charles de Kersaint was made *élève sous-lieutenant* in the engineers in 1811, served with the Grand Army in the 1813 campaign, then at Antwerp, and was made *capitaine-en-second* in the sappers in August 1814. During the next fifteen years he rose no higher than *capitaine-en-second* on the staff. He resigned in December

---

[1] Petition to Min.Int. 22 May 1822 (AN doss. 166(14)).
[2] C.-H.-F. Barthélemy, *Souvenirs d'un ancien préfet* (1886), p. 117.
[3] Sers, *Souvenirs*, p. 146. AN doss. Kersaint, incomplete and muddled with his son's, 165.

1829, was made *maître-des-requêtes* on the Council of State, and in April 1830 prefect of the Orne.[1] In neither case do the dossiers contain a written recommendation from either the duc or duchesse de Duras. She had a salon and a network of her husband's relatives at her disposal; he was a Gentleman of the Chamber. A written petition would have been an unlikely show of pendantry.

With other candidates the relationship or the recommendation exists, but there can be no certainty that they were the basis for the nomination. Barrin was related to Talleyrand, and was a former schoolfellow of the First Restoration Minister of Police, Anglès. Auditor in 1810, sub-prefect in 1811, Barrin became prefect of the Lozère in June 1814. Milon de Mesne, officer in the Carabiniers under the Ancien Régime, and émigré at the Revolution, served for a short time in the artillery on his return to France, before he was made sub-prefect of Porrentruy in 1813. He was related to the duc de Doudeauville, and recommended at the First Restoration by Mathieu de Montmorency and his wife. In June 1814 he became prefect of the Charente. The presumption in both cases is very strong, but presumption it remains, there being no means of linking the relationship or the recommendation with the nomination except by a purely 'post hoc ergo propter hoc' argument.[2]

It is tempting to see another motive at work in the nomination of prefects, that of a reward for loyalty, not merely to a party but to the dynasty itself. The First Restoration prefects include Indy, who as sub-prefect of Bagnères in the Hautes-Pyrénées had rallied to the duc d'Angoulême in the early months of 1814, and Vaulchier, who had offered his services to the comte d'Artois when the latter spent an uncomfortable month at Vesoul (Haute-Saône) in February-March 1814. Above all there was Scey, former aide-de-camp to the duc de Broglie and émigré, indefatigable royalist conspirator under the Empire, who, when made governor of his department by the Austrians during the invasion, worked wholeheartedly for the Bourbons, and acted as host to

[1] Doss. and AAG, CG 1960.
[2] AN doss. Barrin, 156(6). Milon de Mesne, 158(14), 167(24); AAG, CG 2701.

the comte d'Artois at Vesoul.[1] Similarly, the fact that four of the five sub-prefects who followed Louis XVIII to Ghent were subsequently made prefects might also seem a reward for services not necessarily political. Nevertheless, it is impossible to dissociate this reward from the political beliefs of the man concerned or the ministry that nominated him. Of the five sub-prefects, Waters was given a prefecture on his return from Ghent, Foresta and Romain by the second Richelieu ministry in June 1822, and Lestrade only in November 1828 by Martignac.[2] Admitting the difference in age—Waters was thirty-eight in 1815, Lestrade ten years younger—the date of nomination is significant. Simply because he was given a prefecture immediately on his return, Waters' nomination might be considered as a recompense for his loyalty to the Bourbons. In the case of the other three, their return to the administration and subsequent careers make it impossible to consider the journey to Ghent as the sole motive for their promotion, since it cannot be separated from a complex of political attitudes and actions during the interval. Even in an isolated case, that of Dalmas, where the motive was avowedly that of a reward for his past services to the Monarchy, the nomination had political overtones. Advocate and mayor in the Ardèche before the Revolution, *procureur-général-syndic* of his department in 1790, Dalmas was elected to the Legislative Assembly and sat with the Monarchical Right. Vaublanc made him prefect of the Charente-Inférieure in November 1815.[3] Commenting on his nomination in a letter to the duchesse de Richelieu, Vaublanc wrote: 'M. de Dalmas reçoit ainsi la récompense dûe à sa courageuse défense de Louis XVI.'[4] That it was Vaublanc who nominated him was no accident. It would have been a strange gesture for Decazes to make, and Decazes it

[1] AN doss. Indy, 163; Pouthas, *Guizot*, p. 57. Vaulchier, 176(6); Leuilliot, *L'Alsace*, I, 348. Scey, 173(11); AAG, Emigrés, 519(11); Capt. F. Borrey, *La Franche-Comté en 1814* (1912), pp. 11, 13–16.

[2] AN doss. Waters, 177(1); Foresta, 160(10); Romain, 172(15); Lestrade, 166(31), 169(1).

[3] AN doss. 158(1); R+C, II, 244.

[4] Draft of undated (Nov. 1815?) letter to the duchesse de Richelieu (AN doss. Saillard, 173(1)). See also Vaublanc, *Mémoires*, III, 313–14.

was who retired Dalmas in 1819, although with more consideration than was habitual, the measure being motivated, plausibly enough, on the grounds of Dalmas' great age. Villèle was to disregard this and bring Dalmas back to the administration as prefect of Var in August 1823—at the age of sixty-seven. No nomination was outside or untouched by politics.

The group of men, like Scey, made prefects in 1814 might seem an exception to this rule; but the political considerations in this case lay deeper, the difference being more simply an antithesis between those who rallied to the Bourbons and those still loyal to Napoleon, or even between those who had served Napoleon and those, like Scey or Vaulchier, who had not. In one sense this was a question purely of loyalty to the dynasty, but this in itself was the foundation of Restoration political differences; not in theory, since all ministries paid homage to the Restored Monarchy, but precisely as it affected recruitment for any service or administration. The Centre and Centre Left placed experience first. This was trite enough as a maxim, but in so far as administrative experience was concerned, for the first years of the Restoration it was almost exclusively limited to those men who had served Bonaparte. The Right, particularly the Extreme Right, saw loyalty to the dynasty not only as an indispensable qualification but as one sufficient in itself. Dalmas' career symbolizes these attitudes. It is no more surprising that Decazes should have replaced him on the ground of his age than that Villèle should have brought him back in spite of it. The theory mattered less than the men. In all probability Decazes was less concerned with Dalmas' age or administrative ability than with his politics, Villèle less influenced by his behaviour some thirty years before than by his known Right-wing sympathies. In its extreme form the antithesis was not that of two theories of administration, but of two different and mutually suspicious groups of interests and even societies, that of the Revolution and Empire on the one hand, that of the pre-revolutionary Monarchy on the other. It was the misfortune of the ministries in 1814 and 1815 that they had to make their choice of administrative personnel at a time when the antithesis was most evident and most sharply felt.

# CHAPTER 3

# THE PREFECTS IN AN AGE OF CRISIS
## 1814–15

### THE FIRST RESTORATION

When Beugnot became *commissaire* for the Interior in the Provisional Government on 3 April 1814, he was faced by two immediate tasks.[1] The authority of the Provisional Government, formed and in existence for nearly a week before the emperor abdicated, had to be recognized throughout France: and as a corollary, the prefectoral administration, disorganized by the allied invasion and by a change of régime, had to resume its normal functioning. The authority, and indeed the very existence, of the Provisional Government was unknown outside Paris in the early days of April.[2] At Toulouse, Wellington learnt of the change of régime only on the 12th; at Avignon the prefect was told of it by travellers from Lyon on the 14th.[3] Without adequate information, and with no clear lead from above, the prefects could not be certain in whose name they exercised their authority.[4] In the departments occupied by the allies the position was doubly difficult. Napoleon had given orders that, in the event of invasion, the prefect should, whenever possible, take refuge in some fortified place in his department. The remaining civil and religious authorities, from the bishop to the members of the electoral colleges of the *arrondissements*, should retire to the interior of France.[5] Two prefects obeyed, Adrien de Lezay-Marnésia at Strasbourg and Debry at Besançon.[6] The remainder

---

[1] *BL*, 5th ser., vol. 1, bulletin 1.   [2] Vitrolles, *Mémoires*, I, 323, 351–6.

[3] Toulouse: Bertier de Sauvigny, *La Restauration*, p. 65. Avignon: pr. Vaucluse to Beugnot, 27 Apr. 1814 (AN, F⁷ 7028).

[4] Barante, *Souvenirs*, II, 19–29; Pasquier, *Mémoires*, II, 341.

[5] Min.Int. to Roederer, Commissaire Extraordinaire in the 6th Military Division, 4 Jan. 1814, quoted in P. Leuilliot, *La première Restauration et les Cent Jours en Alsace* (1958), pp. 13–14.

[6] Lezay-Marnésia: Leuilliot, *La première Restauration*, p. 14. Debry: *DBF*, VII, col. 587.

of those threatened by invasion preferred, to the Minister of the Interior's annoyance, to retire along with their subordinate authorities. Nor did they always wait until the last moment. Capelle was suspended (later dismissed) and brought before a Commission of Enquiry for his alleged desertion of his post at Geneva. The prefect of the Vosges, Himbert de Flegny, fled from his department in December 1813 at the news of the first skirmish, and was only induced to return by the remonstrances of Caulaincourt and the *commissaire extraordinaire*, Colchen. On 11 January he once again took route for the interior, but with even less success, being captured by Cossacks the same day, and spending the next four months as prisoner of war in Germany.[1] But whether the prefect was blockaded in a fortress or left his department when the allies arrived, the imperial government's intention was the same. The allies were not to be left with an administrative staff that would facilitate their task. Their rejoinder, predictably, was to create a puppet administration. While France was still technically at war, the Provisional Government could have no relations either with the makeshift administrations or with the prefects under siege. But even after the armistice of 11 April, the allies continued to make difficulties. La Vieuville, who had left Colmar in early January 1814, was permitted to return to his department only on 9 May, and to take over the administration on the 15th. Lezay-Marnésia had resumed on 13 May, almost a month after he had hoisted the Fleur de Lys in his *chef-lieu*.[2] In the Haute-Saône and the Rhône the Austrians made similar difficulties and imposed a similar delay. They were not the only allied power to act in this way. In Corsica the royal commissioner accused the English of having engineered, or at least countenanced, a rising that replaced the legally constituted imperial authorities by a junta more to their liking.[3]

[1] See E. Chapuisat, 'La restauration de la république de Genève et le préfet Capelle', *La Révolution française*, LXXII (Feb.–March 1912), 132–47, 214–38. Colchen to Min.War 4 Jan. 1814, quoted in L. Bennaerts, *Les Commissaires extraordinaires de Napoléon Ier en 1814...* (1915), p. 13; AN, F1bII Vosges (4).
[2] Leuilliot, *La première Restauration*, pp. 14, 32, 55, 57.
[3] Haute-Saône, Rhône: AN, F7 7027, 7030. Corsica: report to the king by the *Commissaire* in the 23rd Military Division 4 July 1814 (AN, F7 7030).

In such circumstances, as Vitrolles pointed out, the government's first duty was to establish its own, and thereby the king's, authority.[1] The question of administrative personnel was secondary. Hence the commissioners created by *arrêté* of 22 April were primarily designed to dispel the prevailing uncertainty, to ensure that the administration ran smoothly in the departments, and that it was exercised in the king's name.[2] They had powers to suspend administrative personnel, particularly the subordinate personnel, but when it came to the prefects Beugnot was cautious. His circular to the commissioners stated that prefects could be suspended, but that this should not be done publicly. They should merely be told to report to Paris for the government's orders. In laying down the reasons for which a prefect might be suspended, Beugnot took care to distinguish between acts of harshness or injustice, and errors committed simply through obeying the orders of the imperial government. Few prefects could have avoided such errors, he reasoned: it was a motive for indulgence. In cases when, through obeying these orders, a prefect had become so unpopular that he could no longer serve in his department, the commissioner was to inform Beugnot if he could usefully be transferred to another department.[3] This moderation came naturally from Beugnot, himself a former Napoleonic prefect who had administered the Nord during the last months of the Empire.[4] He admired the Corps, and his memoirs make it clear that he was in the main satisfied with its personnel.[5] His satisfaction bordered on insensitivity. He and Vitrolles had chosen the commissioners as a blend of imperial and royalist names.[6] The gesture was tactful, the choice of their destinations less so. A former Napoleonic general was sent to the duc d'Angoulême's fief at Bordeaux, where his mission was fruitless; a former Napoleonic magistrate to the Vendée, where

[1] Vitrolles, *Mémoires*, II, 56.
[2] *BL*, 5th ser., vol. I, bulletin 5.
[3] Circular of 22 Apr. 1814 (AN, F7 7027).
[4] AN doss. 156(22), defective.
[5] *Mémoires du comte Beugnot, ancien ministre (1783–1815)* (3rd ed., 1889), pp. 406–27.
[6] Vitrolles, *Mémoires*, II, 63.

he had subsequently to be aided and in part superseded by a colleague less suspect of Bonapartism.[1]

The results of the commissioners' missions were to be seen later under the abbé de Montesquiou's ministry. Meanwhile the Provisional Government itself made few changes. Between 21 April and 2 May, ten prefects were replaced, and a successor chosen for Beugnot's former post as prefect of the Nord. The grounds for these dismissals are not altogether clear. Beugnot claimed that he dismissed two prefects only, and those simply because they had left their posts and he had made sure that they did not wish to return.[2] This may refer to Thibaudeau, who had escaped from a riot at Marseille and did not return to his department, and Fréville, who had been transferred from Vaucluse to the Meurthe by a decree of 15 December 1813, had arrived in Nancy on 11 January 1814, and had left the department, along with the majority of the functionaries, on the night of the 12th.[3] Vitrolles wrote that the Provisional Government replaced only five prefects, and those on the grounds of administrative incapacity.[4] He names only those replaced on 21 and 22 April: this does not explain the dismissal of another five on 28 April and 2 May. There is a certain logic in the dismissal of Debry and Thibaudeau, both regicides, of Himbert de Flegny, another former Conventionnel and, in any case, in no position to remonstrate, and of Lamagdelaine, criticized in a note for the comte d'Artois because he had retained the behaviour and principles of a Revolutionary representative on mission. Even the dismissal of Roederer, personally unpopular because of his harshness, might seem explicable on the same grounds, had not Beugnot (or his subordinates) recommended him to the comte d'Artois for the prefecture of the Vosges.[5] The emphasis may

---

[1] Dejean at Bordeaux (AN, F7 7028). Gilbert de Voisins in the Vendée (AN, F7 7029); Barante, *Souvenirs*, II, 69–70.

[2] Beugnot, *Mémoires*, p. 444.

[3] Thibaudeau: Vitrolles, *Mémoires*, II, 57, note 1. Fréville: AN, F1bII Meurthe (5); G. Richard, 'Nancy à la fin de l'Empire. L'entrée des Alliés en 1814', *Le Pays lorrain* (1954), no. 1, p. 23.

[4] Vitrolles, *Mémoires*, II, 56–7.

[5] Debry: R+C, II, 283. Thibaudeau: R+C, V, 396. Flegny: R+C, III, 353. Lamagdelaine: undated note (early April), AN doss. 166(7).

well seem to have been on the new prefects to be chosen, rather than on those who were dismissed. The eleven new prefects (one of whom, Voyer d'Argenson, refused the proferred post[1]) included three men from the prefectoral administration, and three more who had served the Empire in other administrations. Two at least were protégés of the comte d'Artois. Scey and Mique had both rallied to Artois in February-March 1814, before the allies had decided unequivocally for the Bourbons. Among the members of the comte d'Artois' Council, Talleyrand was represented by his cousin, Jaucourt by his friend Riccé, Vitrolles, in all probability, by his former companion in emigration, Casimir de Montlivault. Jules Pasquier was the brother of the prefect of police, Mézy his oldest friend.[2] Beugnot may have attempted to limit the choice to those with previous administrative experience. There are lists of candidates for eight prefectures, submitted by the Ministry of the Interior to the comte d'Artois in April 1814, in the Archives Nationales. Twenty-three of the total twenty-eight candidates were, or had been, members of the prefectoral administration. In the five cases where the prefect was nominated by the comte d'Artois, only twice was he chosen from the candidates submitted.[3] Beugnot had less control over the nominations than future Ministers of the Interior. This was due in part to his position as temporary *commissaire*, and not minister, in a government that was in any case provisional. It was due also to his temperament. Beugnot's abilities were unquestioned, his timidity legendary—'il avait un peu l'épine dorsale brisée'.[4] Both position and character would have exposed him to the influence, the pressure of his colleagues. As a result it is impossible to seek any coherent criterion for the dismissal or choice of prefects, other than a natural desire on the part of members of this government to place their protégés.

[1] Letter of 13 May 1814 to *Commissaire* for Int. (AN doss. 155(6)).
[2] Scey: Borrey, *La Franche-Comté*, p. 176. Mique: Richard, 'Nancy sous la première occupation alliée', *Le Pays lorrain* (1954), no. 2, pp. 61–2. Riccé: *Souvenirs 1785–1870 du feu duc de Broglie* (2nd ed., 4 vols., 1886), I, 76. Montlivault: Pasquier, *Mémoires*, I, 47.
[3] Scey for the Doubs, AN, F1bII Doubs (5); Siméon for the Nord, doss. 173(17).
[4] Broglie, *Souvenirs*, I, 259.

On 13 May the first Restoration ministry proper was formed, with the abbé de Montesquiou at the Interior. On the 24th Guizot became Secretary-General to the Minister of the Interior.[1] The first series of nominations came on 10 June, and between this date and 15 March 1815, thirty-five prefects were replaced.[2] They included Adrien de Lezay-Marnésia and Montagut, both of whom died in office. Three others joined the Council of State. La Tour du Pin returned to a career in diplomacy, Cossé-Brissac was made a peer.[3] In several cases the dismissal followed the advice given by the *commissaires extraordinaires*. Gilbert de Voisins, commissioner in the 12th Military Division, suspended the prefect of the Vendée; in the Midi Jules de Polignac provisionally replaced Bouvier-Dumolard at Montauban; while General Marescot wrote to the minister recommending the dismissal of the prefect of the Tarn.[4] All three were replaced by the ordinance of 10 June. In eleven cases where the commissioner either suspended the prefect or wrote very unfavourably about him to the minister, the prefect was subsequently dismissed.[5] In a further five cases where the commissioners were not altogether favourable, or recommended a transfer, the prefect was likewise dismissed. Beugnot's dividing line between those who should be transferred and those who should be replaced proved difficult to observe.

The twenty-eight prefects replaced without being given alternative employment form two clearly distinguishable groups. Eleven had been made prefects under the Consulate, seven of these from the creation of the prefectoral administration. The

[1] *BL*, 5th ser., bulletins 13 and 18.
[2] A royal ordinance of 15 March 1815 made Vanssay prefect of Vaucluse, Saint-Chamans prefect of Isère (AN, F1a* 95 (2)). Saint-Chamans was never installed, and has not therefore been included among the First Restoration prefects.
[3] AN doss. Lezay-Marnésia, 166(32); Montagut, 167(26). Abrial, Boissy d'Anglas and Maurice joined the Council of State (*Moniteur*, 6 July 1814). AN doss. LTDP, 166(15). Cossé-Brissac, 156(46): Raoul de Warren, *Les pairs de France*, vol. 1.
[4] Voisins, AN, F7 7029. Polignac (10th Military Division), F7 7028. Marescot (20th Military Division) to Min.Int. 26 May 1814 (F7 7030).
[5] AN, F7 7027–7030.

THE PREFECTS

remaining seventeen had been made prefects in or after 1809, and included eleven auditors. Among the first group were a number of deputies from the assemblies of the Revolution or Empire. Beugnot had dismissed two regicides. The remaining two who held office as prefects, Chazal and Richard, were dismissed by Montesquiou.[1] Pougeard du Limbert had been a member of the States General, an Ancient and a Tribune, and had rallied to Napoleon after Brumaire. Roujoux had sat in the Legislative Assembly, in the Ancients and as a Tribune: Boullé had been one of the founders of the Breton Club, a member of the Five Hundred, and a Brumairien.[2] They could be reproached their part in the Revolution, their unpopularity among the royalists of their departments. By origin and formation they were incompatible with the new régime. They represented the generation of *sans-culotte* prefects—the basis of the reproach against Lamagdelaine—whose most famous figure had been Jeanbon Saint-André.

The second group, including Bergognié, Bouvier-Dumolard and Chassepot de Chapelaine, had been characterized by their intemperate zeal and occasional harshness, particularly over conscription and during the invasion.[3] The complaints against them are typified in the reasons given by Gilbert de Voisins for his suspension of Basset de Chateaubourg, prefect of the Vendée: that he was characterized by 'roideur et incapacité, sévérité déplacée ou faiblesse pusillanime...'.[4] The difference in social origin between the two groups was as clearly marked as the difference in their administrative experience. All eleven of the first group were bourgeois by origin, eight of the remaining seventeen were noble. Mere nobility was not enough to prevent dismissal. Nor, in all cases, were previous services to the Monarchy. Angosse and Chassepot de Chapelaine had both emigrated:

[1] AN doss. Chazal, 157(20); R+C, II, 81. Richard, 172(9); R+C, v, 138.
[2] AN doss. Du Limbert, 170(22); R+C, v, 29. Roujoux, 172(18); R+C, v, 204. Boullé, 156(38); R+C, I, 428.
[3] AN doss. Bergognié, 156(18). Bouvier-Dumolard, 156(41); A. Le Bihan, 'Les préfets du Finistère', *Bulletin de la Société archéologique du Finistère*, LXXXV (1959), 189–204. Chapelaine, 157(19).
[4] Letter of 7 June 1814 to Min.Int. (AN, F7 7029).

Méry de Contades was the son of an officer who had fought at Quiberon and was made *maréchal-de-camp* in emigration, grandson of a Vendéen, and great-grandson of a Marshal of France.[1]

The Montesquiou ministry named thirty-six new prefects:[2] of these fourteen came from the prefectoral corps. One was a special case. Vanssay was replaced in June 1814, but given another prefecture in March 1815. Six others had administered departments outside the 1814 frontiers of France, seven had been promoted from inside the Corps. To these fourteen can be added six new prefects who had previously served the Empire in other fields, whether in an intendance abroad like Chabrol-Crousol, in the Cour d'Appel like Brosses, or as an auditor like Brevannes.[3] By contrast, the remaining sixteen prefects nominated had not served the Empire at any but a local level. Seven had been army officers under the Monarchy, an eighth a naval officer, and two had sat in the Parlements. The remainder had held no post under the Ancien Régime.

The total number of nominations given (thirty-six) and the number of former Napoleonic functionaries among them (twenty) differ from those given by M. Pouthas.[4] The difference is significant. M. Pouthas includes the prefects switched from one department to another inside France among the new nominations. The proportion of former Napoleonic officials thereby becomes considerably higher, some two-thirds of the new prefects. The inclusion of those transferred is difficult to understand. Unlike their less fortunate colleagues who had formerly administered posts outside the 1814 frontier, they had never been out of office. In 1814 such transfers had not yet become a recognized ministerial technique, part of a general measure: they had

[1] AN doss. Angosse, 155(6), 158(2); F7 5490. Chapelaine, F7 5706, O3 2571. Contades, 157(31): for his father O3* 2566: for his family *ADLN* (1854), pp. 201–3.
[2] This does not include Valsuzenay, provisionally replaced at Bordeaux in March 1814, but nominated afresh on 11 June.
[3] AN doss. Chabrol-Crousol, 157(13). Brosses, 156(46). Brevannes, 156(44) defective; AN, AF IV 1335.
[4] *Guizot*, p. 57. Forty-three nominations, twenty-nine ex-imperial administrators.

no motive other than administrative convenience. On Adrien de
Lezay-Marnésia's death, Kergariou was moved from the Indre-
et-Loire to Bas-Rhin, Hersant-Destouches from the Haute-
Garonne to the Indre-et-Loire, Saint-Aulaire from the Meuse to
the Haute-Garonne, and Vaines was given the prefecture of the
Meuse.[1] If the nominations are to be examined as an indication
of the ministry's policy, it is misleading to consider Saint-Aulaire,
a Napoleonic prefect maintained at the Restoration and then
merely transferred to another department, as a 'new' prefect.

M. Pouthas' figures lead him to conclude that the Montesquiou
ministry, and particularly Guizot, deliberately chose a large
majority of former Napoleonic administrators, eschewing,
wherever possible, declared royalists. He points out, in confirmation, that only seven émigrés were given prefectures.[2] Yet this
figure includes only those émigrés who had not served the
Empire. The assumption is that where a man had both emigrated
and subsequently served the Empire, the ministry regarded him
solely in the light of his imperial background, and chose him on
those grounds alone. As a result, M. Pouthas can increase the
number of those he regards as former imperial officials still
further and, with these figures to support him, has no great
difficulty in showing that the Montesquiou ministry preferred
such officials. But the total number of émigrés among Montesquiou's thirty-six new prefects was not seven but twelve.[3] The
proportion of émigrés among the prefects with no previous
administrative experience (just under 50 per cent) was certainly
higher than that among the former Napoleonic functionaries
(20 per cent). This latter figure may seem insignificant: it is not
altogether easy to establish its importance, because there are no
self-evident criteria for judging what would be a high percentage
of émigrés. But it is interesting to note that the percentage of
émigrés among the twenty Napoleonic functionaries given
prefectures by Montesquiou was far higher than that among
the prefectoral corps in France as a whole, at the end of the

[1] Ordinance of 13 Oct. 1814 (*BL*, 5th ser., vol. II, bulletin 50).
[2] *Guizot*, pp. 56–8.
[3] See Appendix V, Emigrés given posts in the prefectoral corps, 1 April 1814–
15 March 1815.

Empire: 4 per cent. There are some grounds, therefore, for considering emigration as a motive behind the nomination of prefects. It is logical to suppose that this was so in the case of, for example, Marnière de Guer, an émigré and later a Chouan leader in Morbihan, whose experience otherwise was limited to the membership of his departmental electoral college. It may also have been the motive that prompted the minister to promote Bouthillier or Milon de Mesne.[1] Both had served as sub-prefects under the Empire, but if administrative experience was the most important criterion there was no lack of prefects, particularly from the departments outside France, Du Bouchage, Houdetot, Sainte-Suzanne or Tournon, who had better claims but had not emigrated.[2] The importance of emigration in 1814 does not lie in any anachronistic equation of émigrés and Ultras, but rather in its having been, in the eyes of the ministry, a proof of past services, and a guarantee of future loyalty, to the dynasty. If the majority of new prefects had served the Empire in some capacity, it should not be forgotten that they had also given gages to the Monarchy.

M. Pouthas' conclusion has fixed the image of the First Restoration prefectoral movement. 'Il est difficile de parler de réaction et d'épuration dans l'administration préfectorale.'[3] The statement has been accepted—and exaggerated.[4] It seems over-simplified. There are two ways in which a prefectoral movement can be studied, and they have never been properly distinguished. The first is from the point of view of the departments, of administrative continuity. In this sense the only figure that is relevant is that of the departments which retained the same prefect. The second is to consider the administrative personnel, their social origin as well as their career. The First Restoration

---

[1] AN doss. Guer, 161(21), 167(8); F7* 105, BB¹ 90 plaque 4. Bouthillier 156(41); AAG, Emigrés, 519(1). Milon de Mesne, 158(14), 167(24); AAG, CG 2701.

[2] AN, no personal doss. Du Bouchage: elements in F1bII Alpes-Maritimes (2). Houdetot, 162(7). Sainte-Suzanne, 156(48), 173(6). Tournon, 174(11).

[3] *Guizot*, p. 57.

[4] See, for example, E. Beau de Loménie, *Les responsabilités des dynasties bourgeoises* (4 vols., 1943–63), I, 64.

was not a clean sweep, as were the Hundred Days, the Second Restoration, or the 1830 Revolution. But of the eighty-seven departments which formed France in 1814, only thirty-five had the same titular at the start of the Hundred Days as at the start of the First Restoration. This does not suggest a remarkable degree of continuity. Among the personnel a considerable number had in some sense served the Empire: twenty-six of the forty-six prefects nominated between 1 April 1814 and 15 March 1815. Equally important is the measure of change socially. This is a factor that has been masked by the over-emphasis on the administrative experience of the prefectoral personnel. The number of nobles among the prefects almost doubled. At the end of March 1814 there had been thirty in the eighty-seven departments of First Restoration France. On 15 March 1815 there were fifty-eight. This may not indicate a purge, but it does underline a significant change in the nature of recruitment.

The First Restoration movement was in some sense a compromise. Only 40 per cent of the departments kept the same prefect throughout the period, but if the newly nominated prefects included a high proportion of former imperial functionaries, these were often men who, if they had not themselves served the Monarchy, offered a pledge in their name and family. Any more extreme solution would have been difficult. The change of régime produced, inevitably, a rush of applicants for places in the administration. 'Tous les honnêtes gens qui s'étaient effacés sous Bonaparte voulaient alors des préfectures': so Frénilly thought, who was an unsuccessful candidate.[1] There were émigrés like the comte de Tryon-Montalembert, former officers like the comte de Tilly, members of the magistrature of the Ancien Régime like Victor de Botherel, and pronounced royalists of all shades, from Frénilly himself to Barruel-Beauvert.[2] The commissioners' missions, however tactfully carried out, provoked a stream of denunciations against the administrative

---

[1] *Souvenirs*, p. 356.

[2] Tryon-Montalembert, Barruel-Beauvert, AN, F1dI* 8. Tilly, Botherel, F1a 251. For further evidence of the rush for places, see Barante, *Souvenirs*, 1, 28; *Mémoires du baron d'Haussez, dernier ministre de la marine sous la Restauration* (2 vols., 1896–7), I, 142–52.

personnel. In these circumstances it would have been impossible to have maintained all the prefects in place. Even those who were popular in their department, and praised by the commissioners, found their situation embarrassing. As late as September, Adrien de Lezay-Marnésia, prefect of Bas-Rhin, wrote to the former commissioner in his department:

Après cinq ans d'une administration qui, nécessairement, a fatigué tout le monde, et non seulement les fripons qu'elle gênait, mais l'universalité des adminstrés auxquels elle n'a pas passé une semaine sans lui demander ou son fils, ou son cheval, ou ses denrées, ou son argent, ou ses corvées; après un changement de gouvernement qui a ouvert carrière à beaucoup d'ambitions et à d'ancien ressentiments, il était impossible que, Préfet d'une Préfecture aussi difficile et aussi enviée, chacun ne se jetât sur moi et que le Gouvernement ne donnât pas quelque créance à une réclamation aussi générale...A chaque commandement de ma part, on répond aujourd'hui: à quoi bon, il sera destitué dans huit jours.[1]

As an alternative, it might have been possible to remove or suspend all the existing prefects by one ordinance, re-employing those who were thought suitable. This was what Jules de Polignac, commissioner in the 10th Military Division, had suggested. He pointed out, with some justification, that a general measure of this kind would avoid something of the odium of successive dismissals, since it could be regarded as the result of a deliberately adopted system, rather than the consequence of party bias.[2] The opportunity was there for the Provisional Government. Yet, as Vitrolles had recognized, the government's first duty was to establish its own and the king's authority, and widespread change, by disorganizing an administration already in a state of confusion, would have delayed this. By June the opportunity no longer existed. Partial changes had already been made, and a general measure could no longer have appeared as the inevitable corollary of a change of régime.

[1] Lezay-Marnésia to the chevalier de la Salle 23 Sept. 1814, quoted in Leuilliot, *La première Restauration*, p. 82.
[2] Polignac to Min.Int. 23 May 1814 (AN, F7 7028).

Between these two extremes the government of the First Restoration operated its reshuffle; but a reshuffle that differentiated the prefectoral corps of the Restoration from its imperial predecessor. An aristocratic body with a large proportion of trained administrators: whatever Guizot's influence in the nominations, it is Barante's description of the abbé de Montesquiou's attitude that comes to mind—'la restauration, c'était pour lui l'ancien régime rendu raisonnable'.[1]

## THE HUNDRED DAYS

Jaucourt—whose testimony is not altogether unbiased—alleged that Montesquiou was bitterly disappointed by his new administration, finding the new prefects far inferior to their predecessors and risking the princes' displeasure by an increasingly obdurate defence of those imperial veterans still in place.[2] Whether prejudiced or not, Jaucourt's opinion was premature. Montesquiou's administration was not given time to prove itself. On 20 March 1815 Napoleon re-entered Paris, Carnot was made Minister of the Interior, and during the next three months there was a continued stream of nominations, transfers and dismissals. Carnot believed widespread change to be necessary but, to avoid disorganizing the prefectoral administration, wanted it to be gradual.[3] It became endemic. Between 15 March and 22 June (the date of Napoleon's abdication), only eight departments kept the same prefect. During the same period thirty had three or more titulars, the Hautes-Alpes, Côte-d'Or and Tarn-et-Garonne had five, Hérault had six.[4] Prefects were transferred from one department to another with bewildering rapidity. Le Roy de Boiseaumarie was given three different prefectures within a week. Rambuteau, prefect of the Loire at the start of the Hundred Days, was transferred to the Allier on 6 April, to the Aude on 20 April,

[1] *Souvenirs*, II, 40.
[2] Jaucourt to Talleyrand 25 Jan. 1815 (*Correspondance du comte de Jaucourt... avec le prince de Talleyrand...*, 1905, p. 168).
[3] Carnot to Napoleon 2 Apr. 1815 (*Correspondance inédite de Carnot avec Napoléon pendant les Cent Jours*, 1819, pp. 36–8).
[4] *BL*, 6th ser. (1 vol. only), *passim*.

to the Tarn-et-Garonne on 15 May.[1] In the Ain and Ille-et-Vilaine two prefects were named simultaneously to the same post, but such reduplication was rarer than the prolonged vacancies caused by rapidly succeeding nominations, prefects being changed before they had time to take up the posts to which they had been appointed, or transferred almost immediately after their arrival. The royalist prefect of the Côte-d'Or left Dijon on 13 March. His successor arrived on 1 April, was transferred on the 6th and left on the 10th. The department remained without a prefect until 7 May. Lot-et-Garonne was without a prefect for over a month, the Aude for over two months.[2]

The government's difficulties were as much moral as physical. Royalist prefects took an active part in opposing Napoleon, whether by attempting to organize resistance, or by refusing to leave their posts when replaced: Albertas and Bouthillier in Provence, Harmand d'Abancourt in the Hautes-Alpes, Trouvé, the marquis de Villeneuve and Alban de Villeneuve-Bargemon with Vitrolles in the Midi, Talleyrand with Gouvion-Saint-Cyr at Orléans. Capelle, Vaublanc and ultimately Riccé followed the king to Ghent. Saint-Luc attempted to do so but was arrested and imprisoned.[3] The prefectoral corps showed more energy for the Bourbons in 1815 than it had for the Empire the year before. But those who actively opposed the new régime, or those who immediately resigned their functions, were frequently anticipating a more or less certain dismissal. Capelle had been brought before a Court of Enquiry in January 1814 for his alleged desertion of his post, Vaublanc rode out of Metz as the officer charged to arrest him rode in.[4] 'Ces messieurs aimaient les Bourbons de

---

[1] AN doss. Le Roy de Boiseaumarie, 166(28); *BL*, 6th ser., bulletins 6, 7, 8 (25 March 1815 Moselle, 28 March Hautes-Alpes, 30 March Loiret). Rambuteau, 172(2); *BL*, 6th ser., bulletins 11, 18, 30.

[2] Ain: AN doss. Abrial, 155(1), and P.-J.-M. Baude, 156(9). Ille-et-Vilaine: doss. Bonnaire, 156(32), and A. E. Méchin, 167(15). Côte-d'Or: AN, F1bII Côte-d'Or (5). Lot-et-Garonne: F1bII Lot-et-Garonne (4). Aude: F1bII Aude (3).

[3] AN doss. Bouthillier, 156(41); Harmand, 162(2); Capelle, 157(5); Riccé, 172(8); Saint-Luc, 173(4). No doss. Vaublanc, but R + C, v, 489. Albertas, Trouvé, Villeneuve, V.-Bargemon, Talleyrand: H. Houssaye, *1815, La première Restauration—le retour de l'île d' Elbe—les Cent Jours* (28th ed., 1899) pp. 391, 409 note 1, 430.  [4] Capelle: see above p. 45. Vaublanc: *Mémoires*, III, 209–11.

toute la haine qu'ils portaient à Napoléon et aussi de la peur qu'il
leur faisait.'[1] More significant was the behaviour of former
imperial prefects who had no such reason to fear the emperor.
Malouet was dismissed in spite of his pleas to be maintained,
both Goyon and Sartiges behaved in a manner sufficiently
ambiguous to lead to denunciations at the Second Restoration,
but proved and loyal Bonapartists maintained at the First
Restoration refused to turn their coats again.[2] Barante, Finot,
La Vieuville and Massa resigned.[3] Barante might have been suspect on the grounds of his distant relationship with the abbé de
Montesquiou, but La Vieuville had been an imperial chamberlain,
Finot was a relative of Bassano, the Secretary of State, Massa
the son of the former Grand Judge: 'J'ai exercé ces fonctions sous
le dernier gouvernement', he wrote, 'et ma délicatesse répugne à
manifester dans le même lieu une opinion contraire à celle que
mes fonctions me faisaient un devoir d'énoncer publiquement.'[4]
Unequivocal loyalty to the Empire had not survived 1814. Nor
had unreasoning confidence. His royalist beliefs might lead Du
Martroy to refuse the prefecture he had lost in April 1814. Three
former prefects overlooked and unemployed at the First Restoration likewise refused the departments they were offered during
the Hundred Days, Breteuil the Nièvre, Houdetot the Loiret,
Tournon first Finistère and then Hérault.[5] Among Bonapartists
less hampered by political scruples or family tradition, refusals
were rarer but bargaining was rife. Bessières, moved from the
Aveyron to the Ariège in April 1815, demanded successively the
Isère, a prefecture near Bordeaux, the Aveyron, Lot, and a
prefecture near Paris. Himbert de Flegny refused the Tarn-et-
Garonne on the ground of his age (he was sixty-four), but
wanted the Vosges or the Meuse, alternatively the Tarn-et-

---

[1] Beugnot, *Mémoires*, p. 564.
[2] AN doss. Malouet, 167(4): he was later proposed by Carnot for the Côte-d'Or (report to emperor 26 Apr. 1815, AN, F1bI 150–2). Goyon, 161(16). Sartiges, 173(9).
[3] AN doss. Barante, 156(3) and Barante's *Souvenirs*, II, 71; Finot, 160(6); La Vieuville, 176(11); Massa, 167(11).
[4] Massa to Min.Int. 28 March 1815 (AN doss. Basset de Chateaubourg, 156(8)).
[5] AN doss. Du Martroy, 157(4); Breteuil, 156(43); Houdetot, 162(7); Tournon, 174(11).

Garonne for his son. Lameth, transferred from the Somme to the Haute-Garonne on 6 April, remarked to Napoleon that as he had been responsible for the motion to abolish the Parlements in 1790, he would prefer a department whose administrative centre was not a town which had formerly possessed a Parlement. He remained at Amiens. Waterloo marked the end of this process. On 20 June, Napoleon, hurrying back to Paris, talked briefly with the prefect of the Aisne, Micoud d'Umons. The latter drew his own conclusions. The next day he wrote informing the Minister of the Interior that his deteriorating health might prevent him carrying on. Two days later he left his post.[1]

If refusals and bargaining both multiplied nominations and handicapped the government, it was also hampered by its very consciousness of the urgency of the situation. 'Dans la crise qui se prépare', Carnot wrote to Napoleon, 'ce sont des *forts* qu'il nous faut; et tout fonctionnaire, en acceptant l'écharpe, doit être convaincu qu'il monte sur la brèche.'[2] The breach was not a position the majority of prefects either wished, or were fitted, to occupy, hence the constant inquietude and interference by Napoleon himself, uncertain that even the prefects newly chosen were sufficiently capable. He imposed changes on Carnot: at his demand Jerphanion was replaced in the Haute-Marne, Richard in Calvados, Saulnier in the Tarn-et-Garonne, Fourier in the Rhône, because they were not able or energetic enough for their posts.[3] Nor was Napoleon content merely to dictate dismissals. He chose prefects, not only from the personnel under consideration at the Ministry of the Interior, but from his own entourage. Pons became prefect of the Rhône, Galeazzini, who had also accompanied the emperor from Elba, was given the Maine-et-Loire three days after Carnot had named Viefville des Essarts

---

[1] Himbert de Flegny: AN, F1bI 150–2. Bessières: AN doss. 162(6); F1bI 150–2; F1bII Tarn-et-Garonne (2). Lameth: *Correspondance de Napoléon I<sup>er</sup>* (31 vols., 1858–70), XXVIII, 102. Napoleon to Carnot 15 Apr. 1815 (21812) Micoud d'Umons, 167(22).

[2] Carnot to Napoleon 2 Apr. 1815 (*Correspondance de Carnot*, p. 37).

[3] Jerphanion: 25 Apr. 1815, report to the emperor (AN, F1bI 150–2). Richard: *Correspondance de Napoléon*, XXVIII, 172. Napoleon to Carnot 10 May 1815 (21889). Saulnier: 15 May 1815, report to the emperor (AN, F1bI 150–2). Fourier: Napoleon to Carnot 2 May 1815 (AN, F1a 554).

to the same post.[1] The imperial family was also represented. Ferri-Pisani had been Joseph Bonaparte's secretary at Naples and Madrid, Le Gras de Bercagny had been in Jérôme's service in Westphalia, Cochelet was the brother of a lady-in-waiting to Queen Hortense.[2] But alongside protégés of the emperor or his family, young and enthusiastic Bonapartists like Harel or Combe-Sieyès, inheritors of Revolutionary or Napoleonic names like Petiet or Treilhard, were the veterans of the Revolution itself.[3] Here the influence was clearly Carnot's. Officer in the engineers, Conventionnel and regicide, president of the Directory, exile: every stage of Carnot's career before Brumaire is represented in his nominations. Faipoult had been at the Ecole de Mézières with Carnot, and had also served in the engineers before becoming briefly Minister of Finances under the Directory, and *commissaire* in Italy. Seven regicides were given prefectures, an eighth, Quinette, refused. Faipoult, Ramel, Cochon, and Bourdon de Vatry had been ministers under the Directory, while Desgouttes had befriended Carnot when the latter was an exile in Switzerland.[4] To meet a revolutionary situation Carnot looked deliberately to the men who had played a part in the Revolution. In so doing he marked the logical end of a process that had started during the invasion of 1813–14. Napoleon had then attempted to re-create the patriotic fervour of the Revolution by reviving revolutionary slogans and devices. The imperial *commissaires extraordinaires*, as Fiévée noted, had been imitations of the Representatives on mission.[5] In the Hundred Days Carnot not only re-employed this pseudo-revolutionary measure,

---

[1] AN doss. Pons, 170(19). Galeazzini, 161(2); *Correspondance de Napoléon*, XXVIII. Napoleon to Carnot 25 March 1815 (21709).

[2] AN doss. Ferri-Pisani, 160(5). Le Gras, 156(17). Cochelet, 157(26); Broglie, *Souvenirs*, I, 96.

[3] AN doss. Harel, 162(2). No doss. Combe-Sieyès, but AF IV 438; *DBF*, fasc. 50, col. 359. Petiet, 170(11). Treilhard 174(12).

[4] AN doss. Faipoult, 160(1); R+C, II, 593; M. Reinhard, *Le grand Carnot* (2 vols., 1950–2), I, 42. Ramel, 172(2), defective; R+C, V, 80–1. Cochon, 157(26); R+C, II, 145. Bourdon de Vatry, 156(39); *DBF*, VI, cols. 1458–9. Desgouttes, 158(18), defective; F1bII Drôme (4); Reinhard, *Carnot*, II, 241, 379 note 5. For Quinette's refusal F1bI 150–2.

[5] Fiévée, pr. of Nièvre, to the *Commissaire* for the Interior 5 May 1814 (AN, F7 7030).

but re-employed former Revolutionaries themselves in the prefectoral administration. Yet, at the same time, he attempted to combine revolutionary fervour with administrative experience.

Between the prefectoral corps of the late Empire and that of the Hundred Days the difference was marked. The 'bonapartistes de la bonne compagnie' had almost disappeared as a class. In March 1814 one prefect in three holding office in France had been a noble. In June 1815 the figure was one in nine. Angosse, Flavigny and Rambuteau were exceptions in an administration that was now primarily bourgeois in origin. Yet in spite of this, and in spite of the continued nominations, the recruitment remained highly professional. Only fifteen prefects who had held office under the Bourbons remained in the administration on 22 June, yet sixty-nine of the eighty-seven prefectures were occupied by men with previous experience in the Corps, sixty of whom had been prefects. The largest single group was formed of the prefects who had been dismissed in 1814, and now returned to the administration. A second group consisted of prefects who had administered departments outside France, but had not been employed at the First Restoration. Micoud d'Umons had been a prefect in Belgium, Roggieri in Holland, Doazan and Ladoucette in Germany, Dupont-Delporte, Fauchet and Maurice Duval in Italy.[1] But the proportion of prefects with administrative experience was even higher, since among those new to the Corps were former intendants like Dunod de Charnage, auditors like Eusèbe Dupont, and an ex-Director-General of Police in Tuscany, Lagarde.[2] Among the Conventionnels themselves the majority had more recent—if perhaps not in Carnot's eyes more relevant —claims than their behaviour twenty years before. Cochon had been a prefect until 1809, Chazal until 1813, Debry and Richard until their dismissal by the Bourbons in 1814. André Dumont

---

[1] AN doss. Micoud d'Umons, 167(22); Roggieri, 172(4); Doazan, 158(24); Ladoucette, 166(3); H.-J.-P.-A. Dupont-Delporte, 158(38); Fauchet, 160(2); Maurice Duval, 158(40).

[2] AN doss. Dunod de Charnage, 158(36), defective; F1e 65. Eusèbe Dupont, 159(3), defective: AF IV* 438, AF IV 1335. Lagarde, 166(5) defective; H. Faure, *Galerie administrative ou biographie des préfets...* (2 vols. in 1, 1839), II, 7-9.

had been a sub-prefect until he was dismissed at the First Restoration, Cavaignac had been a Councillor of State in Murat's Naples. The only Conventionnel who had not served the Empire before becoming a prefect during the Hundred Days was Ramel.[1]

This curious insistence on Revolutionaries with proper administrative experience is typical of the timid Jacobinism of the Hundred Days. The *commissaires* were no longer the representatives of l'An II; the former Conventionnels given prefectures were more imperial civil servants than the patriots of 1793. The façade might be reminiscent of the Republic: the foundation was irrevocably that of the Empire.

## THE SECOND RESTORATION, JULY–AUGUST 1815

The prefectoral movements of July–August 1815 bear a certain resemblance to those of the First Restoration. As in 1814, they were carried out against a backcloth of invasion and occupation, of interrupted communications and incomplete governmental control. Louis XVIII re-entered Paris on 8 July, the Talleyrand–Pasquier ministry was formed on the 9th, but the Fleur de Lys was only hoisted at Metz and Toulon on the 24th, at Strasbourg on the 30th.[2] Inevitably, relations with the allied powers lacked even the affectation of cordiality which had characterized the First Restoration. Prefects in the occupied areas, Indy in the Ardèche, Joseph de Villeneuve-Bargemon in the Haute-Saône, found themselves involved in interminable disputes over requisitions. Others, less fortunate, were arrested or deported: Talleyrand's cousin, Pasquier's brother, and Maurice de Gasville, nephew of the Chancellor of France.[3]

[1] AN doss. Colchen, 157(26). Chazal, 157(20), defective; F1bII Hautes-Pyrénées (3); R+C, II, 81. Debry, 156(49). Richard, 172(9). Dumont, 158(36). Cavaignac, 157(11); R+C, I, 615–16, and *DBF*, VII, col. 1490, confuse him with his younger brother. Ramel, 172(2).

[2] Metz: H. Contamine, *Metz et la Moselle de 1814 à 1870* (2 vols., 1932), I, 313. Toulon: H. Houssaye, *1815, La seconde abdication—la Terreur blanche* (44th ed., 1909), p. 447. Strasbourg: Cons. de préf. to Min.Int. 4 Aug. 1815 (AN, F1bI 688).

[3] Indy: J. Regné, 'Les Autrichiens dans l'Ardèche en 1814 et 1815', *Revue historique de la Révolution française...* (July–Sept. 1918), pp. 399–400. Joseph

Even outside the areas under allied occupation, the government found difficulties. At the start of the Hundred Days, and later in June when the allies moved forward into France, the royal government had created several *commissaires extraordinaires.* The habit died hard: and as the imperial régime collapsed, other self-appointed royalist authorities proliferated. At Bordeaux in early July there were four complementary sets of authorities. Besides the official functionaries were the duc d'Angoulême's representatives, those of his wife, and a special royal delegate whose mission consisted of watching his rivals.[1] A return to normality was essential. An ordinance of 19 July put an end to the commissioners' missions and retired their powers. It had no immediate effect on the most important commissioner of all, the duc d'Angoulême, who had hurried to the Midi at the end of the Hundred Days to resume his functions as commander of the 5th Military Division, which he had been given in March. He established what was, in fact if not perhaps in intention, a quasi-autonomous state. A series of administrative appointments were made, supplementing or supplanting the central government's nominees. Rémusat, who had officially been nominated as prefect of the Haute-Garonne on 12 July, was told on arrival that his post was destined for one of Angoulême's protégés, Limairac, and prudently retired. Angoulême had travelled to Paris in an effort to persuade the government that the Midi should be excepted from the general rule laid down by the ordinance of 19 July. He failed, but it was only on 13 August, a month after his nomination, that Rémusat was installed at Toulouse.[2]

It is evident that the main preoccupation of the Talleyrand–Pasquier ministry was to get the prefectoral administration working again as smoothly, above all as quickly, as possible. Even so, the nominations were surprising. The Hundred Days acted as a catalyst on Restoration history. They stripped off the

de Villeneuve-Bargemon, *Souvenirs,* p. 67. Talleyrand, Pasquier: Pasquier, *Mémoires,* III, 366. AN doss. Gasville, 161 (5), 161 (15).
[1] Moulard, *Tournon, préfet de la Gironde,* p. 36.
[2] For this whole episode see J. Loubet, 'Le gouvernement toulousain du duc d'Angoulême après les Cent Jours', *La Révolution française,* LXIV (Feb.–Apr. 1913), 149–65, 337–66.

façade of reconciliation between two mutually suspicious societies which, however abraded, had existed in 1814: 'la catastrophe du 20 mars', Salaberry told the Chamber of Deputies, 'a tracé une ligne de démarcation entre les bons et les mauvais citoyens...'[1] They sharpened the emphasis the Right placed on loyalty to the dynasty, for the Right had seen prefects maintained by the king at the First Restoration forsake him in 1815 as they had forsaken the emperor the year before. '[Napoléon] avait raison de dire que ses aigles voleraient de clocher en clocher,' Chateaubriand wrote, 'il allait de préfecture en préfecture coucher chaque soir, grâce à vos soins, chez un de ses amis'.[2] But if the Right attributed the Hundred Days to the king's concessions to the Bonapartists, the Moderates believed Napoleon's return to have been provoked by the incoherence and inefficiency of the government of the First Restoration. Pasquier drew the moral with melancholy self-satisfaction: the mistakes committed at the First Restoration could have been avoided if only those who alone had experience of men and affairs had been left in place.[3] If the Right wanted a counter-revolution without complaisance, the Moderates wanted a return to tried imperial methods and men. A ministry with Talleyrand at its head, with Pasquier at the Interior and Prosper de Barante as his secretary-general, gave them their opportunity.

Pasquier brought back fifty of eighty-seven prefects in office before the Hundred Days.[4] The thirty-nine newly nominated were characterized by their background of administrative experience, although not always in the prefectoral corps, and by their youth. They make an interesting contrast to Montesquiou's nominations. Sixteen of Montesquiou's new prefects had never rallied to the Empire, had therefore no previous administrative experience other than on a purely local level. Of Pasquier's thirty-nine new prefects all but one, Albert de Lezay-Marnésia, had a background of imperial service. The average age of both

---

[1] Sitting of 28 Oct. 1815. AP, 2nd ser., xv, 155.    [2] A. de Chateaubriand, *De la Monarchie selon la Charte* (Paris, 1816), p. 104.    [3] *Mémoires*, II, 386.
[4] The fifty who returned include Girardin, replaced in Aug. 1815 shortly after his nomination. The thirty-nine newly nominated include Bondy, also replaced by the Talleyrand–Pasquier ministry.

groups was not widely dissimilar (43·5 for Montesquiou's prefects, 41·1 for Pasquier's), but the use of an average is itself misleading. The ministry's complete freedom of choice, and the personal nature of nominations, guaranteed a wide span of age. Among Montesquiou's new prefects Germain was twenty-seven and Frémin de Beaumont seventy, among Pasquier's Gasville was twenty-five and Du Bouchage sixty-eight.[1] But whereas Montesquiou's prefects covered the whole span from thirty to sixty fairly evenly, Pasquier's were far more concentrated, 60 per cent being under forty: the generation that had grown up under the Revolution or Empire. Both as concerns experience and age, Pasquier's recruitment was less haphazard than his predecessor's. The ministry nevertheless made one group of nominations which appear almost deliberately provocative. Pasquier brought back to the administration two prefects who had been replaced by the Bourbons in 1814, and sent one of them, Chassepot de Chapelaine, back to the same department he had administered under the Empire.[2] He also re-employed a group of prefects who had compromised themselves by serving during the Hundred Days. Jessaint was maintained as prefect of the Marne, where he was already something of an institution, having administered the department since 1800. Rogniat and Villiers du Terrage had been made prefects during the Hundred Days: Pasquier maintained them, merely transferring them to other departments.[3] At the time, the most discussed nominations were those of Richard, Bondy and Girardin. Richard had been a prefect from 1800, and prefect of the Charente-Inférieure from 1806 until his dismissal in 1814. Napoleon brought him back to the administration as prefect of Calvados in March 1815, only to dismiss him in May. Two months later Pasquier made him prefect of the Charente-Inférieure once more. It was at least unusual that Richard should be sent back to the department he had administered under the Empire. Given his background as a former Conventionnel and regicide, who had taken office during the Hundred Days, it was

---

[1] AN doss. Germain, 161(10); Frémin, 160(13); Gasville, 161(5), 161(15). No doss. Du Bouchage, but F1bII Alpes-Maritimes (2).    [2] AN doss. 157(19).
[3] AN doss. Jessaint, 164(4); Rogniat, 172(14); Villiers du Terrage, 176(14).

extraordinary. He was a friend of Fouché's, which may account for his nomination but does not explain the continued favour he enjoyed after Fouché's fall. After his resignation in October 1815, Richard was excepted from the law of 12 January 1816 which cancelled all pensions accorded to former regicides who had returned to office during the Hundred Days. He was given an annual indemnity of 6,000 francs, equivalent to the maximum possible pension for a prefect. The law of 15 May 1818 suppressed all pensions or indemnities paid from the funds of individual ministries. Richard was once again excepted. The initial decision to grant him an indemnity had been taken after Vaublanc had reported to Louis XVIII on the subject and Feltre had told the king that when Richard was a Conventionnel on mission in Holland he had, at considerable personal risk, saved over 500 émigrés. There had been, therefore, grounds on which a Right-wing ministry could favour Richard, which makes it less surprising that a Moderate ministry should have employed him. But these grounds would not have been known to the majority of royalists, who might well have echoed Vitrolles' comment on the nomination: [Richard,] 'dont le caractère et la probité étaient intacts, sauf qu'il avait été révolutionnaire violent, et avait voté le mort de Louis XVI'.[1]

Bondy was a personal friend of Pasquier's. He had been dismissed as prefect of the Rhône at the First Restoration, but was made prefect of the Seine on Napoleon's return. Pasquier transferred him to the Moselle. He adduced, as the reasons for this favour, Bondy's moderation and the part he had played in arranging the return of Louis XVIII at the end of the Hundred Days. Girardin had been prefect of the Seine-Inférieure under Napoleon, was maintained by Louis XVIII in 1814, maintained once more by Napoleon in April 1815, and then transferred to the Seine-et-Oise. Pasquier was willing to place him and, although he doubted the wisdom of sending him back to the Seine-Inférieure, gave way when Girardin made it a point of honour. Not unnaturally, these two nominations aroused protests from

---

[1] *Mémoires*, III, 140. AN doss. Richard, 172(9); R+C, v, 138; Vaublanc, *Mémoires*, III, 300.

the Right. Girardin was replaced on 2 August, Bondy on 11 August.[1] Whatever the immediate pretext, it seems likely that Pasquier lost his nerve. The dismissals took place shortly before the elections (14 and 22 August), and the sacrifice of two unpopular prefects may well have appeared a necessary price to pay for electoral support. As it was, the elections of August 1815 produced the *Chambre Introuvable* and led to the formation of the first Richelieu ministry, with Vaublanc at the Interior.

The prefectoral movement of July–August 1815 was the last Restoration movement caused by a change of régime. Once again, large-scale changes of prefects were made with a rapidity that circumstances made inevitable. Yet the Second Restoration movement differed greatly from that of 1814. The façade of reconciliation during the First Restoration had meant that there were few dismissals which could be regarded as automatic. Loyalty to the dynasty had for the most part been assumed among the former Napoleonic personnel. At the Second Restoration it could be proved or disproved. The great majority of prefects who had held office during the interregnum were automatically disqualified from any administrative post during the remainder of the Restoration. Some hundred prefects had served during part at least of the Hundred Days: only ten were maintained at the Second Restoration, or came back to the administration during the next fifteen years.

The question of loyalty to the dynasty being, so to speak, eliminated, the emphasis narrowed to the nuances of political feeling. It is unsatisfactory to use party labels here, if these labels imply any priority of political programme over personalities. Even in 1814 the question had been less how to govern France than who should do the governing. The Talleyrand–Pasquier ministry's desire to limit the extent of the reaction at the Second Restoration was primarily an effort to retain the cadres of Napoleonic society in place, unless they should prove to be too badly compromised. A reaction would not have been limited

---

[1] AN doss. Bondy, 156(31); Girardin, 161(11). For the discussion over their nominations, Pasquier, *Mémoires*, III, 323, 349–50, 382–3; Molé, *Mémoires*, I, 293–4; Vitrolles, *Mémoires*, III, 140, 189–90.

to those who had greeted the emperor's return with enthusiasm: it would have spread to the former Napoleonic administrators as a whole. The ministry therefore took particular care, in its choice of prefects, to nominate only those it thought were moderate: and these moderates it found among the former Napoleonic officials. Similarly, of the one group of the First Restoration prefects who were excluded in July 1815 on the grounds of their alleged extremism and incapacity, none had held office before 1814. Floirac, Guer, Montureux, Saint-Luc, Scey, Terray, and the marquis de Villeneuve were overlooked although their conduct during the Hundred Days had been irreproachable—indeed, their only compensation was to be a letter of thanks for their loyalty.

The Talleyrand–Pasquier ministry's confidence in the moderation of former imperial personnel, precisely because they were former imperial personnel, may seem naïve. It was frequently misplaced.[1] Among the prefects maintained at the Second Restoration were Arbaud-Jouques, Bouthillier and Trouvé, all of whom were to be noted for their Ultra sympathies.[2] Yet in the circumstances it was perhaps inevitable. The ministry's miscalculation lay in its ignorance or disregard of the political temper of the departments, and a correspondingly over-sanguine opinion of its administrators' resilience. 'Mon pauvre ami,' Saint-Aulaire was to write to Barante some years later, 'il ne faut pas nous dissimuler qu'en général les libéraux sont peu héroiques; ils se contentent d'être les plus forts devant Dieu, et il semble que leur royaume n'est pas de ce monde.'[3] The analysis was apposite enough at the Second Restoration. Houdetot had administered Calvados for three weeks only when he complained that the effort was beyond his strength and strained his conscience: he was not equipped, he wrote, to deal with a situation in which political passions precluded the use of reason.[4] With more excuse, Brevannes threw up the administration of Hérault after two

[1] Barante, *Souvenirs*, pp. 177–8.
[2] Arbaud-Jouques and Trouvé: Pasquier, *Mémoires*, VI, 198. Bouthillier: Pouthas, *Guizot*, p. 203; Frénilly, *Souvenirs*, p. 453.
[3] Saint-Aulaire to Barante 18 Sept. 1823 (Barante, *Souvenirs*, III, 126).
[4] Houdetot to Barante 30 July 1815 (*ibid*. II. 185).

months in office. Nominated on 14 July but installed only on 11 August, he had taken over the department from the marquis de Montcalm, Angoulême's commissioner, thus laying a firm basis for his unpopularity: this was real enough for the general in charge of the military division to be obliged to take active steps to protect him.[1] In a letter expressing his complete discouragement, Brevannes described the situation he had found in the department:

La différence des opinions politiques, des croyances religieuses, étaient des causes d'exil, de poursuites, d'emprisonnement et de confiscation. Les haines particulières s'agitaient dans ce désordre. Chacun se faisait la mesure de la satisfaction qu'il avait droit de prétendre, et poursuivait privativement sans le concours de l'autorité, ses préventions ou sa vengeance. Un très grand nombre de fonctionnaires publics, d'agents des contributions, et des administrations financières étaient en fuite. Le peuple ne payait presque rien, se livrait à tout licence et s'applaudissait d'un désordre qu'il regardait comme une espèce de triomphe, et comme un état permanent.[2]

By trying to re-establish order, by carrying out ministerial orders, notably the disarming of the *volontaires royaux*, Brevannes had made his position untenable: he no longer wished to hold it, nor, for that matter, any other post in the prefectoral administration. His Hobbesian picture may seem overcharged, but the prefect's position, particularly in the Midi, was hardly enviable. The ministry might be criticized less for its ignorance of the prefects' political beliefs than for its underrating the pressure that would be put upon them in the departments, and for overlooking that element of calculation any government functionary possesses. A former imperial official might find it safer to compensate for his Napoleonic past by moving to the Right, as Lachadenède did in the Moselle, than by observing a moderation that was not always attuned to departmental feeling.[3] Not for the last time in French history, unimpeachable 'liberals' sent out from Paris adopted a contrary attitude when they had spent some time at their post.

[1] Général de Briche to Min. War 7 Oct. 1815 (AN, F1bII Hérault (5)).
[2] Brevannes to Min.Int. 9 Oct. 1815 (AN doss. Floirac, 158(7)).
[3] Contamine, *Metz et la Moselle*, I, 325.

# CHAPTER 4

## THE PREFECTS 1815–30

The development of the Second Restoration political groupings considerably affected the functions of the prefectoral corps. The Corps had always had a duality of function, political as well as administrative. From 1815 the greatly increased importance of elections emphasized the prefect's political role, often at the expense of the administrative. The prefect was ideally placed to exert the maximum of pressure on the electorate, and in particular on government employees of every kind—'des gens qui mangent au Budget'. The phrase is Stendhal's, and it is Stendhal who, in *Lucien Leuwen*, has left the classic and malicious description of prefectoral election-rigging. An exaggeration so far as the Restoration is concerned, perhaps: but the importance of elections to the prefects was such that they did not tend to be too nicely scrupulous. They might well stake their careers on their success in making the elections for the ministerial candidate, or at least preventing the election of the more obnoxious of the ministry's opponents. Manuel's election in 1818 cost the prefect of the Vendée his place, that of the abbé Grégoire led to the transfer of Choppin d'Arnouville, prefect of the Isère.[1] As a result, voters were subjected to overtly exercised pressure, told which way to vote, as was the electorate of the Seine-Inférieure before the elections of September 1816, threatened with the loss of their employment, or tempted by judiciously timed promises, a method Haussez used with advantage in the Isère.[2] So widespread was the use of these methods that when Guizot and the Society 'Aide-toi, le Ciel t'aidera' organized petitions against the irregularities in the 1827 elections, the Parliamentary Commission of October 1828 found only twelve of the twenty-four prefects accused completely innocent. The govern-

[1] Vendée: AN doss. Kerespertz, 165; Pouthas, *Guizot*, p. 203. Isère: doss. Choppin d'Arnouville, 157(24); Haussez, *Mémoires*, I, 321–2.
[2] Seine-Inf.: Molé, *Mémoires*, II, 289. Isère: Haussez, *Mémoires*, I, 323–34.

ment had already replaced three of the most compromised in March.[1]

The political importance of the prefect made it unwise for a ministry to leave a convinced opponent, or even a lukewarm supporter, in place. The danger of doing so was illustrated by the Minister of the Interior's experience before the elections of September 1816. Whether it was because Lainé, the minister, did not choose to disturb the administration, or because the interval was so short between the dissolution of the *Chambre Introuvable* and the elections, only two prefects were replaced. One of these, Trouvé, had himself distributed Chateaubriand's attack on the ministry (*De la Monarchie selon la Charte*) and had advised his mayors to vote for their former Ultra deputies.[2] Behaviour like Trouvé's became rarer under subsequent ministries, but the theory that 'le préfet ne discute point les actes qu'on lui transmet...'[3] had never been entirely true under the Consulate and Empire, and was less so during the Restoration, when a number of prefects were at the same time members of the Chamber of Deputies. Girardin was not prevented by his post as prefect of Côte-d'Or in 1820 from launching an embittered attack on the second Richelieu ministry in the Chamber. He had a very special reputation as a deputy—'il semblait travaillé par une sorte d'hydrophobie qui le portait sans cesse à mordre'—but as late as 1829 another prefect, Preissac, who was also a deputy, could write to the Minister of the Interior, saying that he never did and never could subscribe to what he called 'la loi ignominieuse', that a prefect should have no opinions other than those of his minister.[4] Girardin was dismissed, Preissac resigned; but understandably no ministry would wish to find itself with an administration hostile, even vocally hostile, to its ideas. Logically enough,

---

[1] Pouthas, *Guizot*, p. 383 and note 4 pp. 383–4.

[2] Duvergier de Hauranne, *Histoire du gouvernement parlementaire en France* (10 vols., 1857–72), III, 510. He lists at least eleven departments where the prefects worked more or less openly against the ministry in the subsequent election (p. 513).

[3] Chaptal to the Corps Législatif 28 Pluviôse An VIII (AP, 2nd ser., I, 230).

[4] Girardin: Haussez, *Mémoires*, I, 405. Preissac to Min.Int. 12 Sept. 1829 (AN doss. 170(25)).

therefore, there grew up during the Restoration the custom that was to mark the prefectoral administration throughout the century, that of a new ministry dismissing or transferring prefects simply because they were not of the appropriate political colour —the 'massacres' and 'waltzes' of prefects.

The first and most striking example was that given by the Decazes–Dessolle ministry. There had been large-scale movements of prefects in 1814 and 1815, but they had been the consequence of a change of régime. Those of 1819 were the more remarkable because the numbers involved and the rapidity of the measures (Guizot as Director-General of Departmental Administration replaced or transferred twenty-four prefects in the first six weeks of the year) threw the principle of political dismissal, never previously acknowledged, into clear relief. On 8 February 1819, after the first two movements, Barante wrote Decazes a letter that is the more interesting in that Barante was himself a former prefect, son of another prefect who had been dismissed by Napoleon.

J'ai pensé à ces abatis de préfets, et je ne puis être entièrement de cet avis. Il y a injustice à destituer des hommes qui ont eu seulement le tort de suivre la ligne que leur traçait le ministre de l'intérieur, ou de partager son esprit d'incertitude...Rabrouez vos préfets, ne leur passez rien, menez-les avec fermeté; mais au nom de la justice et de la convenance, attendez pour les révoquer qu'ils se soient montrés instruments indociles ou insuffisants...Allez doucement quant aux personnes, mon cher ami, c'est par là qu'on fait des plaies incurables...

On gagne à prendre possession d'un homme qui pourrait être ennemi; on perd à jeter dans l'hostilité un homme qui, en tombant, vous donne vingt ennemis de plus par sa famille et ses amis...

Je n'aime ni comme morale ni comme succès durable les opinions bonapartistes; mais je fais grand cas de la conduite bonapartiste quant au personnel. Elle était remplie de ménagements et d'habilité.[1]

A generous and intelligent man, Barante nevertheless overlooked the inevitable difference between the prefectoral administration under the Empire and that under the Bourbons. The nature of Napoleonic rule had ensured a certain stability of

[1] *Souvenirs*, II, 361–2.

personnel. Power was held by one man, and the choice of administrators was his own, as it was never to be Louis XVIII's or Charles X's. Hence a change like that from Consulate to Empire, a change of façade rather than foundation precisely because the central figure remained the same, left the prefectoral corps unscathed. Under the Restoration, successive changes of ministry made prefectoral movements of some amplitude inevitable, although the degree and technique of change varied. The movements are difficult to assess, because of the varying length of the ministries, from Vaublanc's eight months at the Interior in the first Richelieu ministry, to Villèle's six years. Even an estimate based on the average number of movements each month may be misleading, since the majority of such changes would be made immediately on the ministry taking office. As a corrective, the average of monthly movements (dismissals or transfers) during the first year alone of each ministry can be taken. It provides an interesting sidelight on ministerial techniques. At one extreme is the Martignac ministry, with its very rapid changes, an average of 4·5 per month; at the other are Decazes and Siméon, with just over 2. The remainder of ministries are echelonned between.

Martignac's is a good example of a ministry making widespread and immediate changes. During the last eight months of his ministry, from mid-December 1828, not a single prefect was moved. On the other hand, bearing in mind Barante's strictures, the small number of changes Decazes made is surprising. This suggests a second criterion: the proportion of movements during the entire ministry that were dismissals. For Siméon and Martignac, the proportion was around one-third. The two Centre Right compromise ministries characteristically preferred to transfer prefects as a less drastic alternative to dismissing them. At the opposite extreme is Decazes; nearly two-thirds of his total movements were dismissals. So high a proportion reflects a deliberate technique of prefectoral change, one that was adopted by ministries with a sharply defined political colour. Taking the proportion of dismissals among the movements in each ministry's first year, Decazes and Villèle alone dismissed more prefects than they transferred. Although the Polignac ministry is the next in line, it may seem surprising that its proportion of dismissals should be so low: a mere third of the total movements. The reason is less to be found in Polignac's notorious apathy (he was surely the most unready counter-revolutionary in history) than in the nature of Martignac's recruitment, and in his technique of prefectoral change. Martignac's prefects, as Salaberry noted, included not only several of the Decazes squadron, but men like Preissac, Fussy and Lezardière, who had formed part of the extreme Right-wing counter-opposition to Villèle.[1] They were likely, for this reason, to approve Polignac's policy—or at least sympathize with what they might construe his apparent absence of policy to conceal. Again, Martignac's preference for transferring rather than dismissing prefects meant that in August 1829 La Bourdonnaye, the first of Polignac's Ministers of the Interior, inherited sixty-seven of Villèle's prefects, whose political sympathies would be, in varying degrees, favourable to an extreme Right-wing government. Villèle, by contrast, started his ministry with seventy-seven prefects who had served Decazes. The number of prefects a minister dismissed was inevitably conditioned by the political formation of the prefectoral personnel he inherited from his predecessor. Nevertheless, Decazes, who as Minister of Police had been actively concerned in the prefectoral nominations of the previous ministry, replaced nineteen prefects who had served under Lainé. It is worth noting that only four of the nineteen had been nominated, as opposed to maintained, by Lainé, and that one of these, Vignolle, was replaced for reasons other than his political beliefs.[2] Moreover, Decazes' influence had been primarily unofficial during the first Richelieu ministry, based on his favour with the king. With the formation of his own ministry in December 1818, he was in a position to organize prefectoral movements as part of a general ministerial measure and on a large scale. Under Richelieu Decazes had required a particular motive for dismissing, or advising the

[1] *Souvenirs politiques du comte de Salaberry*...(2 vols., 1900), II, 184.
[2] Vignolle, pr. of Corsica, had repeatedly asked to be replaced on the grounds of his ill health (AN doss. 176(12)).

dismissal, of a prefect. At the head of his own ministry, he could dismiss prefects as part of a political programme.

This in turn accounts for the homogeneity of Decazes' prefects. The Talleyrand ministry had frequently been mistaken over the political beliefs of its personnel, the first Richelieu ministry had lacked effective direction and a coherent political outlook. Decazes had both the programme and the power to implement it. His personnel had in the majority of cases been trained under the Empire, and a significant number had remained in office during the Hundred Days. Among the nineteen nominations there were six former prefects. Périer and Didelot had not been employed since the Hundred Days. Girardin and Rogniat had also served during the interregnum, Girardin being almost immediately dismissed at the Second Restoration, Rogniat being replaced by Vaublanc. Five of the eight sub-prefects promoted had likewise been in office during the Hundred Days. The second Richelieu ministry, with Siméon at the Interior, removed the most committed—or compromised—of the squadron: Girardin with some fracas, Didelot, Feutrier and Saint-Aignan more discreetly.[1] The majority of those who survived Siméon succumbed to Villèle: and Villèle's nominations are indeed in marked contrast to Decazes'. Six of Villèle's forty-two new prefects had served in the royalist armies of the west during the Hundred Days, seven in the Midi or south-west; Du Bourblanc, Foresta and Romain had made the 'sentimental journey' to Ghent.[2] It does not follow that their behaviour during the Hundred Days was the sole reason for their nomination, but the contrast in the conduct of the two groups reflects the full measure of their difference. Socially, the major change among the prefects had already taken place at the First Restoration, when the number of nobles in office had nearly doubled. The percentage remained between sixty and seventy-five for the remainder of the Restoration. There was, nevertheless, a considerable difference between the social background of the prefects nominated by the Centre-

[1] AN doss. Périer, 170(9, 10); Didelot, 158(22); Girardin, 161(11); Rogniat, 172(14); Feutrier, 160(6); Saint-Aignan, 173(1).
[2] AN doss. Du Bourblanc, 156(38), 158(29); Foresta, 160(10); Romain, 172(15).

Left ministries (Talleyrand, Decazes) and those appointed by the
Right and Extreme Right (Vaublanc, Villèle and Polignac).
One-half of the Centre-Left prefects, but three-quarters of the
Right-wing nominees, were noble. The latter group were also,
on average, considerably older. Over half of the Centre-Left
prefects, as against a quarter of the Right wing, were aged
less than forty when appointed; one in three of the Right wing
were over fifty, only one in eight of the Centre Left. Two
examples may serve to pinpoint these contrasts. Pelet de la
Lozère was made prefect by Decazes in 1819 at the age of
thirty-three, Calvière by Villèle four years later at the age of
sixty. Pelet had served as an auditor on the imperial Council of
State, and became a *maître-des-requêtes* in 1811. Calvière, by
contrast, had been a junior officer before the Revolution, had
emigrated and campaigned until 1801. He returned to France, but
held no official position until he became a member of the *Chambre
Introuvable* in 1815. Whereas Calvière came from a distinguished
family of the nobility of Languedoc which had numbered general
officers and presidents in the provincial Parlement, Pelet was a
member of an almost archetypal bourgeois dynasty. His grandfather had been a successful merchant, his father was a former
Conventionnel (happily absent during the vote on Louis XVI)
who had rallied to Bonaparte, serving him as a prefect and later
as Minister of Police, before rallying in turn to the Bourbons, as
he was to rally to Louis-Philippe sixteen years later.[1]

Neither socially nor in terms of age and experience was the
homogeneity of these opposed groups entire. The majority of
Pasquier's prefects might be under forty years old, but du Bouchage was sixty-eight, Kersaint sixty-seven. The majority of
Decazes' new prefects had a background of imperial service,
but Jahan and Saint-Aignan were both former émigrés who had
never served the Empire at more than a local level. The Right
might have a preference for members of the old nobility untainted
by Napoleonic training, yet Croze, made prefect of the Basses-
Alpes by Polignac in April 1830, was not only of bourgeois

[1] AN doss. Calviere, 157(3); AAG, Emigrés, 519(12); Chaix, VIII, 133–6. Pelet,
170(7); Révérend, *Restauration*, V, 313–14.

extraction but had been an auditor and sub-prefect during the Empire, and a member of the imperial household during the Hundred Days, at the same time as his father—another former sub-prefect—was elected deputy.[1] Nevertheless, the coherence within each of the two groups of prefects, and the contrast between the groups, suggests the full extent of the dichotomy between the Centre Left and the Right during the Restoration. They recruited in two different societies.

This distinction is masked by the absence of massive prefectoral changes between September 1815 and July 1830. No ministry ever replaced as many as half the prefects in office, and as a result, even after the Decazes ministry's fall in 1820, the percentage of nobles among the prefects in place was still over sixty. It was the First Restoration movement that had radically changed the social background of the prefects. This new social framework, as much as the increased political importance of the prefects and the recurrent movements of personnel, differentiated the Corps during the Restoration from its imperial predecessor.

---

[1] Du Bouchage: see p. 65 note 1. AN doss. Kersaint, 165, defective; Révérend, *Armorial*, 1, 235. Jahan, 164(1); BB[1] 73 plaque 1; F7 5168. Saint-Aignan, 173(1); AAG, Emigrés, 519(3). Croze, 157(37); Alboize, *M. le baron de Croze, ancien préfet* (undated), pp. 2–3; R + C, 11, 227.

# PART II

## THE SUBORDINATE PERSONNEL

CHAPTER 5

# LOCAL RECRUITMENT AND DIFFICULTIES

Throughout the Restoration the majority of sub-prefects and secretaries-general were locally recruited. The explanation can be found in the nature of their functions. The sub-prefects were a link in the chain that ran from minister to mayor, their duty that of ensuring the execution of their superiors' orders: local knowledge and influence were clearly an advantage. The secretary-general's was an unimportant clerical post, and for this reason it would have been illogical to subject him to the added inconvenience of taking up such duties far from home and family. In the 1820s the post began to be used as a means of training young entrants to the administration, and a larger number of secretaries-general held office in departments other than their own, but such cases remained a minority.[1]

The typical sub-prefect or secretary-general was therefore a figure with strong local roots and considerable local influence. One result was a sort of semi-permanence among certain of the subordinate personnel: a career like that of Ruhlière, sub-prefect of Falaise from 1801 to 1830, or Contencin at Mamers from 1802 to 1830, or Dufays at Château-Salins from 1814 to 1848. This influence might go back to the Revolution, the post of sub-prefect or secretary-general being merely the culmination of a long career in local administration. Lom held various positions in the administration of the Basses-Pyrénées almost without interruption from 1795 to his death in 1831. Viville had been a member of the municipal administration of Metz before becoming *conseiller de préfecture* in the Moselle in 1800 and secretary-general in 1804, a post he held until 1830, greeting each change of régime with impartial enthusiasm.[2] His enemies might call him 'un caméléon politique' but the modesty of a sub-prefect's or

[1] See below, p. 134.
[2] AN doss. Ruhlière, 172(8, 21); Contencin, 157(31); Dufays, 148(31); Lom, 155(7), 166(33); Viville, 176(17).

secretary-general's functions, and their local background, made such versatility not merely profitable but probable. Even after a change of régime, the major sufferers were the prefects. The subordinate personnel did not emerge unscathed, but the percentage of survivors was far higher. Some 50 per cent of the prefects in office in April 1814 were still in the prefectoral administration in March 1815, whether in the same department or not: the figure for the sub-prefects and secretaries-general was 70 per cent.

The continuity in administration, exemplified in long careers in local administration, was thrown into relief during the Restoration by the government's occasional nomination of a son to his father's position. This had not been unknown under Napoleon—Coster, for example, took over the sub-prefecture of Vouziers from his father in 1805, Guillaume became secretary-general of the Haute-Marne in his father's place in 1813.[1] Yet it is surprising to find it being continued during the Restoration. The Bourbons and their ministers were frequently accused of wishing to return to the principles and practices of the Ancien Régime, and this type of nomination was, as the ministers were themselves aware, dangerously reminiscent of one of the admitted abuses of the Ancien Régime, 'survivance':[2] the inheritance of administrative functions. As a result of such nominations, certain *arrondissements* were administered for much of the Empire and Restoration by the members of one family. At Avranches Isaac-Julien Lehurey had been a member of the local administration before becoming sub-prefect in 1800, to be succeeded by his son in 1820. At Tournon the La Roque, father and son, administered the *arrondissement* from 1813 to 1830; in the Haute-Marne the Berthot administered Langres from 1800 to the July Revolution.[3] In certain cases the *arrondissement* seems almost to have become family property. The first sub-prefect of Melle was the former marquis de la Coste: he was succeeded in

[1] AN doss. C.-J. Coster, 157(33); F.-V. Guillaume, 161(23).
[2] See drafts of ministerial letter to the pr. Manche 11 Dec. 1820 (AN doss. H.-J. Lehurey, 166(22)).
[3] AN doss. Lehurey; La Roque, 158(10); Berthot, 156(19).

1802 by Jacques-Claude Jard-Panvilliers, who was replaced in 1814 by his nephew Charles-Marcellin, La Coste's son-in-law.[1] The most striking example is that of the Andurrain family at Mauléon. Jean Jules d'Andurrain became sub-prefect of Mauléon in 1821, but resigned five years later in favour of his son Clément. Replaced at the July Revolution, Clément d'Andurrain returned to Mauléon in 1840 and, with a brief interval after the February Revolution, administered the *arrondissement* for over twenty years. As the prefect of the Basses-Pyrénées remarked in 1858:

Parlant la langue du pays, que personne, si ce n'est l'indigène, ne pratique et ne comprend, il exerce une influence absolue dans l'arrond[issemen]t. Héritier de la popularité de son père...la localité n'a jamais connu d'autres administrateurs que son père et lui...la famille d'ailleurs occupe tous les emplois et il vit à Mauléon, comme un patriarche...[2]

Such prestige did not make things easier for a ministry which wished to replace a sub-prefect. A note for the minister in the early 1820s stated that although Fabry, sub-prefect of Gex, had frequently been denounced for his liberal opinions, his own and his family's influence in the *arrondissement* was such that nothing had been done.[3] Lebare, sub-prefect of Pontivy from 1806 to the Second Restoration, and from 1819 to 1830, had likewise been accused of Left-wing views in 1820, but the prefect advised the minister to leave Lebare in place, 'parce qu'il dispose de l'arrondissement à sa volonté'.[4] It appears to have been an accurate assessment. Lebare's dismissal in December 1830 was the signal for an enormous volume of protests. The man suspected of having provoked the dismissal had the windows of the house in which he was hiding smashed by a crowd of workers and National

[1] AN doss. Jard-Panvilliers, 164(3). For the relationship to La Coste, Révérend, *Armorial*, II, 342.

[2] Prefect's report of 1858 (AN doss. C. d'Andurrain, 155(4): for his father see also 158(2)).

[3] Undated note (*c.* 1821–2), AN doss. Louis Fabry, 160(1). Louis Fabry had succeeded his father as sub-prefect in Aug. 1815.

[4] Undated note for the minister quoting the prefect's letter of 10 Oct. 1820 (AN doss. Lebare, 166(17)).

Guardsmen, 'poussant les cris les plus féroces'.[1] The ministry capitulated. Lebare returned to Pontivy in January 1831.

As the case of the Andurrain indicates, local prestige was not only personal, the result of a long period in local administration: it was also a matter of family influence. The Subra-Saint-Martin at Pamiers, the Ruphy at Annecy (when Mont-Blanc was still a French department), the Gondinet family at Saint-Yrieix are examples of clans reminiscent of the Minoret and their relatives at Nemours in *Modeste Mignon*. According to the *commissaire extraordinaire* during the Hundred Days, while Ruphy was sub-prefect at Annecy, one of his brothers-in-law was mayor, another was *greffier* in the tribunal, and other relations worked in the various municipal, financial and charitable administrations of the *arrondissement*. Pierre Gondinet, mayor of Saint-Yrieix and administrator of the district and department, was made sub-prefect in 1800 and held the post until his son François-Marcellin took over in 1825. In October 1819 a note for the minister pointed out that while Pierre Gondinet was sub-prefect, his brother-in-law was president of the tribunal, one son was *adjoint* to the mayor, another a member of the *conseil d'arrondissement*, a third *greffier* to the *juge de paix*.[2] Such proliferation was exceptional, but a large number of sub-prefects and secretaries-general came from families that had held various offices in their *arrondissement* or department well before the Revolution: the Bovis at Lorgues, the Bourayne at Etampes, the Torcy at Vitry-le-François, the Bonnegens at Saint-Jean-d'Angély. Savary de l'Espinerays, secretary-general of the Vendée at the Second Restoration, came from a family that had provided a long series of magistrates and mayors in the *arrondissement* of Fontenay. Augier de Crémiers, a fellow naval officer and friend of Villèle, named sub-prefect of Montmorillon in 1823, had a similar background. His family had been members of the *haute bourgeoisie* of Montmorillon for centuries before the Revolution, and lieutenants of the *sénéchausée* for nearly one hundred years.

---

[1] Undated letter from the victim to Min.Int. (doss. Lebare).
[2] AN doss. Subra-S.-M. 173(21). Ruphy 172(21); Commissaire to Min.Int. 25 Apr. 1815 (F1a 554). Note for Min.Int. 11 Oct. 1819 (doss. Gondinet, 161(14)).

The sub-prefect was the latest of a chain of local administrators whose influence in their *arrondissement* had only been briefly shaken by the Revolution.[1] The principle of local recruitment remained constant throughout the Restoration. It lacked neither disadvantages nor critics. One of the current fears of Restoration ministers was that a sub-prefect or secretary-general might be influenced by personal motives, to the detriment of the administration: political sympathies that ran counter to the ministerial line, personal prejudices that would affect purely administrative action (which was no doubt the reason for the ministerial ban on a sub-prefect or secretary-general exercising another profession simultaneously). This was a danger implicit in the very principle of local recruitment. It was difficult for a local sub-prefect, however willing, to avoid some bias. Even should he try, his family's loyalties and connexions might make his efforts hopeless. The prefect of Corsica noted laconically in 1820 that Petriconi, sub-prefect of Bastia, suffered from the lively enmities aroused by the murders his own and his wife's family had allegedly perpetrated.[2] In a more general sense, it was difficult for a local sub-prefect to avoid taking a stand with one party or the other in departments where political or religious feeling ran high. This being precisely the case in the departments of the Midi after the Hundred Days, there was some justice in Villiers du Terrage's statement in 1820 that the Gard was the last department in which sub-prefects should be recruited locally.[3] A second difficulty was the position of a former émigré who had returned to find his estates sold, and who became a sub-prefect at the Restoration: the experience of Grimaldi at Forcalquier, Marcillac at Villefranche and Cellès at Prades.[4] It could hardly be expected of any

---

[1] AN doss. Bovis, 156(42); Chaix, VI, 300–2. Bourayne, 156(38): Chaix, VI, 128–9. Torcy, 158(21); *ADLN* (1896), pp. 422–3. Bonnegens, 156(33); Chaix, VI, 265–6. Savary, 173(11): Révérend, *Restauration*, VI, 220. Augier, 155(11); H. Beauchet-Filleau and C. de Chergé, *Dictionnaire...des familles de Poitou* (2nd ed., 3 vols. and 4 fascicules, 1891–1915), I, 172–7.

[2] Pr. Corsica to Min.Int. 31 July 1820 (AN doss. Constan, 157(31)).

[3] Villiers du Terrage to Min.Int. 19 June 1820 (AN doss. Saubert de Larcy, 166(11)).

[4] AN doss. Grimaldi, 161(20). Marcillac, 167(6). Cellès, 157(12), defective; AAG, CG 634.

sub-prefect in these circumstances, however disposed he might be to forget and forgive, that he should mix easily with the new proprietors. It was a difficulty the ministry recognized and tried to avoid when forewarned. Giraud des Echerolles, sub-prefect of Saint-Gaudens in 1818, wanted a post near his family in the Allier. A note for the minister in March 1821 advised against such a move: Giraud des Echerolles was believed to have debts in the department which might make him dependent on his creditors, to the detriment of the administration—while the family estates in the Allier had been sold during the Revolution.[1]

In departments where political divisions were deeply felt, locally recruited administrators were those placed in the most awkward position. Yet it was not always possible for a sub-prefect, even if a stranger to his *arrondissement*, to avoid being involved in a faction fight that might well antedate his appointment by years, and in which political beliefs were frequently secondary to local and personal rivalries. The clear-cut division of a provincial town into two mutually hostile parties which Balzac described in the Issoudun of *Les Illusions Perdues* can be found with certain differences in nuance in several *arrondissements* during the Restoration. It was true of Briançon, of Aix, of Bordeaux, where, just as at Issoudun, the mutual hostility of nobility and upper bourgeoisie was emphasized by their occupying different quarters of the city.[2] But the most detailed and striking example comes from Saint-Claude in the Jura. Jean-Baptiste Crestin became mayor of Saint-Claude in 1807, as his father and grandfather had been before him. At the Restoration he was made sub-prefect. In neither capacity did his administration pass uncriticized. The mayor of another commune in the *arrondissement* (Saint-Morez-en-Jura), and Restoration deputy, Jobez, denounced Crestin for his deliberate hostility to Saint-Morez. He alleged that Crestin deliberately caused the commune to pay more than its fair share of departmental expenses, that he

---

[1] Note for minister early March 1821 (AN doss. Bouteland, 156(40)).

[2] Briançon: pr. Hautes-Alpes to Min.Int. 8 Dec. 1815 (copy of letter in doss. Odru, departmental archives Hautes-Alpes, communicated by archivist). Aix: pr. B-du-Rhône to Min. Police 3 June 1818 (AN doss. Foresta, 160(10)). Bordeaux: Moulard, *Tournon, préfet de la Gironde*, p. 74.

produced trumped-up charges of sedition against its inhabitants
and even, under the Empire, attempted to divert a projected
main road from Saint-Morez to Saint-Claude. This attempt had
led him to spend 10,000–12,000 francs at Paris, 'y compris les
joujoux dont il avait fait cadeau à Madame Lætitia Bonaparte
avec de fort jolis petits vers'.[1] Saint-Morez had protested when
Crestin became sub-prefect in July 1814. The commune was no
doubt delighted when he was moved to Poligny in August 1815.
Unfortunately the measure never took effect, and Crestin remained at Saint-Claude. The quarrel now took on an added
dimension. During the Hundred Days a number of the inhabitants of Saint-Claude, under the Bonapartist mayor Colomb, had
shown considerable enthusiasm for the imperial cause, whereas
Crestin had resigned. He took his revenge at the Second Restoration. According to the deputies he used his position to satisfy
his personal animosities, justifying them by signalling his
*arrondissement* as being continually on the verge of revolt, and
in particular accusing all those he disliked of corresponding with
Joseph Bonaparte, then believed to be in Switzerland.[2] Jobez
had written of Crestin's 'aveugle fureur...persécutions achar-
nées...haine invétérée...contre une partie de l'arrondissement...'[3] [Saint-Morez]. Even the more temperate prose of a
ministerial note described Crestin as 'homme haineux, passionné,
qui tourmentait véritablement ses administrés'.[4] In February
1817 he was replaced, but by this time the *arrondissement* was
divided into two camps. On the one hand was the Crestin family,
still powerful, particularly as Crestin's father was president of
the local tribunal, on the other those who had followed Colomb
during the Hundred Days. It was into this situation that the
ministry pitchforked a young sub-prefect of twenty-seven,
Deslandes. A former auditor and imperial sub-prefect, Deslandes
tended toward the Colomb faction, but in the circumstances it
was perhaps hardly generous of the ministry to remark a year

[1] Jobez to Min.Int. 28 June 1816 (AN doss. J.-B. Crestin, 157(36)).
[2] Deps. of Jura to Min.Int. 3 Feb. 1817 (AN doss. Deslandes, 158(19)).
[3] Jobez to Min.Int. (*loc. cit.*).
[4] 23 July 1818, note for Min.Int. summarizing developments at Saint-Claude
since 1815 (doss. Deslandes).

later that he was influenced by 'l'esprit de coterie'. An initial skirmish led to a ministerial condemnation of both the sub-prefect and his opponent. This was followed by a more serious affair. Deslandes removed the mayor of Molinges, a creature of Crestin's, on the ground of financial dishonesty. The Crestin family, and their ally the *procureur du Roi*, protested. The mayor had signed a document acknowledging his misconduct, but he later told the prefect that it was Deslandes' secretary who had put the pressure on him to do so. The affair went before the courts, but, to the great scandal of the ministry, the *procureur du Roi* directed the accusation not against the mayor but the sub-prefect. Deslandes complained: the Garde des Sceaux dismissed the *procureur*, but at the prefect's request Deslandes was trans-ferred to another post.

The labyrinthine politics of Saint-Claude illustrate, exactly enough, the characteristics of the Restoration administration at a local level. Unlike the prefects, the subordinate personnel found themselves in contact with the reality of local politics, pro-portionally the more venomous because personal. Local diffi-culties might not be caused solely by local recruitment, they might arise for reasons initially unconnected with the administra-tion—yet in the microcosm of an *arrondissement* they were both powerful and pervasive.

CHAPTER 6

# THE CHOICE OF SUBORDINATE PERSONNEL

The same motives governed the choice of subordinate personnel as governed that of prefects. The type of influence exerted was similar in essence, but differed in extent. Political reliability still being the main criterion, a minister naturally named his own and his colleagues' protégés. Bardonnenche became a sub-prefect when his cousin La Tour-Maubourg was Minister of War, Jean-Jacques Guizot when his brother was Director-General of Departmental Administration under Decazes, Blouquier de Trélan when his patron Bourmont joined the Polignac Cabinet. Frayssinous, Grand Master of the University and Villèle's Minister of Ecclesiastical Affairs, had a brother and a cousin in the Corps during the Restoration, Chateaubriand had three relatives, and, as might be expected, Decazes had his squadron. Louis Brault had been his schoolfellow, Geffroy de Villeblanche was a personal friend, Babut, Rosily and Laparel de Laboissière were former subordinates in the Ministry of Police.[1]

But because the sub-prefects and secretaries-general were persons of minor importance, patronage was not limited to political figures of the first rank. Individual proprietors, prefects, deputies and peers were also represented. Nor does this exhaust the list. Arros' wife came from a Prussian family. Her husband received a sub-prefecture in 1814 on the recommendation of the king of Prussia. The Russian ambassador, Pozzo di Borgo, recommended Viel for an administrative post at the Second Restoration. La Poix de Fréminville was named sub-prefect in

---

[1] AN doss. Bardonnenche, 156(5). Guizot, 161(25). Blouquier, 156(27): his father had returned from emigration to serve under Bourmont in the Vendée (AAG, CG 350). Frayssinous' brother and cousin, 160(13). For Chateaubriand's relatives: AN doss. Blossac, 156(27), 166(34); Québriac, 171; Ravenel de Boistilleiul, 172(3). Brault, 156(43). G. de Villeblanche, 161(7), 176(12). Babut, 156(1), defective; F7 9780, 9781. Rosily, 172(17). Laparel de Laboissière, 158(6), 166(1), 170(2); F7 9780.

1814 thanks to the Serent family, Perrève was a protégé of Marmont's and Mac-Nab a friend of Macdonald's. Adam became sub-prefect in 1821 on Benoist's recommendation—which did not prevent his dismissal a year later. Kentzinger, secretary-general of the Haute-Loire in 1823, was the nephew of an aide-de-camp to the comte d'Artois: Becquey, sub-prefect two years later, the nephew of an Ultra deputy and former Director-General of the *Ponts-et-Chaussées*. For certain candidates there are lists of sponsors that read like a roll-call of their respective political parties. The young Valsuzenay was recommended for a post under the Martignac ministry by Casimir Périer, Gaetan de la Rochefoucauld, Portal and Rambuteau: a representative gathering of the Centre and Centre Left. The opposite political wing recommended Clock for a sub-prefecture in September 1829: the duc de Polignac, La Bourdonnaye, Curzay and Bouthillier, as well as the duchesse d'Angoulême and the prince de Condé.[1]

A patron's function was not limited to securing his protégé a post. In the conditions of the Restoration prefectoral administration, tenure was precarious and survival might well depend on the support of a vigorous and influential patron. La Roche-Tolay, sub-prefect of Barbezieux from August 1815, was dismissed by Siméon in September 1820. This was the signal for a series of protests from his relative Lally-Tollendal, demanding that the measure be rescinded and justice done to his protégé. The minister had evidently asked the prefects under whom La Roche-Tolay had served for their opinion of him. Reading their letters, it becomes clear that it was precisely justice that had been done when La Roche-Tolay was dismissed. With an impressive unanimity Vaulchier, Alban de Villeneuve-Bargemon, Creuzé de Lesser and Bluget de Valdenuit testified to his mediocre intelligence and abilities. 'Je ne crois pas qu'il soit méchant,' Vaulchier wrote, 'c'est seulement un esprit fort étroit, un pauvre esprit, un

[1] Arros: pr. Moselle to Min.Int. 26 Apr. 1815 (AN doss. Andlau, 158(2)). Viel, 176(11). La Poix de Fréminville: Napoleonic Commissaire in the 6th Military Division to Min.Int. 25 Apr. 1815 (doss. 160(13)). Perrève, 170(10)—he had been in Marmont's Company of the Gardes-du-Corps (AAG, X^AD 26). Mac-Nab, 167(1). Adam, 155(1). Kentzinger, 165. Becquey, 156(12). Valsuzenay, 176(4). Clock, 157(26).

homme fort inconsidéré.'[1] It is a testimony to Lally-Tollendal's
influence that, with so little else to recommend him, La Roche-
Tolay should, nevertheless, have lasted five years in the administration. A more effective testimony was the minister's decision
not to dismiss La Roche-Tolay, but to transfer him. Siméon
offered him the sub-prefecture of Nérac, in the Lot-et-Garonne.
With admirable sang-froid, La Roche-Tolay refused: it was too
far from the Charente where he lived.[2] Meanwhile Lally-Tollendal suggested that the new sub-prefect of Barbezieux should be
transferred elsewhere or that the minister should find another
sub-prefecture in the Charente for La Roche-Tolay. If he was to
be sent to Nérac, then the minister should provide a financial
indemnity. 'Voilà bien des détails, Monsieur le Comte. Ils ne sont
pas tous d'une nature officielle. Mais Saint Louis les eut reçus
dans le bois de Vincennes, Louis XVIII les recevrait dans le
cabinet des Tuileries.'[3] This appears to be very much what
happened, since on 30 September La Roche-Tolay was made
sub-prefect of Châteaulin (Finistère). He celebrated his victory
by issuing a printed pamphlet of farewell to his former *arrondissement*, which was entirely devoted to a eulogy of his administration and was therefore an implicit censure of the ministry which had transferred him. It did not pass unremarked, but
neither did it prevent La Roche-Tolay from obtaining his
transfer to the post of secretary-general of the Charente-Inférieure the next year. Although he was later to claim that he
deliberately leaked ministerial secrets to the Liberal opposition,
La Roche-Tolay appears to have behaved with more discretion
during the first years at his new post. In 1828, however, he was
called as juror in the trial of a woman who had murdered her
employer, a *curé*. According to the Garde des Sceaux, La Roche-
Tolay not only asked unsuitable questions, but made observa-
tions equally unsuitable, disregarding the warnings he was given
by the President of the Court: 'Un nombreux auditoire a été
témoin d'une conduite aussi extraordinaire.'[4] The Minister of the

[1] Vaulchier to Min.Int. 29 June 1820 (AN doss. La Roche-Tolay, 166(12)).
[2] Siméon to Lally-Tollendal 21 Sept. 1820.
[3] Lally-Tollendal to Siméon 21 Sept. 1820.
[4] Garde des Sceaux to Min.Int. 23 May 1828.

Interior agreed that La Roche-Tolay should be punished, and informed the Garde des Sceaux that he would have been, had his family not been known for its distinguished services, and had he not been protected by men of equal distinction—notably Lally-Tollendal.[1] As a result the affair was hushed up, and La Roche-Tolay continued in place until September 1830.

La Roche-Tolay's career was a proof of his patron's influence. It was also a comment on a system in which such protection could enable an administrator unanimously agreed to be incapable, and later proved to be undisciplined, to spend fifteen years in the Corps. An extreme example, most sub-prefects or secretaries-general being better qualified, or at least more discreet, than La Roche-Tolay. Yet it was only the memory of his grandfather's services as intendant, along with the duc d'Avaray's patronage, that kept Mégret d'Etigny in the Corps, and a similar type of protection first secured Jules Ferrand and Du Plessis de Grenédan sub-prefectures, and then smoothed their way in situations in which sub-prefects lacking their connexions could not have been expected to survive.[2] Ferrand's quarrel with the mayor of his *arrondissement* led the prefect to demand that he should be replaced. The note for the minister recapitulating the affair bears the gloss: 'Au lieu de changer M. Ferrand, ce qui est bien difficile, il faut écrire à M. le comte Ferrand...'[3] Ferrand remained. Du Plessis de Grenédan, son of one Ultra deputy and nephew of another, was made sub-prefect in 1823. He was on the worst of terms with the prefect of his department, but the best with Corbière, Villèle's Minister of the Interior. In 1825-6 the prefect continually requested that Du Plessis de Grenédan be transferred. He remained until 1830.

The local background of the subordinate personnel made their choice a matter of concern to the main landowners and to the deputies of their department, as to the prefects whom they were to serve. Perhaps the landowners should include the king, since there is some evidence to suggest that he made the final choice

[1] Min.Int. to Garde des Sceaux 6 June 1828.
[2] AN doss. Mégret d'Etigny, 159(3), 167(16); Ferrand, 160(5); Du Plessis de Grenédan, 158(38).      [3] Note for min. 16 Dec. 1815 (doss. Ferrand).

for posts in the neighbourhood of Paris.[1] They included great noble families like the La Rochefoucauld or Louvois in Champagne, but also members of families whose influence, if more recent, was at least as powerful. This was the case with baron Louis and Gouvion-Saint-Cyr in the Meurthe. Villot de la Tour, sub-prefect of Toul from 1814 to 1816 and again in 1819, was Louis' brother-in-law. On his death in 1820 he was replaced by Husson de Prailly, 'parent, ami, créature de l'abbé Louis', as a hostile prefect termed him, adding despondently that almost all the administrative posts in the *arrondissement* were held by relatives of Louis and Gouvion-Saint-Cyr.[2] Recommended by both, Husson de Prailly continued to administer the *arrondissement* until his not altogether voluntary resignation in 1826. The interrelated Barrère, Dembarrère and Soult families had a similar influence in the Hautes-Pyrénées. As early as 1811 the prefect of the Hautes-Pyrénées had warned the minister that the Barrère–Dembarrère family aimed at occupying all the administrative and judicial posts in the area. The warning was reiterated by ex-senator Péré in August 1815. He was not entirely disinterested: although laying stress on his spirit of Christian forgivingness, Péré held Barrère responsible both for his own imprisonment in 1793 and for his son's removal from the sub-prefecture of Argelès at the Second Restoration. In November 1815 the prefect (a more credible witness) wrote to the Minister of the Interior, as he had previously written to the Minister of War, complaining that comte Dembarrère had enough influence to procure almost all the government posts for his protégés. These included his son-in-law Dauzat, Péré's successor. Dauzat, detested by the major part of his *arrondissement* and derided by the rest, was himself dismissed in January 1816. His father-in-law added a sardonic postscript. Dauzat's dismissal was almost immediately followed by his ennoblement.[3]

[1] See AN doss. C.-A. Walckenaer, 177(1); and 166(1), doss. Laparel de Laboissière for his wife's letter of 16 July 1827 to Min.Int.

[2] Pr. Meurthe to Min.Int. 25 Apr. 1825 (AN doss. Husson de Prailly, 170(24)). V. de la Tour, 176(15).

[3] 'Un rapport du préfet Chazal au ministre de l'Intérieur au sujet de la famille Barrère–Dambarrère (23 Feb. 1811)', *Bulletin de la Société académique des*

The influence of those deputies who rose to ministerial rank, or to a post as director, is self-evident. That of their obscurer colleagues, who formed the mass of any ministerial majority, is more interesting. These deputies often had a background of local office of some kind, whether administrative or judicial, and with their local interests it was natural that the ministry should have consulted them on the choice of administrative personnel in their department. It was equally natural that the deputies should have exerted themselves on behalf of their relatives and protégés. The ministry could regard patronage so bestowed as both retainer and reward, and it is typical of Villèle, with his conception of his role as party manager, that the individual influence of the deputies in matters of patronage should have been greatest during his ministry. Yet such individual favours characterized the period 1815–30 as a whole. Bourdeau, sub-prefect of Roche-chouart in 1819, was the son of a Centre-Left deputy and the son-in-law of another, Verneilh-Puyraseau. Godefroy, sub-prefect in 1822, was the nephew of Potteau d'Hancardie, deputy of the Nord in the *Chambre Introuvable* and from 1818 to 1830. A former member of the local administration of the Dordogne and of the Corps Législatif, Chilhaud de la Rigaudie, rallied to the Bourbons and was elected to the *Chambre Introuvable* in 1815. Président de Chambre in the Royal Court of Bordeaux the next year, he was deputy of the Dordogne during 1816–17 and 1820–7. One of his friends, Denoix-Campsegret, was made secretary-general of the Dordogne in 1820, another (Lavès) succeeded him at Chilhaud de la Rigaudie's request in 1827.[1]

This individual patronage was distinct from the collective denunciations or recommendations made by the deputation of a department as a whole, which characterized the early years of the

*Hautes-Pyrénées* (1956–7), pp. 38–40; Péré to Min.Int. 6 Aug. 1815 (AN, FıbI 688). Pr. Hautes-Pyrénées to Min. War 13 Sept. 1815 (FıbII H-P (5)). Pr. Hautes-Pyrénées to Min.Int. 4 Nov. 1815 (doss. Bégon de la Rouzière, 172(20)). Dauzat, 155(12), 158(5).
[1] AN doss. Bourdeau, 156(39); for his father, Garde des Sceaux under Martignac, R+C, I, 433–4; for Verneilh-Puyraseau, R+C, v, 504. Godefroy, 161(13); for Potteau d'Hancardie, R+C, v, 27. Chilhaud de la Rigaudie: R+C, II, 99; AN doss. Denoix-Campsegret, 157(4). Lavès, 166(17).

Second Restoration, and in particular the Vaublanc ministry. Vaublanc has been accused of fearing the deputies and being over-complaisant toward them.[1] His period in office coincided with the election of the *Chambre Introuvable* in September 1815, with whose Ultra majority he sympathized, being no less eager than the deputies to purge the prefectoral corps of disaffected or disloyal administrators. It was inevitable, therefore, that he should have taken the deputies' views on the administrative personnel seriously and, given the political temper of the time, inevitable that these should rather have emphasized denunciation than recommendation. As in all proscriptions, there were examples of dubious combinations and of mutual horse-trading. The deputies' motives were not uniformly disinterested, whether from prejudice against an individual administrator in place, or the prospect of such a place for themselves or their protégés. As the duc de la Rochefoucauld remarked to the Peers in his long indictment of the excesses which accompanied the purge: 'en dénonçant, je montre du zèle; le zèle donne droit à des emplois; il ne reste qu'à faire vaquer une place, et je l'aurai moi-même. Voilà la logique des temps où toutes les passions sont déchaînées.'[2] In late 1815 the deputies of Lot denounced the secretary-general and one of the sub-prefects, demanding their dismissal. Among the candidates for the former post were two members of the deputation; one of them, Helyot, obtained it. Faydel, who now joined with his fellow deputies in denouncing the sub-prefect of Figeac (Campagne), had previously recommended him. When the minister asked the prefect of Lot for some explanation of this volte-face, the latter replied that the deputies arranged to act collectively, and that as a result their petitions merely showed 'l'accord qu'ils se sont promis pour soutenir respectivement leurs prétentions. "Passez-moi la rhubarbe, je te passerai le séné".'[3]

In such circumstances there was necessarily some tension between prefect and deputies. A prefect, particularly with a

---

[1] Lezay-Marnésia, *Mes Souvenirs*, p. 140.
[2] Sitting of 30 Dec. 1815 (AP, 2nd ser., xv, 635).
[3] Pr. Lot to Min.Int. 30 Dec. 1815 (AN doss. Helyot, 162(4)).

background of Napoleonic service, might fear for his own place, since the deputies' denunciatory ardour was not limited to the subordinate personnel alone. He might not share the political principles of the Ultra majority in the Chamber. And even should the prefect share these principles, he might regret their application to the administration. There were prefects like Alban de Villeneuve-Bargemon who deplored the flood of denunciations, the consequent administrative instability, as well as those who disagreed with the deputies' choice for vacant posts.[1] The prefects' concern was both for their administration and for their own prestige. They were the official representatives of the government in their department, and there were inevitably occasions when the deputies' interference aroused their professional jealousy, the more so because such interference was without precedent in the history of the Corps.

An example of the various pressures at work on the nomination of the subordinate personnel during this period, and in particular of the tension between prefect and deputies, can be found in the Ariège at the Second Restoration. The situation was the more piquant because Chassepot de Chapelaine, named prefect in July 1815, had administered the department under the Empire but had been dismissed in 1814. His return was unpopular, not least with the provisional prefect named by the duc d'Angoulême at the end of the Hundred Days, Fornier de Savignac. The latter handed over the administration to Chapelaine in August, and was almost immediately elected as deputy for the Ariège. Throughout the period of Vaublanc's ministry Chapelaine was being denounced himself (notably by the duc d'Angoulême), and his position was correspondingly insecure.[2] At the Second Restoration the secretary-general of the Ariège, and two of the sub-prefects, had been provisionally replaced by the duc d'Angoulême. The third sub-prefect, Bascle de Lagrèze, had been maintained in office, since he alone had not served during the Hundred Days. Chapelaine wanted the two provisional sub-

---

[1] Alban de Villeneuve-Bargemon to Min.Int. 19 Dec. 1815 (AN doss. Lesseps, 166(31)).

[2] See Min. War to Min. Int. 26 Dec. 1815 (AN doss. Chassepot de Chapelaine, 157(19)).

prefects nominated by Angoulême confirmed, and Bascle de Lagrèze transferred. He also submitted a list of three candidates for the post of secretary-general, since he did not wish the provisional secretary-general, Abat, to be confirmed. Abat's brother was a notary who had married Fornier de Savignac's sister: Chapelaine alleged that Abat's business interests, and those of his family, would prejudice his administration. The minister sent these comments to the deputies. Their reply handled the prefect somewhat harshly. Abat, they stated, was excellent, as were the other provisional administrators. They could not understand why the prefect wanted Bascle de Lagrèze transferred, and were surprised that, supposing that some adequate motive for this transfer existed, Chapelaine had not suggested as his successor the man whom Angoulême had briefly made sub-prefect of the *arrondissement chef-lieu*. Turning to the prefect's candidates, they dismissed one as a stranger to the department, another as a Bonapartist, and the third (Green de Saint-Marsault) as 'tête exaltée, volcanisée, peu propre ou point du tout à une place administrative'. Chapelaine replied by emphasizing his desire to see Bascle de Lagrèze transferred, and asking for a decision on the other administrators: the correspondence had now lasted over two months. The ordinance of 13 November finished the matter and left honours more or less even. The two pro-visional sub-prefects were confirmed, Bascle de Lagrèze dismissed but Abat named secretary-general.[1]

The prefects' own role in the nomination of subordinate personnel was defined by Pasquier's important circular of 6 September 1815. Pasquier explained that the critical situation in July had not permitted him to consult the prefects when naming sub-prefects and secretaries-general, nor to ask them for their own candidates. He had been forced to rely on such infor-mation as he could himself acquire. But in the event of further vacancies he now intended to send the prefect concerned the names of those who had asked the minister directly for a post, so

---

[1] AN doss. Subra-Saint-Martin, 173(24), particularly for Chapelaine's letters of 1 Sept., 4 Sept., 7 Oct., 3 Nov., 10 Nov. 1815, and the deputies' letter of 26 Oct. 1815. Abat, 155(1), defective, elements in doss. Sapia, 173(8). Bascle de Lagrèze, 156(8).

that the prefect could give his comments. He was then to draw up a list of at least three candidates for each place. In all but the most exceptional cases, the minister would make it his duty to pick one of the three names: 'Je ne perdrai pas de vue qu'étant en quelque sorte responsable, vis à vis du Gouvernement, du succès de votre administration, il convient de vous laisser de l'influence sur le choix de vos collaborateurs.'[1]

All this was eminently reasonable, but the Talleyrand–Pasquier ministry fell some three weeks later. Under future ministers the procedure remained the same, but the promised deference to the prefects' opinion was not always evident. Nor was the prefect always consulted before one of his subordinates was replaced. In 1819, for instance, Decazes dismissed Anterroches, Chantreau and Lastic de Saint-Jal without taking their prefects' advice: which, at least in the latter case, would have been hostile to the measure.[2] A textbook example of correct procedure occurred in the nominations to places in the department of the Eure, in November 1815. The prefect, Maurice de Gasville, wanted two sub-prefects and the secretary-general replaced. He submitted three candidates for each post, and in each case the minister took Gasville's first choice: including his brother. Once again, the minister named the first two candidates suggested by Tocqueville for the sub-prefectures of Senlis and Clermont (Oise) in October 1815.[3] The prefect was not always as fortunate. When Lascours was prefect of the Gers he protested against Gounon's nomination as sub-prefect of Mirande (October 1817), and asked if Gavoty could not be given the post instead. The minister would have none of it. To his praise of Gounon he added a request that the prefect should tell Gavoty, if the latter renewed his efforts, 'qu'elles sont au moins inutiles'.[4] In 1822 the place of secretary-general of the Basses-Pyrénées fell vacant, and the prefect strongly recommended his own candidate, Blanc,

[1] *Recueil des lettres*, xv, 184–6.
[2] AN doss. Anterroches, 155(6). Chantreau, 157(16). Saint-Jal, 166(14), particularly pr. Aveyron to Min.Int. 9 March 1819.
[3] Eure: note for Min.Int. (undated but Nov. 1815) (AN, F1bII Eure (6)). Oise: note for Min.Int. 28 Oct. 1815 (AN doss. Ducancel, 158(30)).
[4] Min.Int. to Lascours 8 Oct. 1817 (AN doss. Gavoty, 161(7)).

for the post. A note for the minister added another three candidates, recommending in particular the sub-prefect of Bayonne,
Poublan-Serres. The latter's friends, whose testimony might
appear in the circumstances to have been something less than
impartial, had hinted that Blanc would be unsuitable, his opinions
not being sufficiently royalist for the department. Poublan-Serres
was named. The prefect of the Vienne was equally unsuccessful
in 1828. The secretary-general had died, and the prefect proposed
his own candidate for the post, insisting on his protégé's merits
and on the lack of other suitable candidates. The ministry replied
by drawing up a list of twelve candidates, one of whom became
secretary-general.[1]

Disagreement between minister and prefect over individual
candidates was bound to occur: as was disagreement between
the minister and the candidates' sponsors. Yet throughout the
Restoration a sort of balance was maintained between administrative necessity, as seen by the prefect, and the working of the
patronage machinery through the Ministry of the Interior. The
only threat to this balance had been the collective demands, and
particularly denunciations, made by the deputies under Vaublanc.
They were the product of one specific situation. The great majority of deputies in 1815 had been determined to purge an administration which they believed to have accepted, even encouraged,
the Hundred Days. It was not until 1830 that a similar situation
recurred. Albert de Lezay-Marnésia, one of the few prefects in
office after the Revolution of July who had also administered a
department at the Second Restoration, noted the increased
interference of the deputies in administrative affairs, and made
the comparison with 1815, when 'il fallait opter entre une servile
obéissance ou une destitution inévitable'.[2] His conclusion was
as interesting as his comparison: the situation after 1830 was even
worse.

[1] Basses-Pyrénées: pr. of Basses-Pyrénées to Min.Int. 12 Jan. 1822, note for
min. 6 March 1822, both in AN doss. Poublan-Serres, 170(22). Vienne: note
for Min.Int. (undated but early Feb. 1828) (AN doss. Traversay, 174(12)).
[2] Letter to Min.Int. 16 Apr. 1831 (AN doss. 166(32)).

7-2

# CHAPTER 7

# THE MOVEMENT OF
# SUBORDINATE PERSONNEL, 1814–16

## THE FIRST RESTORATION

The change of régime in 1814 made far less impact on the sub-ordinate personnel than on the prefects. Forty per cent of the prefects in office at the end of March 1814 still held the same post a year later, at the start of the Hundred Days. The equivalent figure was 60 per cent for the sub-prefects, nearly 75 per cent for the secretaries-general. A hundred and thirteen sub-prefects and 23 secretaries-general were replaced. These figures include those who died in office, those who were promoted, and those who left the Corps. Noailles resigned in the hope of finding a place on the duc d'Angoulême's staff, Humbert de la Tour du Pin joined the Maison du Roi, La Bourdonnaye de Blossac, Gasville and Chaudruc de Crazannes the Council of State.[1]

Those dismissed form two separate groups. There were the sub-prefects and secretaries-general named under the Consulate, and those who had joined the Corps in the late Empire (particularly 1811). Among the latter the typical figure was an auditor like François Charrier or Cardon de Montigny.[2] They could be reproached their administrative inexperience and their Bonapartist fervour. The group named under the Consulate was far larger. Nearly 45 per cent of the sub-prefects dismissed and 65 per cent of the secretaries-general had been in office since 1800. The majority had made their mark in the Revolution: certain, like Le Gorrec or Ligeret de Chazey, had even retained

---

[1] AN doss. Noailles, 158(15), 168(3). LTDP, 166(15); Marquise de la Tour du Pin, *Journal d'une femme de 50 ans 1778–1815* (Paris, 1951), intro. pp. xvii–xx. La Bourdonnaye de Blossac, 166(1), defective; AF IV 1335. Gasville, 161(5, 15). Crazannes, 157(20, 36).

[2] AN doss. Charrier, 157(8). No doss. Cardon de Montigny; elements in du Blaisel, 158(28), F1bII Pas-de-Calais (6), AF IV 1334–5.

their revolutionary ardour while serving the Empire. Some had achieved a certain notoriety. Drouet, sub-prefect of Sainte-Menehould from 1800 to 1814, was the postmaster who had been partially responsible for the failure of the flight to Varennes. His dismissal was as inevitable as that of Dumont, a fellow regicide, or Prévost de la Vauzelle.[1] La Vauzelle, secretary-general of the Charente since 1800, was a *ci-devant* marquis who had thrown himself heart and soul into the Revolution: as he had boasted then, '...il prouverait encore qu'il a constamment joui de l'honorable haine des partisans des émigrés, des aristocrates, de prêtres réfractaires et de tous les ennemis de la Révolution...'[2] It was hardly a recommendation in 1814.

Nor could former priests who had left the Church during the Revolution and subsequently married, like Bottin or Bourdon, hope to be maintained in the administration under the new régime. Accusations of immorality coincide with those of Revolutionary or Bonapartist ardour. The commissioner in the 20th Military Division denounced Desprez, sub-prefect of Barbezieux, as 'homme de la révolution, peu considéré, souvent pris de vin'. In the 2nd Military Division the commissioner wanted the sub-prefect of Verdun (Lefebvre) replaced: 'philosophe outré, homme immoral, partisan très prononcé de l'ancien gouvernement, a passé sa vie au billard dans les cafés et peut d'autant plus d'inconvéniences qu'il a beaucoup d'esprit'.[3]

In their place the Bourbons named 145 sub-prefects and 23 secretaries-general.[4] Far fewer had any previous experience in the Corps itself than had been the case among the prefects, although eighteen had previously served in the departments outside France. The proportion of newly nominated administrators

[1] AN doss. Le Gorrec, 161(14), 166(22). Ligeret de Chazey, 166(33). Drouet, 158(27); R+C, II, 411–12. Dumont, 158(36); R+C, II, 481–2. La Vauzelle, 166(17), 170(25).
[2] Undated petition for his removal from the list of émigrés (AN, F7 4991).
[3] AN doss. Bottin, 156(36). Bourdon, 156(39). Desprez: Commissaire Extraordinaire to Min.Int. 25 May 1814 (F7 7030). Lefebvre: Commissaire Extraordinaire to Min.Int. 25 May 1814 (F7 7027).
[4] Certain *arrondissments* had no official titular in March 1814: others had more than one titular during the First Restoration. Hence more sub-prefects were nominated than were replaced.

who had served the Empire in some sense, at more than a local level, was approximately the same as among the prefects. Their previous experience differed widely. Fourment and Forget had been auditors and then intendants of occupied territories. Billiard came from the Ministry of the Interior: Lamorre, Ferrand and Villeron from various posts in the financial administration, Moreau de la Rochette from the police, Huot de Neuvier from the Customs, Giraud des Echerolles from the army, Saint-Martin-des-Islets from the imperial household.[1]

The First Restoration nominations have certain peculiarities. Loyalty to the ministry was the natural prerequisite for a candidate for the administration throughout the Restoration. In 1814 the question was rather that of loyalty to the dynasty: and where was the government to find a guarantee of such loyalty? In a candidate's connexions, perhaps, but also in his own past services to the Monarchy (even if he had subsequently rallied to the Empire), or in those of his family. Boulancy had served in the prefectoral administration since 1808: Prudhomme had administered *arrondissements* in the Saar and in Belgium: Kerespertz had worked in the financial administration of the Côtes-du-Nord: Bonald had been a member of the *Ponts-et-Chaussées*: but all were former émigrés. Digoine had been employed in the *Contributions Directes* under the Empire, but could point to his father, aide-de-camp to the comte d'Artois in emigration. La Corbière, designed for the sub-prefecture of Domfront, could rely on the services of a father who had fought in the Seven Years' War, in America, and under Condé in emigration, to supplement his own otherwise unremarkable qualifications as a member of the financial administration of the imperial army.[2] The proportion of émigrés among the newly nominated sub-prefects and secretaries-general who had not served the Empire was even

---

[1] AN doss. Fourment, 160(10). Forget, 158(7), 160(11). Billiard, 156(24). Lamorre, 166(8), 167(31). Ferrand, 160(5). Villeron, 176(14). La Rochette, 167(30). Huot, 162(8). Des Echerolles, 158(18), 159(1); AAG, CG 1610. Saint-Martin, 173(5).

[2] AN doss. Boulancy, 156(37, 50). Prudhomme, 170(26). Kerespertz, 165. Bonald, 156(30). Digoine, 158(23); for his father, Chaix, XIV, 81. La Corbière, 157(32), 166(2); for his father, AAG, CG 2005. See below, Appendix v.

higher, just over 40 per cent. Recompense for past sacrifices went hand in hand with reliance on past services. Du Blaisel had emigrated in 1792, taking his wife and children with him to England. He returned only in 1814. Quélen and Béville emigrated in 1791, campaigned until 1800, and did not serve the Empire after their return. Castelpers had fought in Spanish service, Pons with the Rohan hussars in Austrian service, until wounded and made prisoner in 1798. Antoine-Joseph Roy, secretary-general of the Charente in July 1814, had been an *avocat* at Angoulême before the Revolution. Deputy to the States General, he opposed all measures of reform, and emigrated in 1791. When he returned in 1801 he had lost the entirety of his own and his wife's fortune.[1]

The governing criteria being past services and sacrifices, there were inevitably some cases where these qualities seem to have stood alone, unalloyed by administrative qualifications. Busquet had spent his active life in the army, which he joined at the start of the Seven Years' War. Fifty-seven years later he made his début in the prefectoral administration as sub-prefect of Sens. It is hard to believe that at the age of eighty he could have displayed the activity demanded of a sub-prefect. Saporta's was a similar case. He had served as an infantry officer from 1758 to 1769, when he left the army. Chamberlain to the Prince Palatine (duc de Deux-Ponts) and then mayor of Apt, he emigrated in 1792. His poor sight prevented his campaigning. As Senator Serrurier described him when petitioning for his elimination from the list of émigrés in 1801, he was an old man, and nearly blind. Thirteen years later, undeterred by his age (seventy-one) and incipient blindness, Saporta became sub-prefect of Apt.[2]

The change of régime made no great difference from the departments' point of view. Nor did it radically alter the social background of the subordinate personnel. The percentage of nobles among the prefects had almost doubled between March 1814 and the Hundred Days. Among the sub-prefects and

---

[1] AN doss. du Blaisel, 158(28). Quélen, 177. Béville, 156(22). Castelpers, 157(10), defective; O³ 2571. Pons, 158(16), 170(19). Roy, 172(13, 20); O³* 772; R+C, v, 217–18.

[2] AN doss. Busquet, 156(50), 158(6, 30); AAG, YB 636. Saporta, 173(8); F⁷ 5766; AAG, YB 181.

secretaries-general the rise was far less marked, from some 22 to just under 30 per cent for the subordinate personnel as a whole. This was due in part to the relatively small number of new sub-prefects and secretaries-general, which ensured that there would be no radical change in the social background of the subordinate personnel. Yet this should not obscure the fact that the proportion of nobles among those who were newly nominated was considerably lower than that among the prefects: 40 as opposed to nearly 90 per cent. Both socially, and in terms of administrative continuity, the First Restoration saw a prefectoral movement that affected, in the main, the upper echelons of the administration.

## THE HUNDRED DAYS

The stability of the administration was rudely shattered by the return of the emperor and the kaleidoscopic changes of personnel that followed. In sixty-six of the eighty-seven departments half or more of the sub-prefects were changed during the Hundred Days, and in twenty of these all were changed. Some sixty of the sub-prefects in office at the end of the First Restoration, and some forty of the secretaries-general, resigned or were replaced. Between 15 March and 22 June, the *arrondissements* of Saint-Quentin, Bergerac, Saint-Pol, Abbeville, and Avallon had four titulars: that of Avesnes had five. The government had wanted a purge of the subordinate personnel. As Carnot wrote in a circular to the prefects:

Plusieurs individus qui, en d'autres circonstances, pourraient continuer leur fonctions, ne conviennent pas maintenant, soit pour avoir été compromis depuis un an, soit à raison de leur faiblesse, soit par la nature de leurs relations sociales...[1]

Commissioners were sent into the departments to examine the conduct of the sub-prefects, mayors and municipal officers, and if necessary dismiss them.[2] Change was therefore inevitable. It became increasingly chaotic. At the same time as the com-

---

[1] Circular of 22 Apr. 1815, AN, F1a 31.
[2] Decrees of 20–22 Apr., AN, AF IV 859 (11, 12).

missioners were empowered to appoint provisional sub-prefects, the ministry continued to nominate them by decree, as it nominated the secretaries-general. Liaison was imperfect. Gengoult-Knÿls, secretary-general of the Allier, was transferred to the sub-prefecture of Saint-Pol by a decree of 25 April. On 6 May the commissioner in the 6th Military Division made him sub-prefect of Montfort. In the Eure-et-Loir the commissioner for the 1st Military Division made Perrigny sub-prefect of Dreux, only to be told by the minister that Petitjean had already been nominated by a government decree, while Perrigny, having been made sub-prefect in the Aube by the commissioner in the 18th Military Division, had left to take up his post. But perhaps the most bizarre incident occurred in the Somme, when an imperial decree transferred Charles-César Romain from Peronne to Abbeville. Romain's father replied: Charles-César was temporarily away from home, he must therefore regretfully refuse the offer on his son's behalf. The next thing the prefect heard was that this prospective imperial nominee had joined the king at Ghent.[1]

The commissioners themselves were handicapped by the necessity to act at great speed. They were appointed on 20 April, and the ministry wished their mission to be completed by 5 May at latest.[2] As a result, Pontécoulant, commissioner in the seven departments of the 10th Military Division (Toulouse), could spend only two days in the Ariège, and his colleague in the 14th Military Division (Caen) spent only five days in Calvados: 'le but de sa mission eut été rempli avec beaucoup plus d'étendue, s'il avait pu y consacrer plus de temps'.[3] Haste would have been no great disqualification had the commissioners not been far more severely handicapped by the instability among the prefects, on whom they necessarily relied for information about the

[1] AN doss. Gengoult-Knÿls, 161(8); F1bII Ille-et-Vilaine (4). Perrigny, 174(1): Commissaire Extraordinaire (1st M.D.) to Min.Int. 13 May 1815 and draft of min's. reply 23 May 1815 (F1bII Eure-et-Loir (4)). Romain, 172(15), and for Abbeville decree 173(6), under Saint-Romain.
[2] Draft of circular, Carnot to the Commissaires 21 Apr. 1815 (AN, F1a 555).
[3] Ariège: pr. to Min.Int. 10 May 1815 (AN, F1bII Ariège (3)). Calvados: pr. to Min.Int. 6 May 1815 (F1bII Calvados (3)).

administrative personnel. Marchand found no prefect at Agen,
Chasset no prefect, secretary-general, or sub-prefect of the *arrondissement chef-lieu* at Tours. From the Midi Pontécoulant wrote
dolefully:

Je ne trouve aucuns préfets [et] pour ainsi dire aucuns fonctionnaires
publics civils ou militaires qui puissent me donner le moindre des
renseignements dont j'ai besoin. A Montauban... il n'y a ni préfet,
ni maire... à Toulouse le préfet n'est point encore arrivé [et] le maire
veut donner sa démission...d'Auch, je me rendrai à Tarbes, si
j'apprends que le préfet y soit arrivé...l'on m'assure que le préfet
de l'Aude n'est point encore arrivé à Carcassonne [et] je crains bien
qu'il n'en soit de même de celui des Pyrénées-Orientales...[1]

Even if the commissioner found a prefect installed, the successive prefectoral movements made it likely that he would be too
recent an arrival to know anything of his subordinates. So
Bedoch found in the Ardennes, Français de Nantes in Calvados,
Costaz in the Nord and Rampon in the Meurthe.[2]

The official criteria for the choice of new administrators had
been laid down by Napoleon in conversation with Carnot, and
were sent to the commissioners by the ministry: 'En général,
l'Empéreur, dans l'état actuel, veut des hommes sûrs: l'état de
choses n'est pas comme il y a deux ans; il faut que les magistrats
soient choisis dans l'intérêt de la population.'[3] Interesting as an
admission of imperial policy in 1813, this is not entirely satisfactory as a guide to the nominations. What it does indicate is the
considerable and deliberate change in the social basis of recruitment. Giving the people what they wanted might involve
eschewing former nobles and émigrés—although not always as
quickly as individual Bonapartists might wish. An anonymous
correspondent complained in March 1815 that the royalist

[1] Marchand (20th M.D.) to Min.Int. 4 May 1815 (AN, F1a 556(2)). Chasset
(22nd M.D.) to Min.Int. 14 June 1815 (F1a 556(2)). Pontécoulant (10th M.D.)
to Min.Int. 30 Apr. 1815 (F1a 555).
[2] Bedoch (2nd M.D.) to Min.Int. 26 Apr. 1815 (AN, F1a 553). Français de
Nantes (14th M.D.) to Min.Int. 25 Apr. 1815 (F1a 555). Costaz (16th M.D.)
to Min.Int. 14 Apr. 1815 (F1a 556 (1)). Rampon (14th M.D.) to Min.Int.
25 Apr. 1815 (F1a 554).
[3] AN, F1a 553.

sub-prefect of Charolles, the former émigré Bruys, was still in place: 'Si Bruys reste sous-préfet, il faudra placer Laroche-Jaquelin au panthéon et Château-briant à l'institut.'[1] But this imperial new look did not involve pandering to any chiliastic revolutionary ardour. The grouping of the nominations, whether they were made by the minister or by the commissioners, is broadly similar to that of the prefects. A number of functionaries dismissed in 1814 returned to the administration, and with them certain sub-prefects and secretaries-general who had served in the departments outside France under the Empire. Andlau, sub-prefect of Metz in June, had formerly administered an *arrondissement* in the Roer: Blanqui had been sub-prefect in the Alpes-Maritimes for fourteen years: Lamothe-Langon was an auditor and former sub-prefect in Italy.[2] Inevitably connexions played their part. Perhaps the most interesting examples of patronage are those by men who became celebrated only during the Hundred Days. Captier was the brother-in-law of Lieutenant-General Clauzel; Gérard was recommended by General Druot, Fabre by Lieutenant-General Gilly, Saivres by La Bédoyère; Las Cases was the brother of the Councillor of State and future memorialist.[3] Particularly among the provisional sub-prefects chosen by the commissioners, there were veterans of local administration. Garreboeuf, a former doctor and member of the local administration of the Haute-Vienne, was made provisional sub-prefect of Saint-Yrieix by the commissioner in May 1815. In Lot-et-Garonne Ménoire became provisional sub-prefect of Villeneuve-d'Agen: aged sixty-six, he had started his career as sub-delegate under the Ancien Régime, and held various posts under both Revolution and Empire.[4]

The search for 'hommes sûrs' naturally led Carnot to recruit from two groups who shared his own experience: Conventionnels and officers. The latter became more important as the Hundred Days continued. A list of twenty-two candidates whom

[1] Undated letter (spelling as in original), AN doss. Bruys, 156(49).
[2] AN doss. Andlau, 158(2); Blanqui, 156(26); Lamothe-Langon, 166(9).
[3] Captier: AN, F1bII Aude (3). Gérard, 161(9). Fabre: F1bII Gard(4). Saivres, 173(6). Las Cases, 166(13).
[4] Garreboeuf AN, F1bII Haute-Vienne (3). Ménoire: F1bII Lot-et-Garonne (4).

the minister himself recommended for sub-prefectures toward the
end of the Hundred Days included five former officers and three
members of the military administration.[1] Espinassy was named
sub-prefect of Trévoux on 10 June, although in his case the
Conventionnel may have overshadowed the general, as General
Mengaud's nomination to Belfort may have been due rather to
his having administered the *arrondissement* from 1804 to 1814
than to his military background.[2] Ulliac, nominated as sub-prefect
of Saint-Omer on 10 June, was a former colonel of engineers:
Cazaux, proposed for Saint-Gaudens on 22 June, and named by
the Provisional Government on 2 July, was a former *chef de
bataillon*: Fabre, Revel and Ropert had been junior officers.
Relatives or protégés of high-ranking officers were similarly
favoured. Alméras la Tour was the brother of a general, as was
Jeannet, Corvoisier was brother-in-law to one general, recommended by another: so that the man who had been replaced as
sub-prefect in 1813, whom his prefect had described as 'nul et
insignifiant... esprit médiocre' triumphantly returned to the
Corps in May 1815.[3]

The Conventionnels did not exhaust the list of former deputies
(both Grand and Hello, for instance, had been members of the
Five Hundred, Garat-Mailla of the Tribune), but it was Conventionnels whom Carnot deliberately recruited. As a result, the
sub-prefects of the Hundred Days included nine regicides who
had not previously served in the Corps, although Hérard had
served in the judicial administration after leaving the Convention,
Mallarmé in both the judicial administration and the *Droits
Réunis*. Roux's experience was more varied. A former priest
who had sat with the Mountain before the 9th Thermidor, he

[1] Undated but pre-20 June list in AN, F1d1 31.
[2] AN doss. Espinassy, 166(30), classified under Lespinassy and defective;
R+C, II, 365. Mengaud, 167(17), 170(26).
[3] Because of the increasingly chaotic situation in June 1815 there is no certainty
that all the titulars were installed—or even notified. AN doss. Ulliac, 175;
AAG, pensions. Cazaux, 157(11); and dossier AAG, communicated individually. Fabre, F1bII Gard(4); AAG, CG 1316. Revel, 172(7); AAG, CG 3297.
Ropert, F1bII Loire-Inférieure(4); AAG, CG 3396. Alméras, 155(3); Révérend,
*Restauration*, I, 28-9. Jeannet, F1bII Aube(2). Corvoisier, 157(32); F1a 553.

had subsequently been elected to the Five Hundred by the department of the Nord. Employed in the Ministry of the Interior under Quinette, and the Ministry of Police under Fouché, he later found a post in the financial administration in Belgium. A decree of 10 June made him sub-prefect of Laon.[1]

With this comparative rigidity of criteria, there were naturally some unfortunate choices. The commissioner in the 16th Military Division suspended Declercq's installation as sub-prefect of Hazebrouck. Declercq, the commissioner informed the minister, might have the reputation of an honest and patriotic man: he was also 'hargneux, tracassier et insupportable'. Fliniaux, who was made sub-prefect of Avesnes by a decree of 15 April, was both a bankrupt and a swindler, the reason for his never being installed—although he preferred to attribute this to a clerical rancour which he feared might follow him to his tomb. Dugué d'Assé, a former Conventionnel and Ancient, was made sub-prefect of Mortagne in May. As soon as his nomination was known, the *procureur impérial* wrote to the prefect that '... sans mœurs, sans probité, sans vêtements, [Dugué] a été, depuis plusieurs années, dans ces contrées, l'objet de la risée publique— par la scandale qu'il a causé, il est devenu la honte de l'espèce humaine...' The prefect informed the minister that he had found a pretext to delay Dugué's installation, the nomination having caused a scandal in the department. Dugué was never installed.[2]

These examples show, in extreme form, the difficulties of recruitment during the Hundred Days. The situation had something in common with that of the First Restoration. Both régimes had so little positive knowledge of their candidates that they depended on certain categories, whether émigrés or Conventionnels, who by the very fact of being émigrés or Conventionnels

[1] Grand: AN, F1bII Dordogne (7); R+C, III, 233. Hello, 162(4), defective; F1bII Côtes-du-Nord (5); R+C, III, 332. Garat-Mailla, 161(4); R+C, III, 106. Hérard, F1bII Yonne(4); R+C, III, 339. Mallarmé, 167(3); R+C, IV, 241–2. Roux, 172 (19); R+C, v, 213.
[2] AN doss. Declercq, 158(6); Commissaire to Min.Int. 9 May 1815 (F1bII Nord (7)). Fliniaux, 160(8). Dugué, 158(33); proc. imp. to pr. 18 May 1815.

might be supposed to have given gages to the cause. To a royalist *Cabinet des Antiquités* that produced Busquet and Saporta, can be added a psuedo-revolutionary pantheon that included Robert and Roux: a former secretary to Danton, a former Conventionnel on mission.

## THE SECOND RESTORATION

The rapid changes of subordinate personnel during the Hundred Days meant that comparatively few of the sub-prefects and secretaries-general in office in March 1815 still held the same post at the end of June. The majority, equipped with the involuntary brevet of royalism that a Napoleonic dismissal conferred, returned to the administration at the Second Restoration. Only 30 per cent of the subordinate personnel, as against 45 per cent of the prefects, failed to return. There is no indication that Pasquier wished to enquire too closely into the conduct of the subordinate personnel. A hundred and eight sub-prefects in office in March 1815 did not return in July: by no means all had been compromised by their conduct during the Hundred Days. Yet a list for the minister, drawn up in early July, showed that 110 sub-prefects had been confirmed in their posts during the interregnum, while another twenty-four had merely changed sub-prefectures.[1] Even had Pasquier wished to purge the administration thoroughly, it would have been ill advised and perhaps even impossible. The immediate priority at the Second Restoration was for the administration, cleansed of its most compromised elements, to resume its normal functioning. This was the reason for the ordinance of 7 July, which enjoined all the sub-prefects who had been in office in March 1815 to return to their posts.[2] In the circumstances the ministry could hardly have expected this ordinance to function smoothly. Nor did it. Every kind of difficulty arose, the result of invasion, occupation, conflicting and quarrelling authorities. In the Marne the former Bonapartist sub-prefect of Vitry was blockaded inside the town he continued to administer,

[1] List of 7 July 1815 (AN, F1bI 153).
[2] *BL*, 7th ser., I, bulletin 1.

while his royalist successor was obliged to exercise his office *extra muros*. In parts of the west it proved difficult to reassert royal authority when the remainder of Napoleon's army fell back behind the Loire: the *tricolore* was still flying in the Vienne on 22 July. There were clashes with the occupying forces, as at Avesnes, where the Prussians not only imprisoned the Hundred Days' sub-prefect, but for good measure his royalist successor as well: one can have a certain sneaking sympathy for the unheroic behaviour of Bain, sub-prefect of Grasse, who retired to bed when the Austrians occupied his *arrondissement*. And in the Midi, ministerially appointed or reappointed sub-prefects had the same difficulties with the duc d'Angoulême's nominees as had their superiors. Balzac had administered the *arrondissement* of Avignon from 1811 to the Hundred Days, when he retired from his post. In July he attempted to return, in obedience to the ordinance of 7 July: only to find that Angoulême's emissary, the duc de Rivière, had given the sub-prefecture to one of his own relations. Balzac went to see Rivière at Marseille, but found him far more disposed to lend Balzac his good offices with Angoulême than to carry out the terms of the ordinance. The commissioners' powers were withdrawn on 19 July. Even so it was only on the 31st that Balzac was reinstalled in his sub-prefecture.[1]

There was, therefore, no time to spare for a detailed enquiry into the conduct of the large number of borderline cases, those sub-prefects or secretaries-general who had spent at least some of the Hundred Days in office. Even now some of these cases remain baffling. Chazelles, for example, sub-prefect of Muret since 1811, had raised a troop of soldiers for the Bourbons in March 1815, at his own cost. They were officially disbanded in April, but Chazelles must have retained some kind of control, since he marched them against Toulouse at the end of the Hundred

1 Marne: J. Bertrand, 'Notes inédites sur les premiers sous-préfets de Vitry', *Almanach Matot-Braine* ... LXVII (1924), 424–5. Vienne: Lantivy, s.pr. Montmorillon to Min.Int. (undated but later July 1815) (AN, F1bI 688). Nord: M. Bruchet, 'L'invasion et l'occupation du département du Nord par les Alliés 1814–18', *Revue du Nord* (vols. 6–7, 1920–1), VI, 288, VII, 57. Bain at Grasse: Siméon, ex-pr.Var to Min.Int. 24 March 1819 (doss. Bovis, 156(42)). Avignon: Balzac to Min.Int. 2 Aug. 1815 (AN, F1bI 688).

Days. A royalist hero—but not entirely unflawed. On 15 April
Chazelles, having already been recommended for Versailles, was
made sub-prefect of Saint-Quentin. He never went there, and
the nomination may seem no more than a repetition of Romain's
experience, stemming from a faulty knowledge of the man concerned, and inadequate liaison among the Bonapartist leaders.
Yet Chazelles was warmly recommended by both duc and
duchesse de Rovigo (Savary) in April, and himself sent Carnot
a letter full of effusive protestations of devotion in June. Perhaps
designed as a cover for his royalist activities: or as a prudent
piece of reinsurance.[1]

As Pasquier had explained in his circular of 6 September, there
had been no time at the Second Restoration to consult the prefects
on the choice of subordinate personnel: they were chosen from
those directly recommended to the minister. It is therefore no
surprise to find, among the new sub-prefects, four who were
related to Pasquier: Vallée, Dortet de Tessan, Le Brun de
Charmettes and Selle de Beauchamps. Desjoberts was a personal
friend, Onfroy de Bréville a former subordinate. La Villegontier,
a friend of Decazes', became sub-prefect of Versailles, a protégé
of the duc de Richelieu sub-prefect of Civray. A former schoolfellow of Barante's was given Baugé, a protégé of his (and
Pasquier's) the sub-prefecture of Tarbes. This latter was not
altogether a happy choice. The new nominee, Gavoty, had asked
for a post during the Hundred Days. If a later accusation is to
be believed he had also, with considerable aplomb, dedicated to
Louis XVIII three volumes of a work originally intended for
Napoleon, after tactfully removing any references which were
likely to indicate 'ses principes atroces'.[2]

In contradistinction to the new prefects appointed by the
Talleyrand–Pasquier ministry, all but one of whom had some

[1] AN doss. Chazelles, 157(21); for his nomination to Saint-Quentin, AF IV
859(10), 6980.
[2] AN doss. Vallée, 176(2). Dortet de Tessan, 158(25). Le Brun de Charmettes,
166(19). Selle de Beauchamps, 156(10), 158(11, 21). Desjoberts, 158(18),
164(5). Onfroy de Bréville, 156(44), 169(2). La Villegontier, 166(17).
Richelieu's protégé: Jahan, 164(1); for Richelieu's recommendation, F1d*1.
Barante's schoolfellow: Persac, 170(10). Gavoty, 161(6).

previous administrative experience, a large number of the sub-ordinate personnel had never served at any but a local level. Some sub-prefects abroad who had not been given places at the First Restoration, like Bonnechose or Ablincourt de Gomiécourt, returned at the Second.[1] A larger number of the new personnel had experience in some kind of administration. Among the sub-prefects who had no previous administrative experience were a number of émigrés. Andrezel, lieutenant-colonel of an infantry regiment before the Revolution, began his new career at the age of sixty-eight. Du Minihy had taken part in the Quiberon expedition, and had fought under Cadoudal from 1796 to 1800: arrested in 1801, he was once again arrested during the Hundred Days. As this suggests, the Hundred Days provided a more recent criterion than emigration. While five of the new sub-prefects had made their administrative début during the Hundred Days, seventeen had distinguished themselves by their devotion to the Monarchy: at Ghent, in the Vendée, with the duc d'Angoulême in the Midi, or as royalist volunteers. Blossac had followed Louis XVIII to Ghent after losing his horse and all his belongings at Béthune, Bessay had been aide-de-camp to Sapinaud in the Vendée (where he had also fought during the Revolution), Lastic de Saint-Jal had raised and equipped a company of royalist volunteers in the Midi at his own cost.[2] The haste with which the nominations were made is reflected in a number of unfor-tunate choices. Montigny-Dampierre, whose nomination to the sub-prefecture of Embrun was due, no doubt, to his relative Lieutenant-General Maison, was completely incapable: while Odru's behaviour during the Hundred Days made his nomination to Briançon at the Second Restoration extremely unpopular.[3] Above all, there was the marquis de Mésillac, sub-prefect of Issoudun by ordinance of 2 August. He came from a family

[1] AN doss. Bonnechose, 156(32); Ablincourt de Gomiécourt, 161(14).

[2] AN doss. Andrezel, 158(2); AAG, Emigrés, 519(12). Du Minihy, 158(35); AAG, CG 2324. Blossac, 156(27), 166(34); and min. note 16 Jan 1816, on the s.prs. of the *arrondissement chef-lieu*, F1bI 82. Bessay, 156(20). Lastic de Saint-Jal, 166(14).

[3] AN doss. Montigny-Dampierre, 167(28). Odru, 169(1); pr. Hautes-Alpes to Min.Int. 24 Oct. 1815 (F1bII Hautes-Alpes (2)).

related to the Talleyrand–Périgord, and his father was a former magistrate whose estates had been sold when he emigrated. Mésillac himself had served in the *régiment de Périgord* before being captured at Leipzig, and had joined the Gardes-du-Corps at Ghent during the Hundred Days. Such at least was Mésillac's story: police and prefectoral investigations revealed another. Mésillac was 'un véritable chevalier d'industrie'. His proper name was thought to be Falyet, and far from being related to Talleyrand, he was 'fils d'un perruquier...et d'une servante actuellement cuisinière à Montpellier'.[1] It appeared that he had made his living by petty thievery and small-time espionage. Vaublanc dismissed him in December. No further steps seem to have been taken, since there are two further petitions in his dossier. The first, signed Mésillac, states that he had been replaced because Vaublanc wanted to give the post to his nephew. The second, from the same address and in the same handwriting, purports to be from the comte d'Hautefort, allegedly the former occupant of a suppressed sub-prefecture. Few other candidates had the persistence or the panache.

Vaublanc succeeded Pasquier as Minister of the Interior on 27 September, and the purge of administrative personnel that the Talleyrand–Pasquier ministry had barely sketched began in earnest. Vaublanc's criteria were summarized in his own post-script to a projected report to the Council of Ministers on Pépin de Bellisle, prefect of the Côtes-du-Nord: 'La chose essentielle à savoir est celle-ci. M. le préfet est-il royaliste décidé? L'est-il avec ce dévouement, cette ardeur qui ne laissent aucun doute? A-t-il jamais la moindre hésitation relativement au service du Roi? Quelle a été sa conduite pendant les cent funestes jours?'[2] Rigid standards, they were rigidly applied. Logically enough, there being no accepted middle position between loyalty and dis-loyalty, Vaublanc made little use of the transfer. Gallois, made sub-prefect of Lure in July 1814, had stayed in place throughout the Hundred Days. This naturally attracted Vaublanc's attention.

[1] Pr. Indre to Min.Int. 24 Dec. 1815 (AN doss. Mésillac, 167(20)).
[2] Postcript 'de la main du M[inis]tre', on projected report to Council 8 Jan. 1816 (AN doss. Louis Pépin de Bellisle, 170(9)).

The prefect of Haute-Saône, Joseph de Villeneuve-Bargemon, admitted that Gallois had done wrong in staying at his post, but attributed it to his weakness rather than to any Bonapartist convictions: in addition, he pleaded Gallois' administrative ability and his large family. If he had to be replaced, Villeneuve-Bargemon suggested that he should be given a post elsewhere. Vaublanc would have none of it: '...il devrait concevoir', he wrote on the prefect's letter, 'qu'il est impossible de...placer [Gallois] ailleurs, après avoir décidé que sa conduite ne permet pas de le laisser à sa place. Ce serait une inconséquence palpable.'[1] Gallois was dismissed.

The purge removed former Bonapartists whose conversion to the Bourbons had been both brief and incomplete. They were symbolized by Royanez, secretary-general of the Ardennes, who had served throughout the Hundred Days and was dismissed in April 1816 after he had arrived at an official meeting wearing a hat whose tricolour cockade was but imperfectly disguised by bands of white satin.[2] But there were cases where the minister (or his informants, including the prefects) acted precipitately. Griffon was dismissed although the prefect had evidence that he had served the royal cause during the Hundred Days, Le Rat de Magnitot although royalists in his *arrondissement* testified that he had protected them.[3] Vaublanc was careful in his choice of new administrators, and particularly correct in his dealings with the prefects: winning a grudging tribute even from Charles de Rémusat. His correspondence with the prefect of Bas-Rhin over the sub-prefecture of Wissembourg, with the prefect of the Hautes-Alpes over that of Briançon, shows him to have been both conciliatory and conscientious.[4] Yet it is difficult to acquit

---

[1] Min.'s gloss on Villeneuve-Bargemon's letter of 3 Apr. 1816 (AN doss. Coetlosquet, 157(27); see also doss. Gallois, 161(2)).

[2] AN doss. Royanez, 172(20). For his dismissal: Min. Police to Min.Int. 23 March 1816 and note for Min.Int. 2 Apr. 1816, both in doss. Mecquenem, 167(16).

[3] AN doss. Griffon, 161(9): for his dismissal, doss. Laffon de Ladebat, 166(4). Le Rat de Magnitot, 166(28).

[4] Bas-Rhin: AN doss. J.-A. Sers, 173(15). Hautes-Alpes: doss. Viel, 176(11). Ch. de Rémusat, *Mémoires de ma vie* (4 vols., 1958–62), I, 295.

Vaublanc of a certain insouciance in his dismissals. His peculiar brand of political manicheism made him a trifle over-ready to believe accusations and to act on them. Certainly such accusations were common enough. As one disabused prefect remarked, all his subordinates had been denounced for one reason or another, and he imagined this state of affairs to be characteristic of the majority of departments.[1] The deputies of Lot denounced their secretary-general, whose political beliefs, they wrote, had always been hostile to the Monarchy: had he not toured the department during the Hundred Days, inciting the population to sign the *Acte Additionnel*, as their only means of avoiding the re-establishment of tithes and seigneurial rights? In the Côtes-du-Nord the military commander and the Lieutenant-General in charge of the 13th Military Division similarly denounced the sub-prefect of Loudéac, a good administrator, perhaps, but 'aussi révolutionnaire qu'on puisse l'être'. But it was the unhappy Bain, at Grasse, who attracted the most detailed and decisive denunciation. He was 'un franc bonnet rouge', a friend of Pauline Bonaparte: worse yet, he was alleged to have said publicly, in April 1815, what many of the Corps must have felt in private: 'Eh, que voulez-vous, la chose est comme cela, il y a huit jours nous criions, Vive le Roi, demain nous crierons Vive l'Empéreur, ainsi va le monde'—and Vaublanc saw to it that Bain went too. Vaublanc's over-hastiness is well illustrated in the case of Le Caron de Fleury, sub-prefect of Senlis. Le Caron, a captain of dragoons before the Revolution, had been a sub-prefect since 1803, but had not served during the Hundred Days. He returned to his *arrondissement* in July, but was dismissed on 6 November. Greatly surprised—he was a friend of the Vaublanc family—Le Caron went to Paris for an explanation. 'Quoi! c'est vous', lui dit M. de Vaublanc, 'je croyais bien que le sous-préfet de Senlis était un prêtre marié ...'[2] Vaublanc's one purely administrative

---

[1] Pr. Gironde to Min.Int. 27 Oct. 1815 (AN doss. Lavergne-Cerval, 158(6)).

[2] Lot: note for min. 21 Dec. 1815 recapitulating the deputies' denunciation (AN doss. Duphémieux, 158(37)). Loudéac: doss. Hillion, 162(6). Grasse: letter of 2 Jan. 1816 from Lieut.-Gen. i/c 2nd M.D. enclosing accusations against the s.pr. (AN doss. Bain, 156(2)). Senlis: Le Caron's own account in petition 10 Jan. 1819 to Min.Int. (160(8)).

measure was as important as the purge of subordinate personnel. The indemnity France had to pay the Allies, and the consequent need for a reduction in government expenses, led to the suppression of the sub-prefectures of the *arrondissement chef-lieu* in December 1815. Eighty-three sub-prefects were left without a post. Vaublanc gave them priority in his nominations to other administrative posts, and the extent of his purge enabled him to place a certain number during the remaining five months of his ministry. The eighty-two new sub-prefects included twenty-nine former sub-prefects of an *arrondissement chef-lieu*, nine other former sub-prefects, and fourteen who had been named provisionally at the Second Restoration but not confirmed by Pasquier.[1] The twenty-two new secretaries-general included three former sub-prefects (one of whom, Saint-Victor, had administered an *arrondissement chef-lieu*) and two former secretaries-general. There were twenty-one émigrés among the new administrators, several of whom, like Du Trésor or La Porte d'Issertieux, had held no administrative office before their nomination. But once again, as had been the case under Pasquier, the Hundred Days served as a more recent reference. Foache and Orfeuille-Foucaud had followed the king to Ghent, Alès had been at Ghent and then in the Vendée, Coetlosquet had accompanied the Maison Militaire to Armentières, Cellès had served under the duc d'Angoulême in the Midi; and with the suppression of the Maison du Roi, a number of former officers entered the prefectoral corps. Perrève had served in the *Compagnie de Raguse*, Coetlosquet and Sagnard de Sasselange in the *Compagnie de Grammont*, Eugène de Gasville in the Black Musketeers.[2]

Vaublanc's eight months' ministry is a convenient dividing line between the time of crisis and the remainder of the Restoration. The purge of administrative personnel did not continue

---

[1] Eighty-seven nominations, but five s.prs. were named to two different *arrondissements* during Vaublanc's ministry.
[2] AN doss. Saint-Victor, 157(10). Du Trésor, 158(40); AAG, Emigrés, 519(3). La Porte, 158(10); AAG, Emigrés, 519(10). Foache, 160(9). Orfeuille-Foucaud, 169(2). Alès, 155(3), 158(1). Coetlosquet, 157(27); AAG, CG 760. Cellès, 157(9); AAG, CG 634. Perrève, 170(10); AAG, X^AD 26. Sagnard de Sasselange, 173(9); AAG, X^AD 29. Gasville, 161(5).

under Lainé, some of whose energy was in fact devoted to redressing the balance and bringing back Vaublanc's dismissed sub-prefects to the administration. There was no rapid and massive movement of subordinate personnel between 1816 and 1830. Moreover, it was Vaublanc who, by suppressing the sub-prefectures of the *arrondissement chef-lieu*, gave the prefectoral administration the form it retained throughout the Restoration. Lainé was to suppress the secretaries-general, but the measure was reversed within four years. The sub-prefectures of the *arrondissement chef-lieu* disappeared forever. From 1816 to 1830, for the great majority of the subordinate personnel, the administration has a well-defined unity.

# CHAPTER 8

# THE SUBORDINATE PERSONNEL 1816–30

It is difficult to gauge the relative importance of the various movements of subordinate personnel between 1816 and 1830. It is equally difficult to interpret them. Because the number of posts changed when the secretaries-general were suppressed, there is no constant standard for a comparison between the various ministries. This purely administrative measure makes it impossible to find any political rationale in either Lainé's or Siméon's movements of personnel. But apart from administrative considerations, the local background of both the sub-prefects and secretaries-general conditioned the extent and technique of these movements. For these reasons it is equally fruitless to search for any political logic in the geographical incidence of the changes. Certain departments saw few changes between 1814 and 1830.[1] The five *arrondissements* of the Aube had twelve titulars during the Restoration, the Eure had ten. The Eure-et-Loir had nine titulars for four sub-prefectures, the Haute-Vienne six, and the three *arrondissements* of the Indre-et-Loir had only five sub-prefects between them in sixteen years. In other departments, the Ardennes or Orne, for example, change was more rapid. Yet the implied homogeneity within a department is often illusory. There was sufficient difference between the various *arrondissements* of the same department to make the department an unsatisfactory unit in calculating the changes. In the Ardennes Vouziers had seven sub-prefects during the Restoration and Sedan had six; but Rethel and Rocroy had three only. In the Cantal Mauriac had three titulars, Saint-Flour had five, but Murat nine. In Bas-Rhin, Schlestadt had two sub-prefects during the Restoration but Wissembourg had seven, in the Var Brignolles had one but Toulon had six. To consider the changes at any but a local level is to oversimplify them: and it is at the local level that political explanation is the least satisfactory.

[1] The figures given omit the Hundred Days.

Characteristics peculiar to the subordinate personnel must shade any generalization that can be drawn from the manner in which the movements were carried out. They do not make such generalization impossible. The ministries which had the highest percentage of dismissals in their movement of prefects recur as those who dismissed, proportionately, the most sub-prefects (Decazes with 75, Villèle with 61 per cent), and, it may be assumed, for the same reasons. That the third is Lainé, with just under 60 per cent, is less easy to explain. The proportion of Lainé's dismissals was in a sense higher than Villèle's, since several of the latter's sub-prefects were made secretaries-general, whereas those whom Lainé removed (except for a handful who became prefects) left the administration altogether. Indeed, for his first year in office, Lainé's percentage of dismissals was in fact higher than Villèle's. This might plausibly be explained on the grounds that Lainé reacted more decidedly against his predecessor's policy than did Villèle. Yet precisely the contrary had been true of Lainé's movement of prefects. The percentage of prefects dismissed, as opposed to transferred, was 36 during his first year in office, but 43 for the ministry as a whole. It might be argued that he preferred to replace rather than to transfer sub-prefects because the suppression of the sub-prefectures of the *arrondissement chef-lieu*, and that of the secretaries-general, gave him a reservoir of trained personnel whose return to the administration was a ministerial priority.[1] Yet, however true this may have been for recruitment, it can hardly have had more than a marginal effect on the treatment of administrative personnel already in place. The only convincing explanation lies in the fact that the transfer of sub-prefects was rare throughout the Restoration, but even rarer at the start of the period. In July 1815 the Talleyrand–Pasquier ministry had brought back 251 of the 359 sub-prefects who had been in office in March. In only 39, or 15 per cent, of these cases did the sub-prefect return to an *arrondissement* other than that which he had administered before the Hundred Days. Vaublanc had replaced eighty-four sub-prefects. He

---

[1] Seventeen of Lainé's sixty-four new sub-prefects had previously administered an *arrondissement chef-lieu*, twenty-six were former secretaries-general.

transferred only fourteen. The emphasis should therefore fall not on Lainé's high percentage of dismissals, as compared to succeeding ministers, but on the greater number of transfers he made than had his predecessors. It was an indication that the period of crisis was over.

Decazes and Villèle shared the habit of dismissal. Their recruitment of subordinate personnel shows the same contrast as does their choice of prefects. Decazes removed known or suspected Ultras, the suspicion often being enough: Belleroche, Bruys, Conny de la Faye, Quatrebarbes, or Suleau.[1] His new sub-prefects included, inevitably, his personal protégés and those of his colleagues. He also brought back to the administration a number of former imperial sub-prefects or secretaries-general who had kept their places during the Hundred Days and had in consequence been replaced at the Second Restoration. Thirty-three of his sixty new sub-prefects had previously served in the prefectoral corps; eighteen of these had not held office since the Hundred Days. One nomination made administrative history: Rougier de la Bergerie, sub-prefect of Issoudun in 1819, had been prefect of the Nièvre during the Hundred Days. This was the only case between 1800 and 1830 of a former prefect returning to the administration as sub-prefect. Chabanon, made sub-prefect of Murat in June 1819, had administered the *arrondissement* from 1800 to August 1815. He was a former Conventionnel and member of the Five Hundred. Cossonier returned to the *arrondissement* of La Palisse, which he had administered from 1800 to the Second Restoration, Dantigny became sub-prefect of Saint-Flour after having been secretary-general of the Haute-Garonne from 1800 until his dismissal by Vaublanc in November 1815. There were former auditors like Pervinquière and Thieullen, both of whom had held office during the Hundred Days, or Cornudet, who came to the administration from the Maison du Roi. Narbonne-Pelet and Imbert de Montruffet had been members of the military administration under the Empire, Boismont had been in Neapolitan service, Bardonnenche was a former naval

---

[1] AN doss. Belleroche, 156(14), 157(19); Bruys, 156(49); Conny, 157(30); Quatrebarbes, 171; Suleau, 173(21).

officer who had been captured at Trafalgar. It was a characteristic gathering of men with a background of Napoleonic service.[1]

Villèle's 119 new sub-prefects and 43 secretaries-general form a decided contrast. Siméon had already brought back eighteen sub-prefects whom Decazes had dismissed. Villèle brought back another eight. Bayne, who had not held a post since his sub-prefecture was suppressed in 1815, returned in 1823 (he was in any case a natural choice for a Right-wing ministry to make, having been denounced during the Hundred Days as a dangerous extremist, in both politics and religion). Ormescheville, who had administered an *arrondissement* in Luxembourg under the Empire, had waited nearly thirteen years for another sub-prefecture when he was given Sarrebourg in 1827. But comparatively few of Villèle's new sub-prefects or secretaries-general had previously served in the Corps (44 of 162) and few came from other administrations, as Du Dresnay came from the Foreign Service or Eugène de Carbonnières from the Maison Militaire. There was an admixture of former, or active, deputies, such as Hersart de la Villemarqué or Regnouf de Vains, but the influence of the deputies is more noticeable in their patronage. Among the newly nominated administrators, Borel de Favencourt, Bengy de Puyvallée, Terrier de Loray and Josse-Boisbercy had brothers who were deputies, Durand du Repaire, Delhorme and Partouneaux were sons of deputies, Dalon, La Marque and Godefroy were close relatives.[2]

---

[1] AN doss. Rougier de la Bergerie, 158(8), 172(17); he became pr. again in 1839. Chabanon, 157(13); R+C, II, 11, v (addenda), 638. Cossonier, 157(32). Dantigny, 155(6), 158(2). Pervinquière, 170(10). Thieullen, 174(6). Cornudet, 157(32); AAG, X^{AD} 26. Narbonne-Pelet, 158(16), 170(7). Imbert de Montruffet, 163. Boismont, 156(29). Bardonnenche, 156(5).

[2] AN doss. Bayne, 156(10); pr. Tarn to Min.Int. 18 Apr. 1815 (F1bII Tarn (5)). Ormescheville, 169(2). Du Dresnay, 158(27, 31). Carbonnières, 157(6); O3* 2249. Hersart de la Villemarqué, 162(5), 176(12); R+C, III, 348. Regnouf de Vains, 172(4); R+C, v, 108. Borel, 156(35); for the dep., R+C, I, 398. Bengy de Puyvallée, 156(15); R+C, I, 251–2. Terrier de Loray, 174(3); R+C, v, 383. Josse, 156(29), 164(6); R+C, III, 427–8. Durand du Repaire, 158(39); R+C, II, 522. Delhorme, 158(12); R+C, II, 320. Partouneaux, 170(3), R+C, IV, 553. Dalon, 155(3), 158(1); son-in-law to Peyronnet, see above, p. 34. La Marque, 158(9); brother-in-law to baron de Cressac, R+C, II, 289. Godefroy, 161(13); nephew of Potteau d'Hancardie, see above, p. 94.

Decazes' new sub-prefects had included a high proportion of former Napoleonic administrators, the majority being of bourgeois extraction. Villèle, by contrast, recruited among a provincial nobility that rarely possessed any previous administrative experience. Over one-half of the subordinate personnel Decazes recruited had previous experience in the Corps, under a third of Villèle's: just over one-half of Villèle's nominees were noble, as against a mere fifth of Decazes'. One of Decazes' 60 nominees had emigrated, 24 of Villèle's 162. Most of these former émigrés were not only new to the Corps, but strangers to any administration at a level other than local. Félix de Bonne returned from emigration to become a member of his *conseil d'arrondissement* during the Restoration, Lestrange became a mayor, Louis de Carbonnières a member of the *conseil général* of Corrèze. Du Boishamon had emigrated in 1791, taken part in the Quiberon expedition and then in the Chouannerie. To save his head he enlisted in the army of Italy and fought at Marengo. After his removal from the list of émigrés, in 1802, there is no trace of his activities until his reappearance during the Hundred Days, in the west, and consequent return to the regular army as *chef de bataillion* in 1817. A few years later he resigned, became a member of the *conseil général* of the Ille-et-Vilaine, and in August 1822 sub-prefect of Ploërmel.[1]

As these examples indicate, the majority of Villèle's new subordinate personnel had a background of local administration, as mayors or *adjoints*, members of the *conseil d'arrondissement* or *conseil général*, even the *conseil de préfecture*. Rocaut d'Anthune had been mayor of Beaune before becoming sub-prefect of his *arrondissement*, Bosquillon d'Aubercourt had been *adjoint* to the mayor of Montdidier before Villèle made him sub-prefect of the *arrondissement* in 1823. Bonchamps had served in the *conseil général* of the Mayenne, Troguindy in that of the Côtes-du-Nord. Rodellec du Porzic, sub-prefect of Châteaulin in June 1822, had previously been *adjoint* and then (in 1817) mayor of Saint-Pol-

---

[1] AN doss. Félix de Bonne, 156(32); O³ 2561. Lestrange, 166(31); AAG, Emigrés, 519(9). Carbonnières, 156(7); AAG, CG 592. Du Boishamon, 156(29); F⁷ 5150; AAG, dossier communicated individually.

de-Léon: as mayor his *adjoint* had been Du Laz, who became sub-prefect of Quimperlé in 1826. Desroys du Roure, sub-prefect of Etampes, had been a member of the municipal council of Versailles and a *conseiller de préfecture* in the department. Des Moutis had served ten years in the Napoleonic army. He resigned in 1813, became a mayor and later a *conseiller de préfecture* in the Orne before being made sub-prefect in December 1825.[1] All these administrators came from the provincial nobility: so far as the subordinate personnel is concerned, Villèle's ministry was the reign of the *hobereaux*.

The social background of the subordinate personnel as a whole had not changed dramatically during the First Restoration.[2] It was never to change as drastically as had the prefects'. Yet between 1814 and 1816 there was a steady increase in the proportion of nobles among those holding office. On 1 April 1814 18 per cent of the sub-prefects and secretaries-general in France were noble; at the start of the Hundred Days 25 per cent; at the end of the Talleyrand–Pasquier ministry 32 per cent; and in May 1816 when Vaublanc left office, just under 40 per cent. For the remainder of the Restoration the percentage fluctuated between 36 and 42. As might be expected the peaks coincided with the end of the three Right-wing ministries, those of Vaublanc, Villèle and Polignac. The outline of the grouping thus suggested, the contrast between the Right on the one hand the Centre Left on the other, is confirmed by the figures of recruitment. Only the three Right-wing ministries had more than 50 per cent of nobles among their newly nominated subordinate personnel. Decazes, with a mere 20 per cent, was at the opposite extreme.

The rapid rise in the percentage of nobles among the secretaries-general in office, from some 5 per cent in 1814 to 20 per cent two years later, is somewhat deceptive, since so few nobles had been secretaries-general under the Empire: only four of the eighty-six in office in France at the start of April 1814. But it is

---

[1] AN doss. Rocaut d'Anthune, 172(11). Bosquillon d'Aubercourt, 156(34, 35). Bonchamps, 156(30). Troguindy, 174(13). Rodellec du Porzic, 172(13). Jégou du Laz, 158(34), defective; F1bII Finistère (7). Desroys, 158(20). Des Moutis, 158(19); AAG, Register of the 18th Dragoons (Cav.), III, An XIII–1814.     [2] See below, Appendix III.

noticeable that after the re-creation of the post in 1820, the percentage of nobles among the secretaries-general was broadly similar to that among the sub-prefects. From the Villèle ministry to 1830, the recruitment for both posts was indistinguishable socially. This suggests, even exaggerates, the parity between the sub-prefects and secretaries-general: but it was less a parity than the evolution of a closer and more formalized relationship.[1]

On the eve of the July Revolution, it was their social background that most clearly differentiated the subordinate personnel from their predecessors of 1814. The difference in age is harder to evaluate, although the contradictory evolution of the sub-prefects and the secretaries-general is at once apparent. The percentage of young sub-prefects declined considerably between 1814 and 1830, that of young secretaries-general increased. The explanation can be found in the history of the two posts. Under the Empire the sub-prefectures of the *arrondissement chef-lieux*, nearly a quarter of the total, were occupied by auditors, young administrators earmarked for promotion. In 1830 there was no comparable group among the sub-prefects. With a certain exaggeration, it might be said to exist instead in the young secretaries-general who had a background of training in either ministry or prefecture. Under the Empire the secretaries-general had been a group apart from the sub-prefects, the places often being held by officials whose administrative career went back almost uninterrupted to the Revolution, and whose hopes of promotion were almost non-existent. Significantly, the secretaries-general had been left untouched by the change in the social background of Napoleonic recruitment. The evolution of the post in the years after 1820 was still incomplete at the July Revolution, as the very high proportion (51 per cent) of secretaries-general aged more than fifty in July 1830 shows. Nevertheless, the reality of this evolution cannot be doubted. Between April 1814 and the July Revolution, the percentage of sub-prefects under the age of thirty who held office had shrunk from 17 to 4 per cent; that of the secretaries-general, by contrast, increased from 2 to 12 per cent. In the case of both sub-

[1] See below, p. 134.

prefects and secretaries-general the percentage over the age of fifty increased between 1814 and 1830. This may be due in some part to the stability of the years 1820–30. The sole exception in a period of otherwise uninterrupted Right-wing rule was Martignac's nineteen-month ministry, but the extent of his changes should not be overestimated. Two hundred and twenty-nine or over 80 per cent of the *arrondissements* kept the same sub-prefect under Martignac as they had under Villèle. The proportion of sub-prefects and secretaries-general over fifty was therefore higher during the 1820s than at the start of the Second Restoration, in the period of crisis.

The stability of the administration during the 1820s is not the only explanation. From 1818 an increasing number of sub-prefects or secretaries-general were given posts when they were already over fifty. In Decazes' case, this was the natural result of his reliance on former imperial administrators replaced at the Second Restoration: thus Cossonnier was sixty-four, Chabanon sixty-one, Lebare fifty-seven, Dantigny fifty-six.[1] From 1820 to 1829, when each ministry averaged 20 per cent or more recruits above the age of fifty, they were in the majority of cases former administrators brought back to the Corps. Martignac brought back Mathieu de Moulon at the age of sixty, after he had been dismissed by Villèle, Siméon brought back Ripert, aged sixty-one, who had been replaced by Vaublanc. Golzart and Traversay, both of whom had left the Corps in 1802 as sub-prefects, returned, the former in 1820 at the age of sixty-two, the latter in 1828 at the age of sixty-six.[2] Another group was made up of the new secretaries-general who had spent most of their administrative careers as *conseillers de préfecture*. Jean-Claude Clément became secretary-general at seventy, Le Porquier-Devaux at sixty-nine, Lavès at sixty.[3]

The change came with the Polignac ministry. Eleven of Martignac's forty-seven new sub-prefects or secretaries-general

---

[1] AN doss. Cossonnier, 157(32); Chabanon, 157(13); Lebare, 166(17); Dantigny 155(6), 158(2).

[2] AN doss. Mathieu de Moulon, 167(32). Ripert, 172(10). Golzart, 161(14). Traversay, 174(12), defective; F1bII Charente-Inférieure (2).

[3] AN doss. J.-C. Clément, 157(26); Le Porquier, 166(27); Lavès, 166(17).

had been over fifty years of age when nominated. Among Polignac's twenty-four there was only one. Approximately two-thirds of Martignac's nominees had been born before 1796 and had therefore come of age before the Restoration. The same was true for barely a third of Polignac's. The majority of his recruits had been too young to have served any régime other than the Restoration. It is tempting to see a contrast between a moderate royalism, whose following was recruited from the generations that came of age under the Revolution or Empire, and an Extreme Right based, broadly speaking, on the generation of the 'enfants du siècle'. But the change was less a deliberate matter of policy than a dramatic illustration of a development that had started in the early 1820s. This was the arrival of a new generation in the administration, and in particular the entry of a second generation of administrators, the sons or nephews of former, or of serving, prefects. Montlivault's nephew became secretary-general in 1824, Martin de Puiseux's son in 1827, Rogniat's in 1828. Valsuzenay's son was made sub-prefect in 1829, Chaulieu's and Pons de Villeneuve's sons became secretaries-general in 1830.[1] If administrative functions were not becoming hereditary, in the sense that places in the pre-revolutionary magistrature had been, a family tradition of service in the prefectoral corps was nevertheless emerging. In the majority of cases it did not survive the July Revolution.

The July Revolution, like the First Restoration, affected the subordinate personnel less than the prefects. Only 5 per cent of the prefects remained in the administration or returned later: nearly 20 per cent of the subordinate personnel. Yet compared to 1814 it was a massive change. In seventy-seven of the eighty-six departments more than half the sub-prefects were replaced. In 1814 the figure had been twenty. Fifteen departments had remained untouched by the change of régime in 1814, one alone (Loir-et-Cher) escaped the general holocaust in 1830.[2] Given

[1] AN doss. Montlivault, 167(28); Martin de Puiseux, 167(10); Rogniat, 172(14); Valsuzenay, 176(4); Chaulieu, 157(20), 172(3); Villeneuve, 173(13).
[2] Ch. Pouthas, 'La réorganisation du Ministère de l'Intérieur et la reconstitution de l'administration préfectorale par Guizot en 1830', *Revue de l'histoire moderne et contemporaine*, IX (Oct.–Dec. 1962), 262–3.

their local background, the wholesale change of sub-prefects was more important than that of the prefects. The prefects' influence derived entirely from the government, or ministry, since the great majority had no roots in the departments they administered. The sub-prefects, by contrast, were as much local figures as government officials, their importance frequently emphasized by an almost hereditary influence in their *arrondissements*. They reflected, in a more permanent sense than did the prefects, the character and strength of the Restoration governing class. Primarily noble, it was based on the provinces and on the provincial nobility. To change the prefects was logical after a change of régime. The massacre of the subordinate personnel made the change of régime revolutionary.

# PART III

## THE PREFECTORAL CAREER

CHAPTER 9

# INTRODUCTORY:
# POLITICS AND ADMINISTRATION

Throughout the Restoration the prefectoral corps was characterized by its informal mode of recruitment and promotion. There
were no official requirements for entry to the Corps, no rules
governing promotion from subordinate office to a prefecture,
and no recognized hierarchy of posts within either level of
administration. The major changes in the career between 1814
and 1830 stemmed, quite simply, from the substitution of a
parliamentary régime for a monolithic military dictatorship.
Under the Empire the Corps' duties had been primarily administrative, since politics, in any but a ceremonial sense, were non-
existent. During the Restoration the political role of the Corps
came to pre-empt all others: politics intruded at every stage and
level of an administrative career. Political patronage was necessary
for appointment, survival, promotion, even a pension. The
Corps' primary function was electoral: and several members
managed in addition to double a parliamentary mandate or seat
in the Peers with an administrative position. A prefect like
Haussez might leave his department for the six months of a
parliamentary session, a peer like Germiny might quite literally
administer his department from the Luxembourg until a politically
unsympathetic ministry intervened—and then to criticize not the
principle involved, but the detailed arrangements Germiny had
made.[1] And if politics refashioned the prefectoral career, making
it increasingly precarious, they also affected the prefectoral
temperament. As Rémusat wrote of former Napoleonic officials
as a whole: 'en face d'une cour, au milieu des partis, sous le
coup de vicissitudes rapides qui changeaient les positions du
jour au lendemain, il fallut bien apprendre l'art de dissiper les
préventions, de calmer les ressentiments, de ménager les opinions,

[1] Haussez: AN, F1bI 82 (Gironde). Germiny, 161 (10), particularly draft of
minister's letter 24 March 1820.

de caresser les amour-propres'.[1] The day of the *préfet à poigne* was—temporarily—over.

The Bourbons made no great contribution to the formal organization of the Corps. Indeed, when they abolished the auditoriat in 1814, they removed part of what little organization already existed.[2] The auditoriat had been created in 1803 as a means of training young men for high posts in all branches of the administration, attaching them to the various sections of the Council of State, with whom they worked. Two decrees, in 1809 and 1811, appointed an auditor to the sub-prefecture of the *arrondissement chef-lieu* of each department, classified them, and provided a means for their gradual promotion. There were three classes of auditor in the prefectoral administration. A minimum of one year's service in the third class was necessary before promotion to the second, and two years in the second before promotion to the first. After a year's service in the administration, first-class auditors could become secretaries-general, or sub-prefects of an *arrondissement* other than that of the *chef-lieu*. But in one sense the use of auditors did not solve but eliminate the problem of promotion. With a minimum quarter of the sub-prefectures reserved for auditors by the decree of December 1809, the ratio of sub-prefectures to prefectures (4 : 1 during the Empire) effectively removed any real chance of promotion for the remaining sub-prefects. The auditors therefore benefited from a scheme of promotion which had the virtue of ensuring that they should spend some time at least in the prefectoral administration before becoming prefects, and the vice of limiting promotion to a group of pre-selected personnel: a curious comment on 'la carrière ouverte aux talents'.

With the return of the Bourbons the auditoriat was suppressed. The institution was regarded, one auditor wrote, as 'la pépinière du despotisme', and this suspicion was no doubt partly responsible for its suppression.[3] The auditors came for the most part from the generation born between 1780 and 1790; they would

[1] Ch. de Rémusat, *Mémoires*, I, 255.
[2] For what follows see Charles Durand, *Les auditeurs au Conseil d'Etat de 1803 à 1814* (1958), *passim*.
[3] Barthélemy, *Souvenirs*, p. 103.

therefore have had no experience of serving a régime other than
the Napoleonic. Not unnaturally there was among them a hard
core of devoted Bonapartists. It was also natural that a corps of
privileged young men, often given considerable administrative
responsibility at an early age, equally often starting their careers
in the departments outside France at a time when the prefect's
major concern was conscription, might produce occasional
figures like Bergognié or Bouvier-Dumolard, whose administrative ability was vitiated by an unimaginative harshness.[1] Fleury
de Chaboulon, auditor in 1810, was made sub-prefect of Château-
Salins the next year. In May 1814 the notables of his *arrondissement* petitioned the Provisional Government for his dismissal.
Their denunciation of the sub-prefect was not only unusually
comprehensive, but provides, almost in caricature, a summary
of the accusations made against the auditors: 'Dureté insupportable, hauteur insultante, prétensions d'un Satrape, orgueil
révoltant, abus continuel de l'autorité, mépris des lois et de la
religion, persécutions contre ses respectables Ministres, con-
cussions, véxations de toutes espèces. Telle est, en raccourci, la
conduite du S$^r$. de Chaboulon.'[2]

But whatever the disadvantages of the auditoriat as an institution, or the defects of the auditors as individuals, the system had
provided, for a carefully selected group of young men, a regulated means of promotion from subordinate office to prefecture.
There was nothing comparable between 1814 and 1830. Nevertheless, there are signs, in the years after 1820, of something
approximating to a pattern of entry to the subordinate posts in
the Corps, and of a more closely defined relationship between
these posts. From 1820 to 1830 there were two parallel developments in the recruitment of the subordinate personnel. A number
of young candidates for the administration spent a preliminary
period either on the staff of a prefecture or in the Ministry of the
Interior as supernumeraries. Arthuys worked in the prefecture
of the Loire under Riccé before becoming sub-prefect in 1827,
Du Lyon worked in the ministry before being made secretary-

[1] AN doss. Bergognié, 156(18); Bouvier-Dumolard, 156(41).
[2] AN, F1bII Meurthe (5).

general of Creuse in 1828. In certain cases a candidate worked in both ministry and prefecture. Jacquelot du Boisrouvray became private secretary to the prefect of Corsica in 1824, before serving under Lamartine when the latter was chargé d'affaires at Florence. He returned to France and worked in the Ministry of the Interior, becoming *sous-chef de bureau* in the personnel department. In December 1829 he was made secretary-general.[1] In the majority of cases, after a period either in the ministry or in a prefecture, the candidate would enter the administration as a secretary-general. Thirty-seven secretaries-general under the age of thirty-five were nominated between 1821 and 1830. Three of these can be omitted, since they were former sub-prefects brought back to the administration. Eighteen of the remaining thirty-four had served in a ministry or prefecture. The only other group of comparable size was that of the secretaries-general who had no previous administrative experience whatsoever.

During the same period the ministries tended increasingly to recruit the sub-prefects from young men who had already spent a certain period as secretaries-general. As a result, and particularly during the Polignac ministry, something like a regular *cursus honorum* had been created. Buchère de l'Espinois, for example, had been a supernumerary in the Ministry of the Interior before being made secretary-general in 1827, sub-prefect in 1829. Puibusque, sub-prefect of Cherbourg in April 1830 after having been secretary-general of the Basses-Alpes, had started his administrative career as a supernumerary, and then worked on Vanssay's and Beaumont's staffs. Collier de la Marlière had worked in the prefecture of the Eure before Polignac made him secretary-general in October 1828, and sub-prefect in May 1830.[2]

The administrative benefits of this kind of training need not be exaggerated. Supernumeraries had no great reputation either for industry or ability (as Balzac showed in *Les Employés*), nor did a year or two as private secretary to a prefect necessarily

[1] AN doss. Arthuys, 155(8). Du Lyon, 158(34). Jacquelot du Boisrouvray, 164(1); N. J. du B[oisrouvray], *La maison de Jacquelot, Anjou–Bretagne 1500–1950...* (1950), p. 131.
[2] AN doss. Buchère, 156(49), 159(1); Puibusque, 170(26); Collier de la Marlière, 166(7), 167(8).

produce a skilled administrator. The *cursus* was never subject to official regulations, and patronage played as large a part in securing a place in ministry or prefecture as it played in entering the prefectoral administration properly speaking. Montlivault worked in his uncle's prefecture, Joseph Leroy in those occupied by his relative Le Roy de Chavigny, Bernardy de Sigoyer was *chef de bureau* to his relative Camille de Tournon before becoming secretary-general and later, in May 1828, sub-prefect.[1] However incomplete this administrative education might be, that it was thought necessary, and even advantageous, indicates a new attitude towards the recruitment of the subordinate personnel. Lip-service to a principle may not prove its efficacy. It does imply its existence.

[1] AN doss. Chas de Montlivault, 167(28); Leroy, 166(29), 170(24); Bernardy de Sigoyer, 173(16).

CHAPTER 10

# THE PREFECTS: PROMOTION AND THE MAKESHIFT HIERARCHY

The original classification of prefectures made by the law of 28 Pluviôse An VIII was designed solely as a means of fixing the prefects' salaries.[1] At no time did this classification, modified in 1810 and subsequently under the Restoration, have an application other than financial. No member of the Corps would have thought in terms of these classes, still less did the government regard them as a formal hierarchy. But unofficially, and to a certain extent in administrative practice, there was a rough division of prefectures. The departments were for the most part of approximately similar size, but their population, and that of their administrative centres in particular, differed widely. Paris apart, Bordeaux, Lyon and Marseille were large cities with some 100,000 inhabitants: Epinal, Montbrison, Saint-Brieuc and Périgeux were by contrast country towns with a population under 10,000.[2] The prefect of the Seine-et-Oise administered a department which could boast six royal châteaux during the Restoration, where the duchesses d'Angoulême and de Berry had acquired land, and which the royal family visited frequently. It was also the home of forty-nine Peers of France, the quarters of four companies of Gardes-du-Corps and three regiments of the Garde Royale.[3] The social standing and obligations of the prefect were naturally somewhat different from those of his colleagues in the Hautes-Alpes or Ardèche, departments with few influential proprietors, whose prefects had no need even of carriages—no one had them at Digne or Privas, the roads making their use impossible.[4]

[1] *BL*, 3rd ser., vol. I, bulletin 17.
[2] Population figures used in this section are taken from the decree of 11 June 1810 (*BL*, 4th ser., vol. XII, bulletin 294).
[3] Pr. Seine-et-Oise to Min.Int. 23 May 1822 (AN doss. Hersant-Destouches, 158(21)).
[4] Pr. Vaucluse to Min.Int. 7 Dec. 1814 (AN, F1bII Vaucluse (5)).

Between the two extremes was a less clearly defined group of departments like Calvados, Haute-Garonne or Loiret, evidently less important than the first, but also clearly differentiated from the mass of what can, for convenience, be called third-class prefectures. The extent of the difference between prefectures, between Nantes (Loire-Inférieure) with its population of nearly 80,000 and Guéret (Creuse) with just under 4,000, made some kind of hierarchy inevitable. It was obvious that to exchange the Creuse for the Ille-et-Vilaine, as Angellier did at the Second Restoration, or ₁0 move from the Sarthe to the Gironde, as Breteuil did in 1822, was promotion. Talleyrand's transfer from the Loiret to the Vaucluse in 1817, Du Martroy's from the Puy-de-Dôme to the Ardennes in 1823, was as clearly disgrace. Both resigned rather than take up their new posts: 'Je ne puis ni ne dois l'accepter', Talleyrand wrote.[1] There were others than Stendhal who disliked the thought of being prefect for 'quatre ou cinq ans dans un trou de 6,000 habitants. . .'. The hierarchy existed even for the government. The Bourbons made 164 prefects. Only seventeen began their careers in any but a third-class department, and nine of these nominations were made during the First Restoration. After the period of crisis was over, the immediate nomination of men from outside the administration to one of the great posts, as Albertas had been made prefect of the Bouches-du-Rhône in June 1814, and Chabrol-Crousol of the Rhône in November of the same year, was never repeated.[2] Yet the extent of this professionalism should not be overstressed. If the government accepted the existence of a makeshift hierarchy, and if the hierarchy provided a theoretical ladder of promotion, this promotion was never regulated. A prefect was not automatically promoted after a certain period of administering a third-class department. Saint-Luc, in a prefectoral career covering twelve years and six different departments, never rose above the third class; the marquis de Villeneuve, so nearly prefect of one of the most important departments in France under

---

[1] AN doss. Angellier, 155(5). Breteuil, 156(43). Talleyrand to Min.Int. 7 Dec. 1817 (doss. 174(1)). Du Martroy, 158(34).

[2] AN doss. Albertas, 155(2); Chabrol-Crousol, 157(13).

Vaublanc, likewise spent his entire career in the third class, and the last seven years of the Restoration in two of the least important departments in France, Creuse and Corrèze.[1] Promotion might come almost immediately—Armand de Beaumont spent only ten months in the third class—or only after long years of administration. Emmanuel de Villeneuve-Bargemon had administered three different departments for a total of nearly eleven years before he was promoted to the Somme in 1826, Wismes had been a prefect for fifteen years when he was given the Côte-d'Or in October 1829. A prefect could also be retrograded. Both Séguier and Talleyrand administered less important departments in 1830 than in 1814. Albert de Lezay-Marnésia finished his career in 1848 as he had begun it in July 1815, in a third-class department, although from 1817 to 1822 he had administered one of the most important prefectures in France, the Rhône.[2] There might be an embryonic hierarchy, even a ladder of promotion, but a prefect's position and progress on this ladder were governed not by administrative regulations but by political influence and opportunity. The very idea of a hierarchy was threatened by local and personal considerations. It was an advantage for a prefect in Alsace to have some command of German, as had Bouthillier or Puymaigre. It was a disadvantage for a prefect in the Midi to be a Protestant, as was the prefect of the Lozère in 1816–17, Fressac (not his only disadvantage, according to his predecessor, who described Fressac as 'presque sourd' and 'fort cassé'); while in Corsica it was almost a rule that prefects should have some kind of military background. Five of the eight prefects the Bourbons sent to Corsica were former officers, one, Vignolle, a full general.[3]

For their part, the prefects did not always adapt themselves to the rapid changes of the Restoration: 'Mieux eussent valu des administrateurs médiocres avec de la permanence dans leurs

[1] AN doss. Saint-Luc, 173(4); Villeneuve, 176(13).
[2] AN doss. Armand de Beaumont, 156(11); Ferdinand de Villeneuve-Bargemon, 173(13); Wismes, 176(16), 177(2); Séguier, 173(12); Talleyrand, 174(1); Lezay-Marnésia, 166(32).
[3] AN doss. Fressac, 160(14); Barrin, pr. Lozère to Min.Int. 10 Dec. 1815 (doss. Barrin, 156(6)). Vignolle, 176(12); AAG, doss. of General Officers (380).

fonctions qu'une rapide succession d'hommes de talent, apparaissant et disparaissant sans avoir le temps de voir germer une seule de leurs idées et encore moins d'en recueillir les fruits.' So Haussez wrote. He would willingly have spent more time in the Landes, where he was prefect from May 1817 to February 1819, and accepted his promotion to the Gard without any great enthusiasm.[1] Tournon, transferred from the Gironde to the Rhône in 1822, at first refused. He had administered the Gironde for nearly seven years, had a thorough knowledge of the department, and had succeeded there. In the Rhône he would arrive as a new prefect, faced with an unfamiliar department, a new set of problems, and the possibility of failure. He decided to accept only because at Lyon he would be nearer his own family and that of his wife.[2] This was a consideration which affected most of the prefects. They were rarely completely successful, because the government was as little inclined to name a prefect to his native department as it was eager to name a sub-prefect to his own *arrondissement*. The exceptions date, for the most part, from the First Restoration, and the majority of these were merely confirmations of choices made, or recommended, by the princes or *commissaires extraordinaires*, or nominations by the Provisional Government. The duc d'Angoulême made Carrère prefect of the Landes in March 1814, and was in all likelihood also responsible for Indy's nomination to the Ardèche. Scey, Pasquier and Mique were named by the Provisional Government, Vaulchier was made prefect of the Jura in September 1814 after having been named provisionally by the commissioner in May.[3] All were in their home departments. For the remainder of the Restoration the majority of prefects could expect at best a post within, or near, the province in which their native department was situated. Saint-Luc came from Rennes (Ille-et-Vilaine), and started his administrative career in two Breton prefectures, Finistère and the Côtes-du-Nord. Replaced in 1819, he returned in 1822 as prefect

---

[1] *Mémoires*, I, 234, 329–30.
[2] Tournon to his wife 3 Jan. 1822, quoted in Moulard, *Tournon, préfet de la Gironde*, p. 221.
[3] AN doss. Carrère, 157(8). Indy, 163; Pouthas, *Guizot*, p. 57. Scey, 173(11). Pasquier, 170(4). Mique, 167(24). Vaulchier, 176(6).

of Lot, moving successively to the Loir-et-Cher and Creuse. He wanted a department near Brittany. The Polignac ministry gave him the Maine-et-Loire. Walckenaer was equally fortunate. A Parisian, his first post was the Nièvre. At his own request, he was moved nearer Paris in 1826, when Villèle gave him the prefecture of the Aisne. But Wismes, whose family came from Cambrésis and Artois, never succeeded in obtaining a prefecture in the north-west or near Paris as he had hoped, and Villiers du Terrage was similarly unsuccessful. From almost the start of his administrative career, in 1815, he had wanted a prefecture near Paris (his family came from the Ile-de-France). Prefect of the Pyrénées-Orientales at the Second Restoration, he was transferred to the Doubs in 1818. In spite of his reiterated demands, the second Richelieu ministry moved him even further from Paris, giving him the prefecture of the Gard (January 1820)—'l'administration la plus dégoutante du Royaume'.[1] The distance of a post from the prefect's home department affected his attitude toward the post and might counterbalance the concept of a hierarchy. It was similarly qualified by the difference in pay and salaries among the prefectures, in private income among the prefects.

[1] AN doss. Saint-Luc, 173(4); Walckenaer and Wismes, 177(1); Villiers du Terrage, 176(16), 177(2).

# CHAPTER II

# THE PREFECTS:
# THE OUTLINE OF THE CAREER

Instability marked the Restoration administration. Inevitably, three changes of régime within eighteen months in 1814–15 left few Napoleonic prefects in place, fewer in the same department. Only a quarter of the eighty-seven prefects who had administered departments inside France in March 1814 survived at the end of August of the next year, only seven in the same department, Jessaint alone had administered without interruption. But even after the great prefectoral movements of the early years, the Restoration administration never achieved the comparative stability of the Napoleonic. Between 1815 and 1830 a prefect could hope to remain in his department only three years: under the Consulate and Empire the average for the same eighty-six departments had been four and a quarter. The problem during the Restoration was not simply to become a prefect but to remain one. Dismissal might sanction administrative inadequacy or ineptitude, or more simply the prefect might be a scapegoat for ministerial loss of face.

It was Frochot, prefect of the Seine, who lost his post after the Malet conspiracy of 1812—not Pasquier, prefect of Police, although his responsibility would seem to have been no less, and his role considerably more ignominious. And when, at Nîmes in 1817, General de Lagarde's murderer was acquitted, the prefect of the department was immediately dismissed. He had taken every possible precaution, packing the jury with government employees, Protestants, and high-ranking officers, all of whom, by sentiment or a proper consciousness of their position, might have been expected to vote the right way: but as the prefect wistfully remarked, 'les arrêtés des tribunaux judiciaires, les opinions des jurés quelles qu'elles soient, sont totalement étrangèrs à mon influence, et au-dessus de mon pouvoir comme de mes efforts'.[1] But the most common reasons for dismissal were political, and the skill necessary for survival was all the greater during the early years of the Restoration because the principle of political movement of personnel was not publicly recognized until the Decazes ministry of 1818–20. The unwary prefect might consequently overlook the dangers of disobeying a new ministry. A considerable number of prefects had worked openly against the ministry in the elections of September 1816.[2] Under later ministries, whose authority was less diffuse and whose control of their personnel was tighter, such widespread disobedience was impossible. As a corollary, it became more difficult for a prefect to avoid committing himself to a definite party programme. This might entail an unpleasantly rapid volte-face when the ministry changed, or should it modify its programme. Argout was made prefect of the Basses-Pyrénées in July 1815, transferred to the Gard in February 1817. Haussez wrote with his customary lack of benevolence: 'Dans le département des Basses-Pyrénées, où [Argout] avait fait son début administratif, il n'avait pas laissé un maire, pas un garde champêtre en place, parce qu'il n'en trouvait pas un dont le royalisme fut à l'hauteur du sien. Dans le Gard, il a destitué des centaines de maires, parce que leur libéralisme n'avait pas assez d'éclat.'[3] Haussez had reason to be scornful. His own progress from Moderate deputy (1815–16) and prefect to a place in Polignac's Cabinet was far more discreetly managed.[4]

Although it was useful for a prefect to have definite political sympathies, it was necessary to temper them with tact and flexibility. Over-enthusiasm would add to the risk of dismissal should the ministry change, indiscretion would alienate even a ministry otherwise well disposed. Carrère suppressed a—possibly imaginary—conspiracy in the Landes with such vigour that he was dismissed. In February 1819 when the marquis de Barthélemy

[1] AN doss. Frochot, 160(14); Pasquier, *Mémoires*, II, 47–9. Arbaud–Jouques, pr. B-du-R, to Min.Int. 24 Jan. 1817 (AN doss. 155(6)).
[2] See above, p. 71.
[3] *Mémoires*, I, 264. AN doss. 162(3), 166(25); R+C, III, 319(20). Haussez had also been recommended for a sub-pr. in the Hundred Days (F1a 556(1)).
[4] R+C, III, 319–20.

put forward his proposal to the peers that the suffrage be restricted, Dugied, prefect of the Basses-Pyrénées, acted with
similar precipitancy, and was likewise dismissed. He had issued
a circular to his department that the Minister of the Interior
judged 'au delà du but et des convenances'. Dugied, the minister
reported to the king, '. . . y parle de *l'opinion*, cette *reine des Rois
et du monde*. . . il va même jusqu'à dire que *l'on sait que le Roi a
hautement improuvé la proposition*'.[1]

The ideal for a prefect was to avoid committing himself, to
drift with events, rather than to find himself faced with the
alternative of dismissal or a drastic change in behaviour. Several
mastered this art. If eighty-three prefects spent less than five
years in the administration between July 1815 and July 1830,
seventeen spent the entire period in office, five changing their
department only once, two administering the same department
throughout. Chabrol de Volvic had been made prefect of the
Seine in 1812 and held the post, with the sole exception of the
Hundred Days, until the July Revolution. Jessaint administered
the Marne without interruption from 1800 to 1838. Their
characters, as their careers, had a certain similarity. Chabrol was
self-effacing, discreet. 'C'est un de ces hommes que personne ne
songe à heurter parce qu'ils évitent de se trouver sur le passage
de qui que ce soit; à qui on pardonne leurs talents réels parce
qu'ils ont grand soin de n'en pas faire étalage. . .' Jessaint, wrote
Barthélemy, who had served under him as sub-prefect '. . . aurait
fait un diplomate accompli; il ne s'engageait jamais, s'avançait
faiblement et savait ne pas se compromettre. . .'.[2] His talents
were nicely displayed in his negotiating Barthélemy's marriage:
equally in his doing nothing to prevent Barthélemy's dismissal.
His acquaintances were perhaps even more useful to Jessaint than
his character. He had been at the Ecole de Brienne with Napoleon;
he was also an intimate friend of the duc de Doudeauville. The
eulogistic account the Napoleonic commissioner gave of him in

[1] AN doss. Carrère, 157(8); Haussez, *Mémoires*, I, 235–6. Min.Int. to Dugied
20 March 1819, and report to king 31 March 1819 (the emphasis is in the
original) (doss. 158(33)).

[2] AN doss. Chabrol de Volvic, 157(13); Haussez, *Mémoires*, I, 399–400. Jessaint,
164(4); Barthélemy, *Souvenirs*, pp. 118, 122–3.

May 1815 finds its echo in the Memoirs of Sosthènes de la Roche-foucauld.[1]

Jessaint's career was exceptional even in his own lifetime. The majority of prefects risked dismissal, or at least a transfer, with a change of ministry. Their situation, once dismissed, was unenviable. Certain were given posts on the Council of State, the more easily if, like Freslon or Fumeron d'Ardeuil, they had served on the Council before becoming prefects.[2] Others became deputies, or continued a career as deputy which they had previously begun. But a prefect who had been dismissed might have no immediate hope of returning to the administration, and very little of starting another career, while the salary he lost might have represented his sole, or major, source of income. 'Votre Excellence n'a pas songé', Auberjon wrote to Martignac after his dismissal in November 1828, 'qu'en brisant ma carrière, vous avez porté un préjudice notable à ma nombreuse famille et à ma fortune...' Lamorélie, dismissed by Villèle in 1823— 'sans état, sans carrière et sans avenir'—at the age of thirty-six, had depended entirely on his salary, having no other source of income except an allowance from his wife's parents.[3]

Inevitably those prefects replaced after a change of régime were in the worst position. Only ten of the hundred involved in the Hundred Days came back to the administration, as prefects, during the Restoration. Only six of the eighty-six prefects in office at the July Revolution were maintained, or returned, under Louis-Philippe. Few of the prefects compromised by their service during the Hundred Days made another career for themselves. Bergognié entered the magistrature, Cochelet the Foreign Service, Harel became a theatrical director and associate of Mademoiselle Georges, Arnault and Chaillou became men of letters.[4] At

---

[1] See Doudeauville to Min.Int. 17 May 1816 (AN doss. Jessaint); Commissaire in 2nd M.D. to Min.Int. 3 May 1815 (F1a 553); *Mémoires de M. le vicomte de Larochefoucauld...* (5 vols., 1837), II, 141.

[2] AN doss. Freslon, 160(14); Fumeron, 160(15).

[3] Auberjon to Min.Int. 3 Dec. 1828 (AN doss. 155(9)). Lamorélie: note for min. Apr. 1824 (doss. 166(8)).

[4] Bergognié: M. Rousselet, *La Magistrature sous la Monarchie de Juillet* (Paris, 1937), appendix I, p. 463. Cochelet: *DBF*, fasc. 49, cols. 65–6. Harel: Pierre Bart, 'Un préfet des Cent Jours, Harel', *Feuilles d'histoire*, XIII, no. 2 (Feb.

the Second Restoration the majority of former Napoleonic prefects, like their Bourbon successors after July 1830, retired from public life, suffering, if not from exile or surveillance, from the moral proscription that drove one prefect to attempt suicide.[1]

Nor were the pension regulations comforting. Based on the decree of 4 July 1806, they stipulated a minimum age of fifty, and thirty years in the state's service, of which ten at least should be in posts dependent on the ministry concerned.[2] The maximum pension was one-half of the prefect's final salary, founded on an average of his salary during the last three years in office. Finally, a dismissed functionary was expressly denied any right to a pension. The regulations, and in particular the last clause, would have debarred the vast majority of prefects from receiving any pension whatsoever. As Patry, the head of the relevant section of the Ministry of the Interior, pointed out in a note of January 1819, the regulations were entirely unsuitable for the prefectoral administration, since they disregarded the importance of the posts, and their essentially precarious nature.[3] But there was in practice a loophole in the 1806 decree. Functionaries with less than thirty years' service could be given a pension if they were incapable, for reasons of health, of continuing their career. This clause was used during the Restoration in certain cases of genuine ill health—for example that of Lachadenède in 1822.[4] It was also used in favour of prefects whose ill health seems to have been the effect rather than the cause of their dismissal. This was particularly true for the pensions given to those prefects dismissed at the July Revolution: Bluget de Valdenuit, Coster, Esmangard, Jahan, Vanssay, Alban and Emmanuel de Villeneuve-Bargemon.[5] There was enough continuity in political personnel between the

1915), p. 118. AN doss. Arnault, 155(7); *DBF*, III, cols. 904–6. Chaillou: *DBF*, VIII, col. 179.
[1] Plancy: see pp. xvii–xviii of the introduction to his *Souvenirs*.
[2] AN, F1bI 287–9.
[3] Note for Min.Int. 26 Jan. 1819 (AN doss. André d'Arbelle, 155(6)). See also the 'Motifs du projet de Règlement Général des Pensions', F1bI 287–9.
[4] AN doss. 166(2).
[5] AN doss. Bluget de Valdenuit, 176(1); Coster, 157(33); Esmangard, 159(2); Jahan, 164(1); Vanssay, 176(5); Alban and Emmanuel de Villeneuve-Bargemon, 176(13).

Restoration and the July Monarchy to make such compensation possible for those with the proper connexions: as necessary to a prefect after losing his post as they had been in obtaining it.

With the pension regulations theory was tempered by administrative practice. For a dismissed prefect, future political events might change his situation. Obviously this would be the case after a change of régime. Twenty-five prefects involved in the Hundred Days and not subsequently employed during the Restoration, thirteen others replaced by Right-wing Restoration ministries, returned under Louis-Philippe, while Suleau, who had left the Corps in April 1830 to become, briefly, *directeur général de l'enregistrement*, returned in January 1849 as prefect of the Eure-et-Loir.[1] It was true also after a simple change of ministry. A prefect might lose his post when the ministry that had nominated him, or which he supported, fell. As a corollary he might return to the Corps should the ministry, or one of the same political colour, itself return. It became habitual for ministers to recruit a certain proportion of their prefects from those dismissed by their predecessors. The seven First Restoration prefects deliberately ignored by the Talleyrand ministry came back under Vaublanc. Decazes dismissed nineteen prefects, three of whom were brought back by Siméon, four by Villèle; Villèle dismissed forty-two, but seven returned to the administration under Martignac. The habit became almost automatic, it being tempting to regard prefects previously dismissed as having by this fact alone given evidence of their loyalties. Haussez wrote of La Bourdonnaye, the first of Polignac's Ministers of the Interior: 'Il choisit avec un tact merveilleux toutes les incapacités dont les précédents ministères avaient débarrassé l'administration, parce qu'il prit pour des motifs de préférence les folies et les exagérations qu'on leur avait reprochées.'[2] Nominations of this type produced careers of a pattern unknown under the Empire. Floirac and Lascours had both served in the army before the Revolution. Floirac emigrated, Lascours stayed in France, and after being a deputy to the Five Hundred and Corps Législatif was made baron of the Empire. Both became prefects at the First

---

[1] AN doss. 173 (21).      [2] *Mémoires*, II, 106.

Restoration. From that moment their careers move in counter-point. Lascours returned to a prefecture at the Second Restoration, but was replaced by Vaublanc. Floirac did not return to the Corps until October 1815, when Vaublanc gave him the prefecture of Hérault, which he administered until Lainé removed him in August 1817—some five months after Lascours had been made prefect of Gers. Villèle dismissed Lascours and recalled Floirac. Martignac dismissed Floirac and recalled Lascours, giving him the prefecture of the Ardennes which he held through the Polignac ministry and until his death in 1835. In short, from July 1815 to December 1828 Lascours served every Centre-Left and Centre-Right ministry, but was replaced by Vaublanc and Villèle, while Floirac served the latter two ministers but was replaced by Lainé and Martignac. Among the other six First Restoration prefects overlooked at the Second Restoration, Montureux and Guer had careers identical to Floirac's, Saint-Luc and the marquis de Villeneuve differed only in surviving the Martignac ministry. Among prefects who served Moderate and Centre-Left ministries, Fumeron d'Ardeuil and Feutrier had careers somewhat similar to Lascours'. Fumeron was first made prefect by Lainé, Feutrier by Decazes. Both were dismissed by Villèle, returned under Martignac, were dismissed once more by Polignac before returning to the administration under Louis-Philippe.[1]

There is a variant to these careers: the case of the prefects who managed to ride a change of ministry at the price of a transfer. The habit of bringing back former prefects to the administration meant a higher level of stability among the personnel than is immediately evident from the figures for the prefectoral movements. The frequency of transfers made this stability largely illusory so far as the departments were concerned. Between 1815 and 1830 sixteen departments had six or more prefects—an average tenure of two and a half years; the Charente, Creuse

[1] AN doss. Floirac, 158(7), 160(8); O³ 2561; AAG, YB 636. Lascours, 166(13), 172(8); AAG, YB 422; R+C, III, 613; Révérend, *Armorial*, IV, 134–5. Montureux, 167(29). Guer, 161(21), 167(8). Saint-Luc, 173(3). Villeneuve, 176(13). Fumeron, 160(15). Feutrier, 160(6).

and Oise had eight, the Vendée ten, Doubs eleven. Thirty-nine of the prefects in office at the end of July 1830 had been prefects for ten years or more. Only thirteen had spent ten years in the department they then administered, as against fifty-eight who had spent less than three years. Even among the prefects who held office without interruption from 1815 to 1830, a career like Maurice de Gasville's, who administered only two departments and was prefect of the Yonne from 1817 to the July Revolution, was unusual. Allonville's and Wismes' four prefectures, Estourmel's and Nugent's five, were more typical.[1]

A prefect might be transferred because, although otherwise admirable, he was unsuited to his department or on bad terms with the military or religious authorities. Montlivault quarrelled with General Donnadieu after the suppression of the Didier conspiracy in 1816 and was transferred from the Isère to Calvados. Bluget de Valdenuit was moved from the Charente to Lozère in 1821 after a series of conflicts with the local authorities, while Auderic's entire administrative career was accompanied, and governed, by his incessant feuds.[2] Alternatively, the ministry might take advantage of a vacancy to carry out a general re-shuffle. Christophe de Villeneuve-Bargemon, prefect of the Bouches-du-Rhône, died in office on 13 October 1829. On the 16th Arbaud-Jouques was moved from the Côte-d'Or to the Bouches-du-Rhône, Wismes from the Aube to the Côte-d'Or, Brancas from the Haute-Saône to the Aube, and the sub-prefect of Coulommiers, Le Brun de Charmettes, was made prefect of the Haute-Saône.[3] But a prefect might be transferred for reasons less administrative than political. Foresta was made prefect by Villèle in 1822, and given the prefecture of the Meurthe in September 1824. On Villèle's fall he was transferred by Martignac to the Vendée, a move he rightly regarded as a disgrace. That his politics would be more to the taste of the Polignac ministry can

[1] AN doss. Gasville, 161(5, 15); Allonville, 155(3); Wismes, 176(16), 177(2); Estourmel, 159(3); Nugent, 168(4).
[2] AN doss. Montlivault, 167(28); Pasquier, *Mémoires*, IV, 116–17. Bluget de Valdenuit, 176(1). Auderic, 155(10), 158(4).
[3] AN doss. Christophe de Villeneuve-Bargemon, 176(13); ordinance of 16 Oct. 1829, *BL*, 8th ser., vol. XI, bulletin 322.

be understood from Frénilly's encomium: 'garçon d'esprit... et nourri jusqu'à l'exaltation de tous nos sentiments...' In April 1830 he moved to a more important department, the Loiret. Another Ultra, Calvière, had been provisional prefect of the Gard under the duc d'Angoulême at the end of the Hundred Days. Elected to the *Chambre Introuvable*, he sat on the Extreme Right, and never took up the official position he had been given as sub-prefect of Grenoble. After eight years as deputy, Calvière was made prefect of the Vaucluse by Villèle (1823), and a year later given the Isère. His politics did not recommend him to the Martignac ministry: he was nevertheless not dismissed but transferred to a far less important department, the Hautes-Pyrénées. Equally naturally, the Polignac ministry promoted him. In April 1830, Calvière was made prefect of the Doubs.[1]

Prefects might be transferred as part of a ministerial programme, or shuffled to meet a chance vacancy. Whatever the motive, the movements imply the existence of some sort of hierarchy among the prefectures.

[1] AN doss. Foresta, 160(10); Frénilly, *Souvenirs*, p. 329. Calvière, 157(3); F1bII Isere (4); R+C, 1, 556–7.

# CHAPTER 12

# THE PREFECTS:
## SALARIES, ALLOWANCES, INCOMES

Throughout the period 1800–30, the system of prefectoral pay was organized on a dual basis. The prefects received a salary based on the classification of their prefecture, and designed as a personal expense and entertainment allowance. They also received a grant for the prefecture and its offices where municipal buildings were not available, the wages of the prefect's staff, the cost of heating, light and printing, the expenses during the yearly meeting of the *conseil général*, and any unforeseen expenditure.[1]

The salaries were calculated, in the law of 28 Pluviôse An VIII, on the basis of the population of the administrative centre of the department. They ranged from 8,000 to 24,000 francs per year, excluding Paris at 30,000.[2] But the very rigidity with which this criterion was employed led to evident injustices. The administrative centre of a department was not always the most populous town. In the Var Toulon had a population four times greater than that of the administrative centre, Draguignan; in the Charente-Inférieure Saintes, with a population of 10,000, was half the size of La Rochelle. The prefect of a large and important department like the Manche (pop. 538,000) received the same salary as his colleague in the Hautes-Alpes (pop. 116,000), the administrative centre of the Manche, Saint-Lô, being a small country town of 7,000 inhabitants.[3] The decree of 11 June 1810 modified the system and raised the salaries. The 117 prefectures were divided into four classes (excluding the Seine), with salaries of 20,000, 30,000, 40,000 or 50,000 francs.[4] The basis of this classification is not entirely clear. The population of the administrative centre was still the determining, but no longer the exclusive, criterion. The Manche and Pas-de-Calais were third-class departments, even though, with administrative

---

[1] Law of 26 Ventôse An VIII, AN, F1a* 88.    [2] *BL*, 3rd ser., vol. I, bulletin 17.    [3] 1810 figures.    [4] *BL*, 4th ser., vol. XII, bulletin 294.

centres of less than 20,000 inhabitants, they were inferior in this respect to several departments in the fourth class. For the border-line cases it seems likely that a combination of criteria were applied: the total area and population of a department, the number of *arrondissements* and communes, the taxes it paid, as well as the population of the administrative centre. The imperial govern-ment did away with the more obvious injustices, but it did not, in the prefects' eyes at least, do away with the anomalies. No classification could have satisfied all the prefects, and the more varied the criteria used to determine the salaries, the more adroit the prefects' reasoning became. Contades argued in 1815 that the only relevant criterion for fixing the prefects' salaries was the population and importance of the administrative centre. His was the only department in the fourth class with an adminis-trative centre whose population was 30,000, which was also a *bonne ville* and possessed a bishopric, academy and lycée. The Puy-de-Dôme should therefore be promoted to the third class. A similar demand was made by the baron de Talleyrand in 1820, for the Aisne. He emphasized a different set of criteria (which was very natural, since the population of his administrative centre was under 10,000): the size, total population and taxes paid by the department. As a final *tour de force* Talleyrand reversed the whole theory that based the prefect's salary on the population of his administrative centre. The cost of living was not lower but far higher in a small town, he alleged: the hotels at Laon being for the most part inadequate, and the prefect being the only government official of any importance there, he was re-sponsible for all and every kind of entertainment.[1] Apart from every prefect's natural desire to be given a higher salary, the basis of these complaints was justified less by the inadequacy of the criteria applied to the classification of prefectures than by the inelasticity of the classification. There were too few classes, and the difference in salary between the classes was too great. This was adjusted by the one important measure concerning the prefects' salaries that the Bourbons introduced. The ordinance

[1] Contades to Min.Int. 17 Feb. 1815 (AN, F1bII P-de-D (4)). Talleyrand to Min.Int. 26 Aug. 1820 (F1bI 83(1) Aisne).

of 15 May 1822 established seven different salaries (excluding the Seine), graded between 18,000 and 45,000 francs. Although the divisions between prefectures were less rigid, the outline of this classification is similar to that of 1810, very broad at the base and narrow at the top. Nearly 70 per cent of the prefectures were in the two lowest brackets, approximately the same percentage as the fourth-class prefectures represented in the 1810 classification.[1]

If the salaries of the individual prefects were scaled down during the Restoration, the reduction was by no means drastic. The total paid in salaries in 1822 was just over two million francs yearly: 2,072,000 francs. In 1810, for the same eighty-six departments, the total had been only some 90,000 francs more. But these figures are largely theoretical. Early in the Second Restoration, the government's financial situation led to its introducing a graded tax on salaries above 500 francs. So far as the prefects were concerned, the deductions were considerable. At 20,000 francs (the lowest level of salary in the 1810 classification) the tax was 24 per cent; at 40,000 26 per cent; at 100,000 (the prefecture of the Seine) 31 per cent. Although the tax was halved in 1819, any benefit the prefects might have enjoyed disappeared with the scaling down of salaries after 1822.[2] Similar economies were made on the prefectoral allowances. Minor costs previously paid by the government or department became the responsibility of the prefect, minor perquisites given the prefects disappeared. The expenses arising from the passage of the emperor or imperial family had been paid by the department. During the Restoration the entertainment of the royal family was the prefect's responsibility. Their visits were infrequent but expensive. One single fête Tournon gave for the duc d'Angoulême during his visit to Bordeaux in January 1816 cost him 8,000 francs.[3] A more important measure was the withdrawal of the governmental grant toward the expenses of a prefect's new establishment, whether he was newly nominated or merely transferred. This had been paid at a sum equivalent to three months of the prefect's

[1] *BL*, 7th ser., vol. xiv, bulletin 524.   [2] Law of 28 Apr. 1816. *BL*, 7th ser., vol. ii, bulletin 81. Cut of 17 July 1819: *BL*, 7th ser., vol. ix, bulletin 295.
[3] Moulard, *Tournon, préfet de la Gironde*, p. 94.

salary. The grants were withdrawn in January 1816—a considerable saving, as Girardin pointed out, now that the prefects had become merely the ministry's commercial travellers.[1] The hardship it caused the prefects is more difficult to gauge, there being no figures available which would illustrate the cost of a first establishment. But the expenses incurred in this way must have been considerable, bearing in mind both the frequency of Restoration prefectoral movements, and the widely admitted insufficiency of the governmental grant for travel expenses. This had been fixed in 1800 at ten francs per post (about eight kilometres). Auderic calculated the expense of his journey from the Basses-Alpes to the Vendée in April 1830 at 3,000 francs over and above the travel grant. Malartic reckoned that he had spent four times as much as the grant when moving from Paris to Nyons (Drôme) in 1829, Decazes that he had spent six times as much on moving from the Tarn to Bas-Rhin in 1819.[2]

These economies were made on the government grants that had been independent of the allowance for prefectoral expenses. These latter were cut at the very start of the Restoration, in February 1815, and subsequently throughout the period.[3] The total allowances paid in 1810 for the eighty-six departments that made up Second Restoration France had been over three and a half million francs. At the end of the Restoration the figure was two and three-quarter million. The Charente-Inférieure had been reduced from 50,000 francs in 1810 to 37,250 in 1829, Corrèze from 30,000 to 20,900 francs, the Basses-Pyrénées from 45,000 to 31,350 francs, the Yonne from 40,000 to 28,500 francs. Inevitably the reductions aroused protests from the prefects. As Malouet wrote, with an eye for consequences as fine as Scythrop's:

Si nous partons du principe, comme le prétendent certains orateurs, que les Préfets sont gorgés d'or, on fait très bien de réduire des abonnements qui alors ne sont entre leur mains qu'un supplément de traite-

---

[1] Ch. of Deps. 15 June 1821 (AP, 2nd ser., XXXII, 174).

[2] AN doss. Auderic, 155(9). Malartic to Min.Int. 28 Feb. 1829 (F1bI 84 (Drôme)). Decazes, 157(12).

[3] Ordinance of 4 Feb. 1815 (AN, F1a* 95 (2)), 27 May 1818 (F1a* 98(4)), 15 May 1822 (*BL*, 7th ser., XIV, bulletin 524), 25 Jan. 1829 (*BL*, 8th ser., vol. x, bulletin 275).

ment. Mais si nous admettons, ce que l'expérience a assez généralement prouvé, que ces administrateurs, loin de s'enrichir, consument dans leurs places une partie de leur fortune personnelle, pour le fragile honneur d'une existence politique qui ne leur assure ni présent ni avenir, consentons un moment à croire qu'ils emploient l'abonnement qu'ils reçoivent en dépenses réelles de l'administration. Or, toutes les fois que l'abonnement éprouve une reduction, il faut que les employés la supportent: de là naît l'instabilité des bureaux, le défaut de zèle, l'absence de talent, et souvent le découragement de ceux qui les habitent.[1]

As allowances were cut, employees were dismissed: a process which a deputy with administrative experience like Girardin could detail and deplore—'toutes ces réformes, toutes ces diminutions ont un grand inconvénient: c'est qu'en dernière analyse, elles retombent sur la classe très malheureuse des employés de préfecture'.[2] The Ain had a staff of twenty-two in 1816, seventeen in 1829: Morbihan had twenty-eight in 1813, eighteen in 1829: the Seine-et-Marne twenty-four in 1813, twenty-one in 1817.[3] The prefects were quick to point out that the consequences were dangerous for the administration. The first reductions came in February 1815, so that the prefects were forced to cut down their staff at a time when the pressure of extra work, dating from 1813 and accentuated by invasion, occupation and a change of régime, made it necessary rather to increase their numbers. Successive reductions made matters worse. In the Aisne in 1821 the prefecture was still dealing with affairs dating from 1814–15. A year later the prefect of the Oise wrote that the latest cut in his allowance would not only make it impossible to catch up on the backlog of work that existed already, but would so increase this backlog that there would be no hope of ever eliminating it.[4] Those of the prefect's staff who were not replaced had their wages frozen or reduced: and these

[1] Malouet, pr. Seine-Inférieure, to Min.Int. 7 June 1819 (AN, F1bI 87(2) Seine-Inf.
[2] Ch. of Deps. 17 June 1820 (AP, 2nd ser., xxviii, 574).
[3] AN, F1bI 83(1) Ain; 86(3) Morbihan; 87(2) Seine-Inf.
[4] Pr. Aisne to Min.Int. Feb. 1821 (AN, F1bI 83(1) Aisne); pr. Oise to Min.Int. 23 Sept. 1822 (86(4) Oise).

wages were in any case insufficient. In the Somme they were lower in the 1820s than they had been under the Directory. In the Seine-Inférieure Malouet was obliged to lodge one of his *chefs de bureau* and feed the other, to help eke out their salaries. Ill paid and insecure, the quality of the employees' work naturally suffered: 'la composition des Bureaux de Préfecture est, en général, une chose pitoyable...'. In a long note for the minister in 1823, the clerk summed up Puymaigre's description of his staff in the prefecture of the Oise:

Les employés ont vieillis dans les bureaux. Presque tous ont 25 ou 30 ans de services. A l'exception de deux, ils sont sinon incapables, du moins au-dessous de leur emploi. Parvenus du grade de copistes à celui de chefs de bureaux, ils sont dépourvus des connaissances spéciales au service qui leur est confié [et] ne savent pas sortir de l'ornière dans laquelle ils se sont traînés depuis de longues années. Avec de pareils collaborateurs, il est impossible que l'adm[inistrati]on du dép[artemen]t de l'Oise reçoive une impulsion rapide [et] régulière...[1]

Obviously over-age or avowedly incapable employees should have been replaced by educated and intelligent young men. Unfortunately the paucity of their allowances made it difficult for the prefects to offer a salary high enough to offset, in some measure, the disadvantages of so precarious a career. The situation of the prefectoral staff, and its effect on the administration, presents the obverse side of the much praised Restoration economies.

The effect of the cuts in allowances on the prefects themselves is more difficult to judge. Under the Empire and early Restoration they were under no obligation to produce accounts: salary and allowances were given them without any government control of their spending. As a result, when the Decazes ministry asked the prefects for details of the present and past administrative expenses of their prefectures in 1819, many were unable to supply them.[2] The ordinance of 15 May 1822 made it obligatory

---

[1] Pr. Somme to Min.Int. 8 June 1825 (AN, F1bI 87(2) Somme); pr. Seine-Inférieure to Min.Int. 7 June 1819 (87(2) Seine-Inf.); note for min. 1823 (86(4) Oise).
[2] Circular to prefects 21 Apr. 1819 (AN, F1a 34).

for the prefects to spend a minimum two-thirds of their allowance on the wages of their staff alone, and during the 1820s a detailed account of the manner in which this sum was spent was sent yearly to the Minister of the Interior. Unfortunately these figures give no indication of a prefect's total expenditure. Between 1824 and 1827 the prefect of the Ardèche spent an average 1,500 francs per year more than the allotted sum for the wages of his staff, but it is impossible to find whether this meant a deficit on the total allowance, or whether it was covered by the grant for the remainder of his expenses. Such few figures as exist for the spending of the allowance as a whole cover only the period 1813–18. There is one exception. The figures for the Gironde are available for the years 1824–8 as well as 1816–18, the allowance remaining 50,000 francs throughout the Restoration. From 1816 to 1818, the prefect spent under 49,000 francs, but from 1824 to 1828 the total allowance was overspent by 3,000–5,000 francs per year, although the staff had been reduced from thirty-three in December 1816 to thirty in December 1828. It is interesting to compare these figures with those for the Rhône, a prefecture of the same rank and with the same allowance. From 1816 to 1818 the prefect of the Rhône exceeded his allowance by sums varying from 1,500 to 4,500 francs, although here also the number of employees was cut, from twenty-four in 1813 to twenty-one in 1817. Generalization is difficult from department to department: the prefect of the Loire-Inférieure, with an administrative centre almost as populous and commercially important as Bordeaux or Lyon, had a surplus of between 500 and 1,150 francs yearly from 1815 to 1818.[1] Nevertheless, the figures available indicate that the successive reductions in the allowances which were made throughout the Restoration made it extremely rare for a prefect to show a profit on his administration. There would certainly seem to be little enough justification in the perennial accusation made by parliamentary oppositions throughout the Restoration, that the prefects built

[1] AN, F1bI 83 (2) Ardèche; 85 (2) Gironde; 86 (5) Rhône, and Albert de Lezay-Marnésia's remarks, *Mes souvenirs*, p. 157; pr. Loire-Inférieure to Min.Int. 31 Aug. 1819 (85 (5) Loire-Inf.)

their fortunes on their vast and superfluous salaries. Several found it difficult enough to balance their budgets. The prefecture of the Aisne showed a deficit of over 13,000 francs for the years 1816–18, the prefect of the Oise overspent his allowance by 2,250 francs in 1817 and 4,500 in 1818, the prefect of the Loiret overspent his by 5,000 francs in 1817 and 8,000 in 1819.[1] In theory a deficit might be paid from the prefect's salary, but the very nature of this salary made such a possibility unlikely. It was designed to cover the expenses a prefect incurred in the course of his duty: less a salary than an entertainment and living allowance. As one prefect put it, 'un directeur, un chef de service *a tout ce qu'il a*, c'est à dire que son traitement n'est grevé de presqu'aucune charge de représentation, tandis qu'un préfet à 20,000 fr. et 30,000 fr. a la charge de dépenser environ 20,000 et 30,000 fr., sous peine de servir mal et de perdre, au désavantage du Gouvernement, son influence...'[2] This belief was common. Tournon could not conceive the possibility of saving on his salary while a member of the administration: '...la dépense de cet argent est un moyen d'administration sur lequel le gouvernement a le droit de compter.' A certain display, a hint even of grandeur, was expected of a prefect. In the words of one Minister of the Interior, 'que nos premiers administrateurs aient une représentation sans luxe, mais noble et décente'. Austerity might be mistaken for avarice: Estourmel was accused of selling the vegetables from the garden of his prefecture.[3] This pressure on a prefect to spend, even to overspend, his salary meant, that far from paying for any deficit there might be in the allowance, the salary might merely provide another source of debt. There was therefore an evident need for a prefect to possess an adequate private income.

The Bourbons made 164 prefects. Some kind of data exists in the dossiers for estimating the private income of 124. The extent

[1] AN, F1bI 83(1) Aisne; 86(4) Oise; 85(5) Loiret.
[2] Creuzé de Lesser, pr. Hérault, to Min.Int. 2 Apr. 1822 (AN, F1bI 85(3) Hérault).
[3] Tournon: quoted in Moulard, *Tournon, préfet de la Gironde*, p. 550, note 1. Vaublanc to Ch. of Deps. 26 March 1816 (AP, 2nd ser., XVI, 702). Anon. and undated letter (AN doss. Estourmel, 159(3)).

and accuracy of this information should not be over-estimated. It was provided by the prefects themselves, as part of the personal information that every member of the Corps supplied (at least in theory) when taking up an administrative post, whether he was newly nominated or merely transferred. Lamagdelaine calculated that almost all the declarations made under the Consulate were inaccurate, the administrators deliberately underrating their personal income—as he had—in view of a still problematic future.[1] The declarations were no doubt more accurate under the Empire and Restoration, but bearing in mind the frequency with which members of the Corps were mistaken over the date of their birth, another item of information they were obliged to supply, there is no reason to give unlimited credence to their estimates of their incomes. In the great majority of cases, these figures are given baldly, without any details. They are figures for gross income, and make no mention of taxes—or of debts. The figures given for Vanssay's income, for example, make no mention of the 5 per cent annual interest he was paying on a loan of 73,000 francs. Similarly with Scey. He was credited with a private income of 100,000 francs in 1814, a very considerable fortune by contemporary standards, but an anonymous note written in October 1815 states that Scey had lost most of his fortune in running a banking concern, and the remainder in a settlement with his brother-in-law.[2]

A more satisfactory index to the prefects' financial situation would be the taxes they paid. Here again there are the problems of the availability and interpretation of the evidence. The major source is the series F1cIII of the Archives Nationales; but the evidence varies in value from department to department, for the most part consisting of lists of those eligible to stand as deputies, with the taxes they paid.[3] These lists have a preliminary defect, that they concern only those prefects who paid 1,000 francs or more in taxes, the criterion for eligibility as a deputy,

[1] These remarks are in an undated form, probably late Empire (AN doss. Lamagdelaine, 166(7)).    [2] AN doss. Vanssay, 176(5); Scey, 173(11).
[3] See A.-J. Tudesq, 'Les listes électorales de la Monarchie censitaire', *Annales* . . ., XIII (Apr.–June 1958), 277–88, for an expert evaluation of this source, on which the following account is based.

and since they do not exist for every department, absence from the lists cannot be taken as negative evidence, as proof that the prefect concerned paid less than 1,000 francs. In the second place it is difficult to consider the taxation figures as an accurate index of wealth: and this for two reasons. Taxation was heavily biased toward landed rather than invested wealth. Although the majority of prefects probably had a private income which derived entirely from land, there are indications of incomes of another pattern. Commercial or industrial interests, those of Angosse or Cintré, for example, appear to have been exceptional, but investment in government stock or bonds and interest-bearing loans to private individuals played a not unimportant part in some prefectoral incomes. Part of Houdetot's *majorat* in 1809, all of Germain's, was in 5 per cent government bonds; in 1810 Roussy had an income of 24,000 francs made up in part from land, but also from government bonds and loans on private individuals, and the same balance can be found with Feutrier ten years later, with estates in Gard, Hérault and Lozère, a third share in a plaster quarry at Montmartre, and 3,000 francs in the 5 per cents.[1]

Again, even if the uneven nature of taxation is disregarded, the ratio of taxes to income differed between departments. It was calculated in 1831 that 300 francs of taxes meant an income of 3,047 francs in Corsica, 3,049 in the Bouches-du-Rhône, 3,085 in the Var, 3,260 in the Ariège, 3,478 in the Basses-Pyrénées, but under 2,000 francs in fifty-six departments, and a mere 1,569 in the Seine.[2] Nevertheless, a weighted average for France as a whole works out at about 1:7—1,000 francs in taxes representing a gross income of some 7,000; and this figure of 1,000 francs in taxes may be less meaningless than most, as it entitled a man to stand as deputy. Using the taxation figures where available

---

[1] The Angosse were ironmasters in the Basses-Pyrénées: see AN, AF IV 1335, details of Casimir d'Angosse's income as an auditor in 1810. Cintré, 157(24). Houdetot, Germain: N. Batjin, *Histoire...de la noblesse de France* (1862), pp. 411, 420–1. A *majorat* (a Napoleonic innovation conserved by the Bourbons) was a guaranteed and inalienable income attached to, and transmitted with, a title: the size of the *majorat* depending on the title. Roussy, AN, AF IV 1335. Feutrier, 160(6).

[2] AN, F1cII 53. I owe this reference to M. Tudesq.

(62 prefects), and the 1:7 ratio to convert figures for gross private income to probable taxes, it is possible to establish the financial situation of 137 of the 164 prefects the Bourbons named. Given the nature of the evidence, the conclusion can be no more than tentative. It is nevertheless surprising. Eighty per cent of the prefects had a private income sufficient for them to stand as deputies: and this in a country where the total number of eligibles was around 15,000. That some prefects had a minimal private income, or none at all, is certain. At the start of his prefectoral career Christophe de Villeneuve-Bargemon had only 1,550 francs per year; toward the end of his, in 1820, Malouet had only 1,500: 'je suis de tous les préfets du Royaume celui dont la fortune personnelle est la plus nulle'. Xavier de Choiseul, prefect of Corsica in April 1830, had no private income whatsoever. He had served in the English army while an émigré, and was entitled to 2,400 francs per year half-pay as a former lieutenant in the 27th Foot. Unfortunately this was seized by his creditors in London. At the Restoration he had been recommended for a pension of 2,000 francs per year from the Maison du Roi, a sum above the average, on the grounds of his services, his wife's poverty, his inability to find a post—'et le nom qu'il porte'. The Maison du Roi only allowed him 1,200 francs as pension, which naturally ceased being paid when Choiseul joined the prefectoral corps in 1822. To Palmerston's surprise and the Minister of the Interior's displeasure, Choiseul then applied to the War Office for a military allowance equivalent to his half-pay.[1] On the whole, however, the prefects seem to have been men of substance, and some, by French standards, very rich indeed: Germain, from a family of Parisian bankers; Terray, who paid over 5,000 francs in taxes in 1816, over 10,000 in 1830; Breteuil, who in spite of having lost his anticipated inheritance from his uncle, bishop of Montauban under the Ancien Régime, had a private income— after his mother's death—of 70,000–80-000 francs.[2] At first sight

[1] AN doss. Christophe de Villeneuve-Bargemon, 176(13). Malouet to Min.Int. 7 June 1819 (F1bI 87(2) Seine-Inf.). Choiseul, 157(23), including Palmerston to Min.Int. 20 Apr. 1822; O3* 768.

[2] AN doss. Germain, 161(10). Terray in 1816, F1cIII Côte-d'Or (5); in 1830 Aube (7). Breteuil, 156(43).

this relative prosperity seems the more surprising in the case of
Boula de Colombiers and Brevannes, whose fathers had been
in the pre-revolutionary magistracy and might therefore have
been expected to suffer considerable financial loss from the
abolition of their offices;[1] and in that of former émigrés. La
Vieuville alleged that the majority of his family estates in Anjou
and Brittany had been sold when he emigrated, so that he had
been reduced to a single estate at Châteauneuf; he was nevertheless able to exercise his functions unpaid during the first years
of the Restoration, and pay just under 8,000 francs in taxes in
1820.[2] On a more modest scale, an émigré like Kerespertz bought
back enough of his former estates to give him a solid income of
some 20,000 francs, Lestrade and Puymaigre acquired a similar
prosperity after the indemnity paid to the émigrés.[3] Neither
Revolution nor emigration would seem to have destroyed the
prefects' fortunes entirely. There were prefects who weathered
the storm unscathed, like Raymond Delaitre, whose considerable
private income came in all probability from Robillard and Company, the tobacco firm he directed for eighteen years: and others
who made a good thing out of the Revolution. Albertas could offer
to serve without pay in 1814 the more easily, perhaps, because
he had considerably enlarged his fortune by successful speculation
since 1789: while Mortarieu's fortune (he paid 5,000 francs of
taxes in 1818) led his detractors to contest the origin of the
prefect's family as well as his fortune, casting him in the role
Malin de Gondreville played toward the Simeuses, with a background allegedly little more august than Malin's.[4]

Fragmentary though it is, the evidence is suggestive. A few

[1] Boula paid between 1,750 and 2,100 francs in taxes between 1828 and 1830
(AN, FICIII Vosges (6)). For the family, H. Diné, *Une famille... sous l'Ancien
Régime et la Révolution. Les Boula* (1957). Brevannes, nearly 2,500 in 1820
(Seine (8)). R. de Clavière, *Les assemblées... de la sénéchaussée de Beaujolais
en 1789* (1935), pp. 634–7.

[2] AN doss. La Vieuville, 166(17), 176(11); FICIII Ille-et-Vilaine (4); Vaublanc
to Ch. of Deps. 26 March 1816 (AP, 2nd ser., XVI, 702).

[3] AN doss. Kerespertz, 176; Lestrade, 166(31), 169(1); Puymaigre, 170(26),
and his *Souvenirs*, p. 268.

[4] AN doss. Raymond Delaitre, 158(9), 172(3). Albertas, 155(2); R+C, I,
30–1. Mortarieu, 167(31); FICIII Tarn-et-Garonne (2).

prefects excepted, the majority had private incomes which could supplement any financial loss they might incur during their administrative careers, however much they might legitimately dislike it. If a prefect's preference for a certain department might be based on its proximity to his home and family, it would also be influenced by his income and probable expenditure. Montli-vault was too poor to accept the Gironde, one of the most coveted posts in France. A glance at the prefects of the Gironde from 1815 to 1830 suggests that a considerable income was necessary: Tournon had 20,000–30,000 francs a year, Breteuil 80,000, Haussez 40,000, and Curzay 25,000.[1] This might appear to put a brake on promotion, the personnel being preselected, as it were, by their incomes as well as their politics, and only the richest being able to hold the top posts. The Gironde would nevertheless appear to have been an exception. Malouet and Vanssay administered the Seine-Inférieure, Malouet and Vaul-chier the Bas-Rhin, although their incomes were under 7,000 francs per year, and these were prefectures almost as impor-tant as the Gironde.[2] It was not simply that a more important department meant increased expenditure, or that promotion necessarily meant the prospect of a greater loss. Departments of the same rank differed in their allowance and in the expenditure necessary to administer them: Locard found the Indre more expensive than the Cher or Vienne. Malouet claimed that under the Empire the Meurthe had been known as a good prefecture for a poor man, it being possible to save 10,000–15,000 francs yearly on the allowance, and early in the Second Restoration Joseph de Villeneuve-Bargemon found it possible to save a considerable part of his allowance in the Haute-Saône.[3] It is doubtful whether this would have been possible later in the Restoration—the allowance for the Meurthe was cut from 50,000 francs per year in 1810 to 37,250 in 1829, the Haute-Saône from

---

[1] Montlivault: Haussez, *Mémoires*, II, 4. AN doss. Tournon, 174(11). Breteuil, 156(43). Haussez, 166(25). Curzay, 156(38).
[2] AN doss. Malouet, 167(4); Vanssay, 176(5); Vaulchier, 176(6).
[3] Locard to Min.Int. 29 Oct. 1829 (AN, F1bI 85(3) Indre). Malouet to Min.Int. 7 June 1819 (see above p. 160 note 1). Joseph de Villeneuve-Bargemon, *Sou-venirs*, p. 76.

35,000 to 25,650—but there is some evidence that departments with very different characteristics existed. The Gers was not a department for a prefect who had to calculate his expenses too nicely, the Oise could not be run on its allowance and prefects would use its convenient proximity to Paris to obtain another and more economical department: '...si le département de l'Oise a vu tant de préfets se succéder...c'est que chacun en sentant le désavantage de sa position...a profité des avantages de cette même position, pour obtenir un changement...'[1] It has been possible to discover the incomes of ten prefects of these two departments. Only one had an income under 10,000 francs. Five had over 20,000.

The difference between departments did not necessarily debar a poor prefect from promotion, nor did it destroy the existence of a makeshift hierarchy; but by introducing yet another criterion by which the prefect judged his post, it qualified his attitude toward this hierarchy. In a career not remarkable for security of tenure, in which promotion was problematical, minor differences between departments became, by compensation, the more important.

[1] Conseiller de préfecture Gers to Min.Int. 24 May 1819 (AN, F1bI 85 (1) Gers). Pr. Oise to Min.Int. 17 Oct. 1825 (86(4) Oise).

CHAPTER 13

# THE SUBORDINATE PERSONNEL

The subordinate personnel and sub-prefects in particular had
one major advantage over their superiors: security. They were
more likely to survive a change of ministry, even, as the Hundred
Days and July Revolution showed, a change of régime. There
were exceptions. 'Il revient pour nous déshonorer tous', Barante
had said on learning of Napoleon's return.[1] Certainly the
Hundred Days imposed a severe strain on those administrators
whose royalism had been none the less exuberant, in 1814, for
its being recent in origin. The Hundred Days was studded with
their convolute and often contradictory manœuvres. Izos, for
fifteen years an imperial sub-prefect, emerged as an enthusiastic
royalist in 1814, only to swing noisily into reverse during the
Hundred Days, which saw him 'livré comme un fou à toutes les
sottises de ce temps', and led to his dismissal at the Second
Restoration. Farnaud had been maintained as secretary-general
of the Hautes-Alpes by the Bourbons, and employed his inconsiderable literary talents to endearing himself to the new
government: he enlivened a prefectoral dinner with royalist
couplets (sung to the tune of 'Plaisirs et Sciences'), and inflicted
his 'Epistle in honour of the comte d'Artois' on the assembled
conseil général. Then Napoleon landed, and Harmand, recipient
of these lucubrations, was forced to leave his prefecture. Farnaud,
by contrast, met the emperor, and extracted his nomination as
provisional prefect of the department. He was precipitate. The
next day, 7 March, Harmand returned, and forced him to give
up his post, burn his nomination and publicly abjure his errors
by taking an oath of loyalty to Louis XVIII. But at the end of
the month Harmand was once again obliged to leave Gap:
Farnaud, as might have been expected, 'retomba dans son
premier égarement', installing himself as prefect. He was transferred back to his post as secretary-general by the emperor, but

[1] Rémusat, *Mémoires*, I, 198.

even after this less than ambiguous conduct, retained his post until January 1816, and returned to it in 1820.[1] Others of the subordinate personnel, Liégeard, Chazelles or La Roque, took even the Hundred Days in their stride. La Roque had been an officer before the Revolution, campaigning with the Marines in the American War. He emigrated in 1791, fought in the army of the Princes, and then retired to London where he spent his time translating Jenner's pioneering work and practising or propagandizing vaccination. Returning to France in 1803, La Roque became sub-prefect of Tournon in 1813, and was maintained at the Restoration. At the start of the Hundred Days he came out strongly against Napoleon. The move was premature: although La Roque later recognized Napoleon as emperor, and pleaded to keep his post, he was replaced. Then came Waterloo and the brusque renaissance of La Roque's royalism. He marched on his former sub-prefecture with a handful of National Guards, took it by main force, and celebrated his reinstallation by carrying out a severe purge of those officials in his *arrondissement* he suspected of Bonapartism.[2]

Politics apart, the subordinate personnel faced the same dangers and obeyed the same imperatives as their superiors. For both the risk was a demonstration of untimely zeal or aberrant enthusiasm. It might be pure bad luck. At the Second Restoration Grassin was sub-prefect of Mayenne, an *arrondissement* in which the proscribed General Lefebvre-Desnouettes was thought to be hiding. Grassin threw himself heart and soul into the search, twice sending the *gendarmerie* to ransack a local château. Unfortunately it belonged to a Peer of France, whose influence was sufficient to put paid to Grassin's career.[3] Noue's was a different case. Disliked by his *arrondissement*, coating private quarrels with a political veneer, his royalism was of a brand too unquiet for his prefect, and even for Vaublanc: 'il ne rêve que correspondances criminelles, associations secrètes, démarches téné-

---

[1] AN doss. Izos, 163: partic. pr. Pyrénées-Orientales to Min.Int. 9 March 1816. Farnaud, 160(2), partic. pr. Hautes-Alpes to Min.Int. 24 Apr. 1816.

[2] AN doss. Liégeard, 166(33). Chazelles, see above, pp. 111–12. La Roque, 158(10) partic. note for min. 13 Sept. 1820: AAG, Emigrés, 519(14).

[3] AN doss. Grassin, 161(18).

breuses, il est toujours au moment de tenir les fils d'une grande conspiration...'[1]

These were dangers common to both levels of the administration, but perhaps less acute for the subordinate personnel, whose secondary rank was in some sense a protection. But there were certain additional difficulties inherent in the local nature of the subordinate personnel's recruitment and administration. They relied, from their very position, on their local influence as much as on their prestige as government agents. Personal failings of any kind might destroy this influence. Such failings ranged from the obsessive avarice that lost Chassoux his post at Bourganeuf, to Stephanopoli's alleged complicity in his brother's kidnapping of the mayor of Bastia's daughter and Durbois' abduction of a local girl who reappeared, to the scandal of his *arrondissement*, in the sub-prefecture.[2] The nature of the posts held by the subordinate personnel was such that a great deal depended on their good relations with other local officials, and with their own superior. When such relations did not obtain, the sub-prefect or secretary-general might find himself replaced. Joseph Leroy's personal feud with the Director of Posts at Prades led to his transfer, Carbon-Prévinquière's public quarrel with the tax inspector at Millau to his dismissal.[3] A prefect's relations with his subordinates might be strained for a variety of political or personal reasons. Tessières, secretary-general of the Côte-d'Or at the Second Restoration, was on such bad terms with his prefect, Maxime de Choiseul, that the latter demanded his dismissal. He was unsuccessful, and when Choiseul was himself transferred shortly afterwards, Tessières proudly—and publicly —attributed the move to his own exertions; thus attracting a ministerial thunderbolt: 'Je suis très bien informé de la manière scandaleuse avec laquelle vous avez annoncé par toute la ville [Dijon] que vous étiez enfin parvenu à faire chasser le préfet...'[4] There are cases where prefect and sub-prefect were tempera-

[1] Pr. Aisne to Min.Int. 27 Feb. 1816 (AN doss. Selle de Beauchamp, 156(10)). Doss. Noue, 158(15).
[2] AN doss. Chassoux, 157(19); Stephanopoli, 173(20); Durbois, 158(40).
[3] AN doss. Joseph Leroy, 166(29); Carbon-Prévinquière, 157(6).
[4] Min. to Tessières 17 Feb. 1816 (AN doss. 174(3)).

mentally or politically antipathetic but condemned nevertheless
to co-exist: the consequence of a political recruitment which
might subordinate a Centre-Left sub-prefect to a Right-wing
prefect, or vice versa, and produce an uncomfortable state of
administrative oxymoron. Gorjon de Verville became sub-prefect
of Doullens in 1816. A year later Allonville was made prefect of
the department. Their association, though protracted, was punc-
tuated by a series of unfortunate disagreements. In 1819 Verville
took the side of a Protestant schoolteacher against the *curé* of
Doullens, who wished to prevent her, as a non-Catholic, from
teaching. Significantly, Verville took this stand against Allonville's advice. The minister approved the sub-prefect's attitude,
on the ground that parents, even if Catholic, should be free to
send their children to any school they wished. The next year,
however, the *curé* announced the imminent arrival of a new
schoolteacher, a sister from a Catholic order. He invited his
parishoners to send her their children, and threatened to bar
young people who had not been taught by a Catholic from
Communion. Verville complained to the prefect: it was an act
of overt intolerance, an infraction of the previous ministerial
ruling. Allonville objected to the form of Verville's report. The
quarrel intensified, with both prefect and sub-prefect writing to
the minister. Allonville alleged insubordination on Verville's
part, and wanted him transferred. Verville accused Allonville of
wishing to reduce him to the status of a mere 'commis de
préfecture'. The minister was inclined to blame Allonville and
caution Verville only as a matter of form. Such action proved
unnecessary. The minister suddenly received a letter from
Allonville, eulogizing Verville's behaviour during the elections,
and retracting the previous complaints. The honeymoon was
brief. Some three months later (February 1821) another quarrel
broke out. Verville had written direct to the minister on a matter
concerning the electoral college of his *arrondissement*. Once again
Allonville scented insubordination. Once again the minister
inclined to Verville's side, and hinted as much. Allonville returned
to the charge later in the year. Verville had written to him about
another religious matter, in a way the prefect found disrespectful.

There is no indication of the sequel: but in December 1821 the Villèle–Corbière ministry came to power. Six months later Verville was transferred to another and inferior sub-prefecture. He resigned rather than accept this post. Allonville continued his prefectoral career unscathed until the July Revolution.[1]

There was a wide range of reasons, not necessarily political, which might lead the minister to replace a subordinate member of the administration. The manner in which they were replaced reflected the local background of the subordinate personnel, transfers being far rarer than among the prefects. The reason is clear. A great part of the subordinate personnel's utility lay in their local influence. There was therefore little to gain in transferring them. Although such transfers did take place, they were frequently limited to an exchange between two sub-prefects, often within the same department. Cussac moved from Murat to Mauriac in May 1816, exchanging with Lalo. Clément Frayssinous moved from Villefranche to Millau in November 1818, exchanging with Du Lac de Montvert.[2] A train of transfers, on the pattern of the prefectoral movement of 13 October 1829, was exceptional. As a result, although the total administrative experience of the prefects and sub-prefects in office in July 1830 was not dissimilar, the sub-prefects tended to have spent longer at the same post. Just over half of the sub-prefects, just under half of the prefects, had more than ten years' experience in the Corps in July 1830: but 30 per cent of the sub-prefects, as against 15 per cent only of the prefects, had spent more than ten years in the post they then held.

Not all the subordinate personnel found this to their taste. There were sub-prefects who disliked their *arrondissements* (Wildermeth referred to Vouziers as 'la Sibérie de la France'), who despaired of their situation in a system in which promotion was so unlikely. 'Enfin je suis un sous-préfet forcé', Le Caron de Fleury complained in November 1817, 'né et condamné à mourir sous-préfet, après l'avoir été presque depuis la création de ce

[1] AN doss. Gorjon de Verville, 161 (4).
[2] AN doss. Cussac, 157 (38); Lalo, 166 (7); Frayssinous, 160 (13); Du Lac, 158 (34).

monde, depuis 1803...'[1] For someone with a lively consciousness of his own worth, the position was peculiarly frustrating.
The baron de Beaumont had asked to be made sub-prefect of
Morlaix, his home *arrondissement*, in April 1814, while still
serving in the army. Retired on 1 June 1820, he demanded the
sub-prefecture of Vico three weeks later. Posted to Calvi in September, he had spent only two years in the *arrondissement* before
he wanted a post nearer Paris. To his annoyance he was transferred
to the Drôme: to be transferred to the Loire-Inférieure in 1824.
It was a move he viewed with disrelish. The minister might think
it promotion, he wrote, but for an erstwhile lieutenant-colonel
who had already administered two sub-prefectures, it was
difficult to see a transfer to a town of only 1,800 inhabitants
(Savenay) in the same light. He still wanted a post near Paris—
particularly as he found that Savenay was having a deleterious
effect on his health. Which was no doubt the explanation of his
escalating claims: in 1828 he demanded the prefecture of Corsica.
Finally, after nine years of continued complaints, the Martignac
ministry made him sub-prefect of Meaux. Beaumont was obstinately unimpressed. He sent the minister a routine letter of thanks,
but could not resist adding that the move was in no sense
promotion.[2] For men like this, the price of security might seem
too high, might seem to be stagnation.

[1] Wildermeth to Min.Int. 9 Feb. 1818 (AN doss. 177(2)); Le Caron to head of
1st Div. Min.Int. 19 Nov. 1817 (doss. 160(8)).
[2] AN doss. 156(11); AAG, CG 209.

CHAPTER 14

# THE SUBORDINATE PERSONNEL: SALARIES, ALLOWANCES, INCOMES

For a prefect a private income was useful: for a sub-prefect it was imperative. As the ministry realized—'le Ministre pense qu'une sous-préfecture [oblige] toujours celui qui l'occupe à des dépenses plus considérables que ses émoluments...'[1] The difference can be illustrated by the disproportion between the prefects' and sub-prefects' salaries. The latter had been based by the law of 28 Pluviôse An VIII on the population of the town in which the sub-prefecture was situated. Towns with under 20,000 inhabitants carried a salary of 3,000 francs, those with over 20,000 one of 4,000 francs.[2] The secretaries-general were given, in principle, one-third of the salary their prefect received, but their minimum salary was fixed at 3,000 francs, and their maximum at 6,000.[3] Even in 1800 the minimum prefectoral salary (8,000 francs) was double that of the best paid sub-prefect. But whereas prefectoral salaries were considerably raised in 1810, and the minimum during the Restoration was around 18,000 francs, those of the subordinate personnel remained basically unchanged, so that the ratio between the lowest prefectoral post and the highest sub-prefecture shifted from 2:1 to something nearer 5:1. The division between the two levels of the administration was evident in their functions and background: it was exaggerated by the disproportion in salaries and allowances. The sub-prefects, like their superiors, were given allowances for expenses and entertainment. In 1815 the majority of sub-prefectures had an allowance of between 3,000 and 5,000 francs. Certain commercial centres, Bordeaux, Marseille, Lille and Dunkirk, for example, had 6,000 or over, Dieppe had 9,500 and Le Havre 10,000 francs. The highest allowances went to sub-prefectures in the Paris

---

[1] Draft of Min.Int. letter (12 March 1821) to duc d'Aumont (AN doss. Constan, 157(31)).  [2] *BL*, 3rd ser., vol. I, bulletin 17.
[3] Law of 17 Ventôse An VIII (*BL*, 3rd ser., vol. XIII, bulletin 90).

area, both Saint-Denis and Sceaux having an allowance of over 13,000 francs.[1] The precise criteria on which these grants were based are predictably difficult to discover. It seems most likely that they were the result of a combination of factors, the population of the *arrondissement*, the number of its communes, perhaps the taxes it paid. Even so, there are apparent, and inexplicable, inequalities. In the Loire-Inférieure Paimbœuf had 25 communes and just under 42,000 inhabitants, Ancenis 28 and some 50,000, Châteaubriant 37 and 60,000, Savenay 51 and nearly 110,000: but each *arrondissement* had the same allowance, 3,000 francs. There were similar discrepancies in the Sarthe. La Flèche had 80 communes and a population of over 90,000, Saint-Calais 60 and a population of 72,000, Mamers 144 and some 130,000 inhabitants. Yet whereas the sub-prefect of La Flèche had an allowance of 4,000 francs, his colleague at Saint-Calais had 3,000 and the sub-prefect of Mamers a mere 3,600.[2]

There was one outstanding anomaly. Should a sub-prefect have governmentally owned lodgings in the town he administered, he paid no rent. But if such lodgings were unavailable, not only did the sub-prefect have to rent them, but the government did nothing to indemnify him. When Nicholas-Charles Besson was moved from Parthenay to Issoudun in 1820, his salary was cut from 4,000 to 3,000 francs: and in addition, whereas his establishment at Parthenay had been rent-free, at Issoudun he had to pay 1,000 francs yearly. Given the sub-prefect's salary scale and small allowances, this was a considerable sum. At Vendôme Armand de Beaumont spent 6,000 francs of his own money on renovating the sub-prefecture only to be obliged to hand it over (almost without compensation), to the Ministry of War, and rent another building at 1,200 francs a year.[3] In these circumstances there was a certain naïvety in the prefect of Cantal's horror when he discovered one of his subordinates administering

[1] These figures are taken from an undated (Hundred Days) list in AN, F1bI 82.
[2] Loire-Inférieure: pr. Loire-Inférieure to Min.Int. 11 Nov. 1829 (AN, F1bI 85 (5) Loire-Inf.). Sarthe: s.pr. Mamers to Min.Int. 10 July 1829 (87(1) Sarthe).
[3] AN doss. N.-C. Besson, 156(21). Beaumont: F1bI 85 (4) Loir-et-Cher, partic. note for min. 1823.

his *arrondissement* from an inn, 'où il n'a qu'une seule chambre à laquelle on ne parvient qu'en traversant la cuisine'.[1]

This meant that in the same department there would be very considerable discrepancies, both in the allowances and in their relative sufficiency. In Calvados, for example, the sub-prefects of Vire, Bayeux and Lisieux all had the same allowance of 4,000 francs, but the latter two sub-prefects had rent-free lodgings whereas the sub-prefect of Vire paid 1,000 francs a year.[2] It is not surprising that the anomalies in the allowance, and its alleged inadequacy, led to a stream of complaints. From 1822 a sub-prefect had to spend a minimum half of his allowance on the salaries of his staff. But in a large number of *arrondissements*—Charolles, Compiègne, Gien, Narbonne, and Trévoux among others—the sub-prefects spent far more.[3] This might mean that there were insufficient funds remaining to pay for other expenses, and that the sub-prefect would be forced to devote some part of his salary, and at the worst, his private income, to eking out the allowance. It is easier to assess how far this may have been the case with the subordinate personnel than with the prefects, because there is more evidence for their total expenditure, at least during the 1820s. At Ploërmel in 1825, at Joigny in 1826–7, the sub-prefect overspent his total allowance. At Gannat the same occurred every year from 1821 to 1829. The sub-prefect of Avallon spent his whole allowance on salaries in 1828, leaving nothing for material expenses like heating, light or paper, while the sub-prefect of Château-Salins in the Meurthe paid 3,900 francs on salaries to his staff out of a *total* allowance of 3,400. At Saint-Quentin the situation was even worse. In the 1820s the sub-prefect's total assets, including his salary, came to 7,700 francs. His expenses were 7,800 francs. As the prefect of the Aisne remarked, this was forcing a government employee to carry out his functions unpaid.[4]

[1] Min. extract from pr. Cantal's letter 24 July 1816 (AN doss. Lalo, 166(7)).
[2] AN, F1bI 83(2) Calvados, partic. note for min. 14 Aug. 1826.
[3] AN, F1bI 87(1) Saône-et-Loire; 86(4) Oise; 85(5) Loiret; 83(2) Aude; 83(1) Ain.
[4] Ploërmel: AN, F1bI 86(3) Morbihan. Joigny, Avallon: 87(3) Yonne. Gannat: 83(1) Allier. Château-Salins: 86(2) Meurthe. Saint-Quentin: 83(1) Aisne, partic. pr. to Min.Int. 7 Nov. 1822.

There were perhaps *arrondissements* which were cheap to administer: those of the Basses- and Hautes-Alpes, for example, sparsely populated and economically undeveloped. A sub-prefect's position was worst in those *arrondissements* or towns where industry or commerce flourished, as at Dreux, with its 120 factories and mills, or Mayenne, where the sub-prefect over-spent his total allowance in 1825, 1826 and 1827. As he pointed out, Mayenne was a commercial centre, the cost of living was high, rents were excessive. A note for the minister concurred. The author noted that commerce and industry had developed greatly since 1814 in both *arrondissement* and town: 'Mayenne est une ville où règne le luxe.' The same was true of Saint-Etienne, where, as one of the deputies wrote to the minister in 1826, the population of the *arrondissement* had increased sharply since the Restoration, and that of the town had doubled. The town was predominantly a manufacturing centre, and the manufacturers could pay their employees well. The sub-prefect, on the other hand, could afford to pay only the same wages as he had in 1814, although rents had doubled since the Restoration.[1] A rise in prices, in rents, even in printing costs ('le renchérissement toujours croissant du papier', the sub-prefect of Saint-Gaudens noted in 1825, 'devient ruineux pour les administrations')[2]— these were less important than the difficulty of recruiting or retaining suitable staff, at salaries lower than they could find elsewhere. At Louviers the sub-prefect could pay only 800 francs a year. As he remarked, no capable employee would seek so ill paid a post, 'ils se font de préférence commis de fabrique, emplois très lucratifs dans ce pays'.[3] In 1814, the staff of the sub-prefecture of Le Havre worked from nine in the morning until four in the afternoon, and again from six to eight, nine, or even eleven at night. All this for 1,000 francs a year. Added to this was the new prosperity peace had brought to the town,

---

[1] Dreux: form for expenses of s.pr. in 1824 (AN, F1bI 84 Eure-et-Loir). May-enne: s.pr. in form for expenses in 1825; note for min. 31 Dec. 1827 (86(2) Mayenne). Saint-Etienne: Fournas, dep. Loire, to Min.Int. 6 Sept. 1826 (85(4) Loire).

[2] Form for expenses of s.pr. in 1824 (AN, F1bI 85 (1) Haute-Garonne).

[3] Form for expenses of s.pr. in 1825 (AN, F1bI 84 Eure).

so that a clerk with a good hand could get 2,000 or 2,500 francs a year in any private business.[1] It was logical therefore that sub-prefects should use members of their own families as office staff. Carbon-Prévinquières excused the use of his two sons on the grounds that he could find no other employees sufficiently capable, honest, or of the proper moral calibre for the posts. Other sub-prefects, Blacas-Carros at Arles and later Lodève, Borel de Favencourt at Compiègne, Renard de Saint-Malo at Céret, found such an explanation superfluous. At Bazas Pierre Descures used three members of his family on his staff in the 1820s. The paucity of trained personnel (or inadequacy of the allowance) must indeed have been remarkable, as one of Descures' sons was only thirteen when he joined his father's staff.[2] The insufficiency of the allowance was another argument in favour of sub-prefects administering their own *arrondissements*, and against transfers. The cost of setting up as sub-prefect, when doubled by travel expenses, might be prohibitive. Hermann spent more than a year's allowance on moving from Paris to Perpignan in 1814. Rouzé, transferred from Chalon-sur-Saône to the post of secretary-general of the Seine-Inférieure in June 1828, spent between 8,000 and 9,000 francs. Once again, more than a year's allowance: and within two years he was transferred to the Bas-Rhin, which meant not only further travel expenses, but the precipitate sale of the 5,000 or 6,000 francs' worth of furniture he had bought at Rouen.[3]

Guillaume, who spent eighteen years in subordinate posts in the administration between 1813 and 1831, wrote early in his career of the sub-prefects: 'ces fonctionnaires semblent recevoir de leur place une sorte de prééminence sur les autres administra-tions de leur *arrondissement*; mais les avantages pécuniaires ne leur permettent pas de soutenir cette position à moins qu'ils n'y consacrent leur fortune privée'.[4] Such data as exist for the private

---

[1] S.pr. Havre to pr. Seine-Inférieure 2 May 1814 (AN, F1bII Seine-Inf. (5)).
[2] Carbon-Prévinquières: form for expenses of s.pr. Millau in 1826 (AN, F1bI 83(2) Aveyron). Blacas: 83(2) Bouches-du-Rhône, 85(3) Hérault. Borel: 86(4) Oise. Saint-Malo: 86(5) Pyrénées-Orientales. Descures: 85(2) Gironde.
[3] Hermann to Min.Int. 16 July 1815 (AN, 162(5)); Rouzé to Min.Int. 14 May 1830 (172(20)).    [4] Guillaume to Min.Int. 25 March 1816 (AN, 161(23)).

incomes of the subordinate personnel (and they are subject to the same reservations as with the prefects) suggest that sub-prefects and secretaries-general were hardly equipped to occupy posts which, far from enriching them, would in all probability make inroads into their own resources. And these, on average, were slender: whatever the reservations necessary, the contrast between the private incomes of the prefects, on the one hand, and of the subordinate personnel, on the other, is immediate and brutal. There is some evidence for the income of 428 of the sub-prefects or secretaries-general given their first post in the Corps by the Bourbons. Only two-fifths had a private income which would have enabled them to stand as deputies, as against four-fifths of the prefects. Twenty per cent of the prefects could be called very rich in their own right, with a private income of 20,000 francs or more, but a mere 1 per cent of the subordinate personnel. Sub-prefects like Moreau de Bellaing or Bouteville, with an income of 20,000 from their industrial interests, were doubly exceptional, as was Duplaa, most of whose fortune had disappeared with the loss of Saint-Domingue, but who nevertheless had a private income of around 15,000 francs a year.[1] Small or non-existent incomes were, on the other hand, common enough. There were émigrés like Geffroy de Villeblanche or Joseph de la Tour du Pin who were entirely reliant on their salaries, or Du Blaisel, who lost his sub-prefecture in the administrative reform of 1816, and whose sole means of support was a pension from the Maison du Roi. Bellefonds had not emigrated, but his father, so badly wounded at Quiberon that the Republicans had thought it superfluous to shoot him, had: and lost a fortune of 30,000 a year.[2] A bachelor with an income of under 3,000 might find himself in difficulties—but what of an administrator in the position of Formey de Saint-Louvent, with ten children, or Maudet, with twelve, both of whom had an income of only 2,400 francs? One former prefect, Garnier, was reduced to the indignity of selling his books ('le dernier de mes sacrifices').

[1] AN doss. Moreau de Bellaing, 156(14); Bouteville, 156(40); Duplaa, 158(37).
[2] AN doss. Geffroy de Villeblanche, 161(7), 176(12); O³* 776. La Tour, 166(15); AAG, Emigrés, 519(6). Du Blaisel, 158(28); O³* 2595. Bellefonds, 156(14); for his father, O³ 2561.

There is no record of a prefect being imprisoned for debt in Sainte-Pélagie, like the former lieutenant-colonel and sub-prefect in the Doubs, Huot de Neuvier.[1]

The disproportion between the salaries paid the prefects and those of the subordinate personnel was naturally reflected in their respective pensions. Since the subordinate personnel's salaries were so much smaller than the prefects', their pensions were insignificant, the maximum awarded being some 1,500 francs. As one sub-prefect put it:

J'ai servi trente ans et plus en qualité de sous-préfet. Au lieu d'aug-menter mon faible patrimoine dans ces fonctions pénibles et peu retribuées, je l'ai diminué. J'ai essayé tous les chagrins, tous les tourments attachés à l'administration pendant les divers orages poli-tiques qui depuis 18 ans ont travaillé la France, et notamment pendant deux invasions. J'ai failli être tué dans une émeute populaire, et pour récompense de tant de travail, et de tant de peines, vous m'annoncez …que le Roi m'a accordé une pension de retraite de cinq cent vingt trois francs.[2]

The conclusion is paradoxical. The great majority of the sub-ordinate personnel had private incomes so small that a salaried post was indispensable. Yet the posts they occupied were such that a private income was a prerequisite.

[1] AN doss. Formey de Saint-Louvent, 160(10). Maudet, 167(12). Garnier to Min.Int. 16 Jan. 1828, doss. 161(4). Huot de Neuvier, 162(8).
[2] Contencin, s.pr. Mamers, to Min.Int. 7 Apr. 1832 (doss. 157(31)).

# PART IV

# CHAPTER 15

# THE NOBILITY AND THE PREFECTORAL CORPS

The most important feature of the recruitment for the Restoration prefectoral corps was the large number of nobles given posts in the administration. As much as the increased political importance of the prefects and the consequent political movements of personnel, it was the difference in the social background of the Restoration administration that distinguished it from the Napoleonic. The Bourbons named 164 prefects. A hundred and eighteen, or just over 70 per cent, came from families that had been noble before the Revolution. Excluding those who later became prefects, and those who were never installed, they named 536 sub-prefects and secretaries-general, of whom 219 were noble. In April 1814 21 per cent of the Corps holding office in France itself were nobles. In July 1830 the figure was just under 45 per cent.

Any classification of these families is handicapped both by their heterogeneity and by the inadequacy of the standards normally applied. The families who possess a known principle of ennoblement are habitually classified according to this principle. Ennoblement would either be by letters patent or by means of offices that conferred nobility: certain municipal offices, financial charges, or posts in the magistrature.[1] In the strict sense, this classification is limited to the means whereby a family acquired nobility. It has no relevance for the family's subsequent activities. But this is so restricted that, by a natural extension, the same terms have come to be used as labels for those members of the nobility who pursued careers in municipal administration or in the magistrature. It is obviously unsatisfactory to classify the Frotté, a military family who provided the celebrated Chouan as well as his relative the Restoration prefect, as 'financial' nobility, on the ground that the family was ennobled in 1523

---

[1] For a useful outline of the methods of ennoblement, see Du Puy de Clinchamps, *La Noblesse*, pp. 16–34.

12-2

by the office of Secrétaire du Roi. The same classification applied to the Bertier de Sauvigny, who provided several councillors in the Parlement of Paris and two intendants of the city, is equally unsatisfactory.[1] Yet the labelling of families by their favoured career, the use, for example, of the term *noblesse de robe* to describe families with members in the Parlements, is technically indefensible.[2] It also encourages the simplification, even syncopation, of a family's services, producing a kind of unsubtle antithesis between 'robe and sword'.

For the families without a known principle of ennoblement, there is no universally accepted classification. Confusion abounds. Divisions and subdivisions proliferate according to the historian's whim, the terminology is used contradictorily and emptied of meaning: 'noblesse de race', 'noblesse d'extraction', 'noblesse chevaleresque'... If there is a rationale behind these divisions, it may be found in the emphasis on the date to which a family's filiation can be proved. Here, as with the comparable emphasis on an ennobled family's origin, there obtrudes the genealogist's almost obsessive preoccupation with a family's antiquity. It reflects the nobility's own preoccupation, an interest in ancestry that did not hesitate, where necessary, to invent ancestors. Leaving aside the false nobility, French history has no lack of examples of recently ennobled families who grafted themselves on to more famous homonyms, as the Riquet de Caraman persuaded contemporaries to accept their descendance from the far older and more illustrious Riquetti de Mirabeau, although the Riquet owed their fortune and ennoblement to the Canal de Midi (1666).[3] Among families with representatives in the Restoration prefectoral administration, the Coussy claimed descent from the celebrated Champagne house of Coucy, the Bonne yoked themselves to the Bonne de Lesdiguières who had provided the last Constable of France.[4] A family's antiquity had some rele-

---

[1] AN doss. Frotté, 160(15); Chaix, x, 328–30. Bertier: J.-F. Bluche, *L'origine des magistrats du parlement de Paris au XVIIIe siècle* (1956), p. 88.

[2] *Ibid.* p. 15 note 1.

[3] J-F Bluche, *Les magistrats du parlement de Paris au XVIIIe siècle (1715–1771)* (1960), pp. 95, 101 note 21.

[4] AN doss. Coussy, 157(34); Chaix, xII, 217–18. Bonne, 156(32); Chaix, v, 241–3.

vance in the eighteenth century, governing admission to the Orders of Chivalry, to the military colleges, to the Estates of certain provinces, to commissions in the Gardes-Françaises or Gardes du Corps, and to the Honours of the Court—although only 462 of the 942 families admitted to the Honours of the Court between 1715 and 1790 possessed the genealogical qualifications required in theory.[1] It is not that antiquity is irrelevant in a discussion of the nobility, but that it is insufficient as a classification, and inadequate as the sole criterion of a family's importance. In the words of the best modern French historian of the nobility: 'tout classement de la noblesse en fonction de l'ancienneté seule est un leurre'.[2] Applied as a criterion to the families which provided members of the Restoration prefectoral corps, it yields disturbing results. Old and obscure families of provincial nobility, the Dreuille in the Bourbonnais, the France in Artois, the Freslon de la Freslonnière in Brittany, whose lineage is as unimpeachable as their services were undistinguished, appear more important than dynasties of government servants like the Colbert or the Terray. The Dreuille could prove their filiation from 1404. The Restoration sub-prefect was the son of a captain in the *chevaux-légers* of the Guard, the grandson of an officer in the *régiment de Beaujolais*. The France provided a bishop of Saint-Omer in the seventeenth, a colonel of cuirassiers in the eighteenth, and a sub-prefect in the nineteenth centuries.[3] The contrast to the two more recently ennobled families is instructive. Boula de Coulombiers, prefect from 1815 to 1823, came from a Parisian family ennobled only in 1705, and then by the 'savonette à vilain'. Yet the family was of some importance in the eighteenth-century magistrature. Five members, including the prefect's father and two uncles, became councillors in the Parlement of Paris between 1735 and 1780. Another was *avocat-*

[1] Du Puy de Clinchamps, *La noblesse*, p. 46; J.-F. Bluche, *Les honneurs de la cour*, I.

[2] Bluche, *Les magistrats*, p. 94.

[3] AN doss. Dreuille, 158(6, 27); Chaix, XIV, 224–7; Woelmont, V, 382–9. France, 162(5); comte Adrien de Louvencourt, *Notices sur les familles nobles... de la Somme* (1909), pp. 385–8. Freslon: Chaix, XIX, 250–3. H. Frotier de la Messelière, *Filiations bretonnes...*, II, 383–92.

*général* in the Cour des Aides. Among the councillors were two *maîtres-des-requêtes*, including Boula de Nanteuil, intendant of Poitiers from 1784 to 1790. The Terray had emerged from obscurity at the end of Louis XIV's reign, and had been ennobled in 1720. The Restoration prefect was the son of an *intendant des finances* and the grandson of a *maître-des-requêtes*, one of whose brothers was the abbé Terray.[1]

The only satisfactory classification of the nobility of the Ancien Régime is by its political importance. At a national level, this was limited to a group of the great court dynasties, to the top of the military and ecclesiastical hierarchies, to the more powerful government servants, from ministers to intendants, and to the presidents of the Parlements. At a provincial level, it included those families possessing a local prestige, which depended on a tradition of local administration, whether in the provincial Estates or its Parlement. But even here reservations should be made. The branches of one family might differ considerably in achievement and importance. Blacas-Carros, officer and later sub-prefect, was a member of one of the great noble houses of Provence, which provided the Restoration minister and duke. Yet the sub-prefect's branch had divided from the ducal as early as the thirteenth century. The prefectoral administration also included a Séguier, member of perhaps the most famous of all families in the magistrature of the Ancien Régime, which could count, by the late 1750s alone, a chancellor, five *présidents à mortier*, thirteen councillors in the Parlement of Paris, two *avocats généraux*, and a number of *maîtres-des-requêtes*. The Séguier in question came from an undistinguished branch and was the son and grandson of officers in the *régiment de Limousin*.[2] 'Les parents de mes parents sont mes parents': but how far the more important branch would have served their less distinguished kinsmen, and how far these latter would have enjoyed a reflected prestige or influence, remains uncertain.

[1] AN doss. Boula de Coulombiers, 156(37); H. Diné, *Les Boula*. Terray, 174(3); *GA*, VI, 279; Bluche, *L'origine*, pp. 394–5.
[2] AN doss. Blacas-Carros, 156(24); AAG, CG 328; Chaix, IV, 322–4. Séguier, 173(12); Bluche, *L'origine*, p. 386; J. Villain, *La France moderne...* (3 vols., 1908–13), III, part II, 1429–42.

Judged by standards of national and even of provincial political importance, the majority of families under consideration were of modest status—'à peine une étincelle a reluit dans leur cendre'. Many had an honourable if undistinguished military tradition, like the Antin from Bigorre, the Cresolles from Brittany, or La Fitte de Montagut from Gascony.[1] René-Charles de Gigord, sub-prefect of Troyes in 1814, had two brothers who had served in the *régiment de Neustrie* before emigrating. Their father had also served in the regiment, their grandfather and great-grandfather had likewise been officers. Pierre Aucapitaine, the Restoration secretary-general, came from a family that had provided three generations of officers in the *régiment d'Aquitaine* in the eighteenth century alone. Pierre had served from 1774 to 1792, his brother from 1771 to 1789, their father had been pensioned in 1763 after twenty-nine years' service, and Pierre's son was *sous-lieutenant* at the Revolution. The military tradition, the humble rank (none rose above that of captain): the Aucapitaine are almost the type of small provincial nobility.[2]

A second and smaller group of families enjoyed considerable prestige in their provinces, or distinction in their chosen careers, but tended to be confined within these limits. The Coetlosquet in Brittany, the Du Puy-Montbrun in the Dauphiné, the La Grange-Gourdon de Floirac in Quercy and the Yzarn de Freissinet in the Rouergue were important provincial families. The Bengy de Puyvallée had a tradition of local administration in Berry, the Carrière in Languedoc: the Restoration prefect was the son and grandson of secretaries to the Estates. The Jacquelot de Boisrouvray had supplied eight successive generations of councillors to the Parlement of Brittany. The two Lezay-Marnésia who became prefects were the sons of a *maréchal-de-camp*, the grandsons of a captain, and the great-grandsons of a

[1] Antin: Chaix, addenda XVI, 387–91; Woelmont, VIII, 31–46. Cresolles: Chaix, XII, 271–2; Woelmont, addenda VII, 991–5. Montagut: Chaix, XVIII, 159–60; Woelmont, I, 390–1.
[2] AN doss. Gigord, 161 (11); R. de Gigord, *La noblesse... de Villeneuve-de-Berg, en 1789* (1894), pp. 226–43. Aucapitaine, 155 (10), 158 (4); AAG, YB 169, 398.

brigadier of infantry.[1] At the summit of this group are families whose importance transcended their province—the Estourmel in north France, the La Bonninière de Beaumont in the west—although still falling short of national importance. To these there can be added certain families who had once possessed such importance, but who had lost something of their dynamism in the eighteenth century. The Bouthillier-Chavigny had sprung into prominence in the shadow of Richelieu. Two members became secretaries of state in the seventeenth century, a third became archbishop of Sens. Well established in the Ancien Régime, their political influence had nevertheless waned. A similar case is that of the Longueil de Maisons. They had been ennobled by office in the Parlements at the end of the fourteenth century, and had provided several presidents in the Parlement of Paris. The tradition died with the last president (1731), and with it much of their importance.[2]

The group of families with real political power includes the Le Clerc de Juigné, represented by an archbishop of Paris and two *maréchaux-de-camp* in the late eighteenth century: the Chastenet de Puységur, distinguished by the Marshal, as well as by an archbishop of Bourges in 1788 and a Minister of War in the same year.[3] Among the imperial prefects re-employed by the Bourbons, Breteuil came from a family that had provided two secretaries of state in the eighteenth century, Nicolay from a dynasty that had held the *premier présidence* in the Cour des Comptes at Paris from 1506 to 1791, and could also count a Marshal of France.[4] The great court families were represented in

[1] Coetlosquet: Chaix, XI, 147–9. Du Puy-Montbrun: Woelmont, VI, 917–28. Floirac: Woelmont, I, 395–8. Freissinet: H. de Barrau, *Documents historiques et généalogiques...du Rouergue* (4 vols., 1853–60), II, 9–37. Bengy: Chaix, III, 337–9. Carrière: N. Viton de Saint-Allais, *Nobiliaire universel...* (21 vols., 1872–7), III, 465–74. Jacquelot: N. J. du B[oisrouvray], *La maison de Jacquelot...* (1950). Lezay: Woelmont, V, 780–4.

[2] Estourmel: Woelmont, VI, 500–7. Beaumont: Chaix, V, 216–20; comte Charles de Beaumont, *La maison Bonnin de la Bonninière de Beaumont* (1907). Bouthillier: Chaix, VI, 160–3. Longueil: Bluche, *L'origine*, pp. 285–6.

[3] Juigné: Saint-Allais, *Nobiliaire universel...*, XII, 74–86. Puységur: Chaix, X, 109–15.

[4] Breteuil: *GA*, VI, 323; Bluche, *Les honneurs*, II. Nicolay: Bluche, *L'origine*, pp. 326–7.

the prefectoral administration by two Choiseul, a Castellane, a La Rochefoucauld, a Brancas and a Narbonne-Lara:[1] families whose claims all but M. de Charlus would have accepted. The gulf that separated these families from the small provincial nobility under the Ancien Régime was immense. Indy, prefect of the Ardèche in 1814, came from a family of the Vivarais which had a strong military tradition. He had been at the Ecole Militaire before the Revolution, and was the son, nephew and grandson of officers, none of whom ranked higher than captain.[2] Maxime de Choiseul's family also had a military tradition, since, in addition to the cardinal and several ambassadors, it had provided four Marshals of France and some thirty general officers. The Castellane had produced two lieutenant-generals and half a dozen *maréchaux-de-camp*, as well as eleven archbishops and bishops. Between the Castellane and the Cromot, between the La Rochefoucauld and the La Roque, the sole link was their common nobility: and in the years before 1789 it may well have seemed a tenuous one.[3] Over thirty years after the disappearance of the Ancien Régime, M. de Montbron recalled the life of the provincial nobility in a speech part of whose interest lies in its very exaggeration:

Le noble de province vivait sous-lieutenant, et s'il vivait longtemps, bien longtemps, il mourait capitaine, ou bien retiré dans son rustique manoir qu'il aurait volontiers appelé son château, s'il avait pu prononcer ce mot sans rire, il jouissait de ses *privilèges*. A ce mot, nous savons qu'il faut frémir d'indignation. Que faisait donc cet individu classé par Buffon, comme autre chose, sous le nom de gentilhomme à lièvre? Ce petit tyran, objet de l'envie et de la haine des philosophes, avait l'odieux privilège de placer une girouette sur sa maison pour savoir d'où venait le vent qu'il sentait déjà trop bien dans son intérieur,

---

[1] Choiseul: Chaix, x, 363–73. Castellane: P. Meller, *Armorial du Bordelais...* (3 vols., 1906), I, 213. La Rochefoucauld: *GA*, VI, 32–3; Bluche, *Les honneurs*, II. Brancas: Chaix, VI, 352–7. Narbonne-Lara: *GA*, 144–5; Woelmont, VII, 691–703.

[2] AN doss. 163; Villain, *La France moderne*, II, 497–501.

[3] Cromot: R. de Roton, *Les arrêts du grand conseil portant dispense du marc d'or de noblesse* (1951), pp. 243, 369. La Roque: vicomte G. de Jourda de Vaux, *Nobiliaire du Velay et de l'ancien diocèse du Puy* (7 vols., 1924–31), VI, 85–6.

il avait le droit d'élever des pigeons et d'appeler *braconniers* ceux qui se permettaient le plaisir de la chasse sans le partager avec lui. *Inde irae*. Si le souvenir de ses aïeux, quand il en avait (et cela commençait à devenir bien rare)...lui inspirait quelque ambition, il allait à Paris supporter, lui tout seul, le mépris des courtisans, toujours prêts à se consoler d'une bassesse par une impertinence. Je dis *lui tout seul*, car dès lors ces mêmes courtisans se montraient affables avec les gens de lettres, les baladins, les savants, et surtout avec les banquiers... Ordinairement il n'obtenait rien, et revenait un peu frondeur, comme vous voyez...[1]

As the disparity amongst those families who provided members of the prefectoral administration during the Restoration suggests, the Revolution cut across the previous divisions within the nobility. Its first effect was the political and economic emasculation of many of the great court families. The effect was heightened by the contrast between the new court and the old. The Restoration Court was no longer the centre of political life, and the end of Versailles meant, not least, the end of the old generosity over pensions and debts. The old divisions did not entirely disappear. Even when anodyne the Court nobility remained antipathetic, a feeling accentuated by the apparent neglect of the Vendéens, and the disproportionate share certain court families received from the *Indemnité aux Emigrés*. The distrust persisted during the Restoration, when the Court was no longer the centre of power. It persisted also after the Court's disappearance in 1830. A matter of historical memory, perhaps: of political disagreement as well: and, as courtiers declined into the *gratin*, of social differences. At base the contrast was that of a whole way of life, between the provincial and the Parisian, the squirearchy and the socialites, the Cambremer and the Guermantes. The Restoration saw the evanescent triumph of the rural squirearchy. 'Il avait fallu cette fin du monde de la Révolution pour arracher Hylas de Fierdrap à ses bois et à ses marais': and whether from choice or necessity, the same was true for many of the provincial nobility who joined the prefectoral corps. *Hobereaux* like La Villegontier and Limairac became prefects while a La Rochefoucauld and La Tour

---

[1] Montbron to Ch. of Deps. 9 March 1821 (AP, 2nd ser., XXX, 311.).

du Pin remained in the decent obscurity of a sub-prefecture 'insuffisante à notre existence, et ... au-dessous de ce qui nous sommes, et des services de tous les nôtres'.[1] Fussy and Vendeuvre were given prefectures immediately, and those in departments above the third class. Woldemar de Brancas, descended from a ducal family of the Ancien Régime, and son-in-law of the comtesse de Colbert spent ten years as sub-prefect, before he was given Saône-et-Loire. A La Rochefoucauld-Bayers and a Narbonne-Lara failed even to enter the Corps.[2]

It might therefore seem arbitrary to use nobility as a criterion during the Restoration, when the status had been robbed of its sanction, and the greater part of the nobility's privileges had disappeared. Yet, in particular so far as the higher posts in the prefectoral administration were concerned, noble extraction would seem to have been a real advantage. Forty per cent of the subordinate personnel named during the Restoration were of noble extraction; but over 70 per cent of the prefects.

The nobility had two initial advantages. The recruitment of the Corps was a matter of patronage, in which connexions were of great importance. A member of a distinguished noble family could work on the complex web of relationships his family would possess. Hervé de Tocqueville, the Restoration prefect, married a Le Peletier: his father had married a Damas-Crux. Through these two marriages Tocqueville was related to the Hennequin d'Ecquevilly, Lamoignon, Menou, Mesgrigny, Chateaubriand and Montmorency-Luxembourg.[3] The Blocquel de Croix de Wismes, one of whose members became a prefect in 1814, were related to the Allonville, Pracomtal and Rougé.

[1] Comtesse de la Tour du Pin, wife of the s.pr. to Min.Int. 13 Feb. 1820 (AN doss. Joseph de la Tour du Pin, 166(15)): for the family, *GA*, VI, 333–4; *ADLN* (1848), pp. 295–322. La Rochefoucauld, 166(12). La Villegontier, 166(17): for the family Frain de la Villegontier, Chaix, XIX, 176–8. Limairac, 166(33); Villain, *La France moderne*, III, part II, 1564–5.

[2] AN doss. Fussy, 160(15), 161(5); for the family Gassot de Fussy, Chaix, XX, 214–16. Vendeuvre, 176(7); for the family Le Forestier de Vendeuvre, Chaix, XVIII, 341–3. Brancas, 177(2). La Rochefoucauld-Bayers, 166(12). Jacques de Narbonne-Lara, 168(1).

[3] AN doss. Tocqueville, 174(8); Bluche, *L'origine*, pp. 271–2; *ADLN* (1852), p. 525; *ADLN* (1895), p. 336.

Through the Rougé alone they had connexions with the Croy d'Havré, Choiseul, Robert de Lignerac de Caylus, Crussol d'Uzès, and Rochechouart-Mortemart.[1] These relationships did not always mean, as prosopographers are too fond of imagining —if the word is permissible—identical political beliefs. Among members of the prefectoral corps alone, Ferdinand de Bertier was related to Jules Pasquier, while the brother of another extreme Right-wing prefect, Curzay, had been partly responsible for Lavalette's sensational escape on the eve of his execution in 1815.[2] But a relationship could mean an interview, a contact, a recommendation. It should not be forgotten how small Parisian society was during the Restoration; the small world, not of Beau de Loménie's *dynasties bourgeoises*, but of Balzac's Faubourg, where the Grandlieu, Navarreins and Chaulieu were all vaguely cousins. This would have been no advantage had not the Faubourg possessed a measure of real power, as it did during the Restoration and in particular when Right-wing ministries were in office. It had enough influence in or on these ministries to name its protégés, and naturally enough the aristocracy's protégés tended to be connexions of their own, or drawn from their own class.

A subsidiary advantage, so far as the sub-prefectures were concerned, was the inherited prestige a noble family frequently possessed in its own province. The position and functions of a sub-prefect made it desirable that he should possess considerable local influence.[3] A candidate who could capitalize on his family's local prestige started with a not inconsiderable advantage. During the Restoration a tradition of intermarriage, emphasized where the families derived from the same province and possessed a similar background, produced clusters of interrelated families. In Guyenne the interrelated Casamajor de Charitte, Capdeville, Duplaa and Nays-Candau families, all of whom had a background of service in the Parlement of Navarre, provided four Restoration

[1] AN doss. Wismes, 176(2); Woelmont, III, 46–51; *ADLN* (1880), pp. 301–9.
[2] Pasquier, *Mémoires*, II, 14; Broglie, *Souvenirs*, I, 321–2.
[3] See above, chapter 5.

sub-prefects.[1] A group of families from the Lyonnais, the Forez, and the north of Languedoc produced two Restoration prefects, Du Peloux and Saint-Genest, and three sub-prefects, Sagnard de Sasselange and the La Roque (both father and son).[2] Another group from the Franche-Comté and Burgundy were represented by Scey, prefect from 1814 to 1818, and three sub-prefects, Esperoux, Jouffroy and Montrond. All but Esperoux held their posts in the Doubs.[3] Panat, member of the Brunet de Castelpers de Panat and prefect in 1828, was related to two other prefects, Auderic and Bastard, and to three sub-prefects: Domézon, Neffiès and Armand de Villeneuve. Neffiès had been a member of the *conseil d'arrondissement* of Béziers and later mayor of the town before becoming secretary-general of the Aude in May 1830; Villeneuve was sub-prefect of Béziers from 1824 to the July Revolution.[4]

If these were the advantages a noble would possess should he wish to join the Corps, they do not explain why he should so wish. The motives seem to have been mainly negative: it is at once evident how few nobles began their career in the Corps, and how few made it their first choice. To a certain degree this was inevitable, a matter of age. One hundred and eighty nobles who subsequently served in the Restoration Corps had been born before 1776, and could therefore have served the monarchy of the Ancien Régime. Just under 130 had started their careers: some already had a long career behind them at the Revolution. Riccé had been a page before joining a dragoon regiment in 1774. Transferring to the

---

[1] AN doss. Charitte, 157(17); Capdeville, 157(5); Duplaa, 158(37); Nays-Candau, 168(1). A. de Dufau de Maluquer, *Armorial de Béarn, 1696–1701* (2 vols., 1889–93), I, 75–8, 91–8, 118–24, 162–74.

[2] AN doss. Du Peloux, 158(16, 37); Saint-Genest, 157(34), 173(3); Sagnard de Sasselange, 173(9); La Roque, 158(10). *GA*, VI, 164–5. Jourda de Vaux, *Velay*, VI, 85–6, 113–21. H. de Jouvencel, *L'Assemblée de la noblesse...de Forez en 1789* (1911), pp. 234–43, 347–51; L. de la Roque, *Armorial...de Languedoc* (2 vols., 1860–3), I, 47–8.

[3] AN doss. Scey, 173(11); Esperoux, 161(10); Jouffroy, 164(6); Montrond, 167(29). Woelmont, II, 338–45, 405–21, 973–80; R. de Lurion, *Franche-Comté*, pp. 557–8.

[4] AN doss. Panat, 170(2); Auderic, 155(10), 158(4); Bastard, 156(8); Domézon, 158(24); Neffiès, 168(2); Villeneuve, 176(13). Chaix, XIV, 129–31. Woelmont, IV, 160–7.

infantry, he became colonel in 1788, *maréchal-de-camp* in 1792.
Cromot de Fougy, prefect of the Aude in September 1816, had
started his administrative career in 1779 as councillor in the
Parlement of Rouen, becoming *maître-des-requêtes* in 1784.
Albertas had become a member of the Cour des Comptes in the
Parlement of Provence in 1771; he became president in succession
to his father four years later, and held the post until the Parlements were abolished.[1] The Revolution cut across these careers:
92 of the 190 emigrated, in some cases with their entire families.
Charles de Beaucorps, the future secretary-general, left France
in 1791 and campaigned until 1798. Three of his brothers also
emigrated, a fourth was wounded while fighting in the Vendée.
Beaucorps' marriage to a relative of 'Monsieur Henri' was in
keeping with the tradition.[2] Helyot allegedly contented himself
with running a rare-books business at Hamburg, Milon de Mesne
at one time owned an inn at Altona, Georges de Montureux
produced evidence to show that he had engaged in no more
warlike pursuit than acting in vaudevilles at Brussels with his
wife; but the majority of émigrés had been trained as officers and
played a more active part, campaigning in Condé's army or that
of the Princes, or in various formations in foreign service.[3]
Charitte fought with the Spanish army, Reinach with the
Austrian: Puységur entered Prussian service after taking part
in the Quiberon fiasco: Armand de Beaumont and Orfeuille-
Foucaud became officers in the 60th line, Joseph de la Tour du
Pin a captain of Marines on board the frigate *La Surprise* at Saint
Domingue.[4] There were émigrés who must have found, in the
genteel haven of an administrative career, a curious contrast to
the vicissitudes of their exile, Albert de Lezay-Marnésia, for
example, who had followed his formidably eccentric father to

---

[1] AN doss. Riccé, 172(8); AAG doss. communicated individually. Cromot,
157(37), defective, personal communication from the archivist of the Aude;
Roton, *Marc d'Or*, pp. 243, 369. Albertas, 155(2); marquis de Boisgelin (ed.),
*Chronologie des officiers des cours souverains de Provence...* (1904), p. 197.
[2] AN doss. Beaucorps, 156(10); AAG, CG 202.
[3] Helyot: AN, F7 5243. Milon de Mesne: F7 3331, but AAG, CG 2701. Montureux: F7 5319, but AAG, Emigrés, 519(16).
[4] AAG, Emigrés, 519(3), Puységur and Reinach; 519(5), Orfeuille-Foucaud;
519(6), La Tour du Pin; 519(7), Charitte; 519(9), Beaumont.

America, to found a semi-commercial, semi-religious 'Asylum', or Robinet de Plas, who was arrested on his return from emigration in June 1798, condemned to death, and only avoided the guillotine by breaking out of prison two hours before he was due to be executed, killing one of the concierge's children in the process.[1]

Those who returned under the Consulate were faced by a problem at once moral and practical. First, there was the decision whether or not to serve Napoleon. Ambition, boredom or penury might make necessary the post that principle deplored. Pasquier's first and hasty thoughts of entering imperial service had been temporarily checked by the judicial murder of the duc d'Enghien. It took him all of two years to recover. Even then he hesitated, rightly fearing the reaction his move would evoke among his less flexible acquaintances. But, as he explained in his memoirs, the only way of defeating the Revolution was to surround and staff its government with men hostile to it: 'lorsque le gouvernement sentait le besoin d'un tel rapprochement, était-il sage de repousser ses avances?'[2] There was a second difficulty, that of finding a career. For the elder generation, whether they had emigrated or not, the career they had started under the Monarchy might no longer be practicable. For obvious reasons Chabrol-Crousol, La Tocnaye and Marmiesse de Lussan did not return to the Church for which they had been trained. There was no longer a Parlement de Paris in which Dupleix de Mézy might serve, a Cour des Aides to which Camusat de Thony or Delbreil de Scorbiac could return.[3] The career might be closed to them, on the ground of their age or poverty. This was the case for many of the émigrés. Sixty-two of the ninety-two had been officers under the Ancien Régime. Few rejoined the army. A

[1] For Lezay-Marnésia, see the early part of his *Souvenirs*. F.-B.-E. Robinet de Plas: AN, F7 4991 (1); AAG, Emigrés, 519 (1). Emigrés had no monopoly of such exploits. Sartiges was captured after the fall of Pondicherry, and despatched to England with his fellow prisoners in the *Kent*. They overcame the crew and escaped to Mauritius—an episode reminiscent of 'The Gloria Scott' (AN doss. Sartiges, 173 (9)).

[2] *Mémoires*, I, 221–2.

[3] AN doss. Chabrol-Crousol, 157 (13); La Tocnaye, 166 (15); Marmiesse de Lussan, 167 (8); Mézy, 167 (22); Camusat de Thony, 157 (4); Delbreil de Scorbiac, 158 (11).

question of scruple, perhaps:[1] equally one of age. Agrain des
Hubas joined the staff, Milon de Mesne served in the artillery.[2]
They were exceptions. A former lieutenant-colonel of infantry
became inspector of weights and measures, a former captain of
dragoons joined the imperial tax administration, a former captain
of artillery became intendent to the Empress Josephine after her
divorce, and a former naval officer joined the imperial administration in Holland.[3]

In one sense, the moral problem involved in rallying to the
Empire might be avoided, or at least obscured, by occupying a
minor position. There were former émigrés who held prominent
posts under the Empire. Goyon and La Vieuville had a similar
background and similar careers: both belonged to the Breton
nobility, served in the Gardes Françaises before the Revolution,
and were among the four Breton officers who resigned their
commissions in 1788 as a protest against ministerial 'persecution'
of their provincial estates. Both emigrated. Both lost their
fathers during the Revolution, Goyon's dying in prison, La
Vieuville's being executed in April 1794. Goyon returned to
France to become, in 1804, one of the first auditors nominated.
Sub-prefect two years later, prefect in 1808, he ended the Empire
as baron and prefect at Livorno. La Vieuville rose higher.
Chamberlain and Count of the Empire, then prefect of Stura, he
was transferred to Haut-Rhin in 1813.[4] The majority of émigrés,
however, returned only to a post as mayor, like Cassaignau de
Saint-Félix, Montrichard or Tocqueville, or became members of
the *conseil-général* of their department, like Barrême or Terray.[5]

---

[1] See Puymaigre, *Souvenirs*, p. 113.
[2] Agrain des Hubas: AAG doss. communicated individually. Milon de Mesne:
AAG, CG 2701.
[3] AN doss. Husson de Prailly, 170(24); AAG, YB 374, 398; Emigrés, 519(16).
Kerespertz, 165; O3 2565; AAG, YB 107. Montlivault, 167(28); AAG, list of
lieutenants of artillery 1768–91 (under Diziers); Vitrolles, *Mémoires*, I, 47–8.
Geffroy de Villeblanche, 161(7), 176(12); O3* 776.
[4] AN doss. Goyon, 161(16); BB¹ 72 plaque 13; AAG, YB 27; Révérend,
*Restauration*, III, 215–17. La Vieuville, 166(17), 176(11); F7 5610; AAG, YB 27
Révérend, *Restauration*, I, 136–7.
[5] AN doss. Cassaignau de Saint-Félix, 173(3); O3* 762. Montrichard, 167(29);
O3* 2595. Tocqueville, 174(8); F1cI 26. Barrême, 156(4, 6); AAG, CG 164.
Terray, 174(3); F7 4890 (3).

A minor post in the prefectoral corps might have seemed merely an extension of this local administration, combining the advantages of a salaried position with the opportunity of recovering an hereditary, if diminished, local prestige, but not involving too direct or dramatic a commitment to the régime.

For the younger generation, both principle and opportunities differed. The decision whether or not to serve the Empire was easier for the generation born between 1776 and 1792. The Empire was well established when most of them started their careers, the Monarchy at best a childhood memory. Lacking their elders' experience, they often lacked their prejudices. The elder generation might regard a Restoration as improbable—when Vitrolles mentioned the possibility to Casimir de Montlivault as late as February 1814, 'il en parut aussi étonné que si je lui eusse parlé de la résurrection de Louis XIV'—but with the exception of those whose enthusiasm for the usurper had been more than usually indiscreet in its ostentation, they could hardly fail to find the idea attractive.[1] It was a very different affair for the younger generation. To talk to them of the Bourbons was, as Chateaubriand found, 'comme si j'avais fait le dénombrement des enfants de l'Empereur de la Chine'.[2] The imperial régime had immense prestige: it also promised the chance of rapid advancement, not least in the administration. Molé became a prefect at twenty-six, a Councillor of State at twenty-eight, a minister at thirty-two. His career was exceptional—'jamais courtisan de Louis XIV n'est parvenu plus aisément'—but Barante and Plancy were prefects at twenty-seven, Houdetot was given Brussels at thirty, Tournon given Rome at thirty-one.[3] That all were auditors was no accident. The auditoriat had been designed as a means of training young administrators. It was also a deliberate attempt at social fusion. Among the auditors, the Ancien Régime jostled the Revolution: Victor de Broglie

---

[1] Vitrolles, *Mémoires*, I, 47–8; Rémusat, *Mémoires*, I, 133.
[2] *Mémoires d'Outre-Tombe*, ed. M. Levaillant and G. Moulinier (3 vols., n.d.), II, 215.
[3] Molé: Raoul de Warren, *Les pairs de France*, II; Rémusat, *Mémoires*, I, 263. AN doss. Barante, 156(3). Plancy, 170(17). Houdetot, 162(7). Tournon, 174(11).

and Henri Beyle; Brosses, Nicolay, La Tour du Pin, Saint-Chamans; Boissy d'Anglas, Garat, Petiet, Regnier, Treilhard.[1] The auditoriat's prestige was undeniable: Vendeuvre might refuse the place he had never solicited, but Terray was only prevented from accepting the offer of a place as auditor by his passionately Royalist uncle; Molé did not wait for an offer but wrote to the emperor asking that he and his friend Houdetot be made auditors.[2] So was its success in attracting young members of the old nobility. It is ironical, in view of the Bourbons' alleged dislike of the institution, that the proportion of prefectures held by former auditors should have remained, between 1815 and 1830, at or above the level it had been at in April 1813: about one-quarter.[3]

Under the Bourbons the prefectoral career seems more than ever to have been a second choice, a *pis aller*. In the heady days of 1814 many of those who sought a place in the Corps—and few contemplated starting other than in a prefecture—would have preferred to serve in the army, particularly the Maison du Roi or the military household of one of the princes. Jacques de Narbonne-Lara's petition records a common desire, and a common failure: 'Rendu à notre Roi légitime, désireux de me ranger sous ses drapeaux et de marcher sur les traces de mes ancêtres, je me rendis il y a quelque temps à Paris pour demander du service à Sa Majesté; mais n'ayant pas la taille requise aux Gardes, ni assez de fortune pour soutenir une place des Mousquetaires (la Révolution m'ayant tout ravi) je ne peux rien obtenir...aujourd'hui j'essaye de parvenir à une place d'administration...'[4] Brancas was likewise prevented by his poverty from joining the Maison du Roi as he would have wished, Thuisy was too old, Juigné both too old and too poor. Even Ferdinand de Bertier, who had succeeded in joining the duc d'Angoulême's staff at the First Restoration, was forced to leave it at the Second, because of his insufficient financial resources.

[1] AN, AF IV 1334-5; Ch. Durand, *Les auditeurs*, Annexe I, pp. 187–91.
[2] Vendeuvre: AN, AF IV 758. Terray, Molé: Barante, *Souvenirs*, I, 145–6.
[3] The 1813 figure: Durand, *Les auditeurs*, p. 24.
[4] Undated (*c*. Aug. 1814) petition to Min.Int. (AN doss. 168(1)).

The same difficulties occurred at a less exalted level. Justin de Bonne, the future sub-prefect of Saint-Pons, had been made *chef de bataillon* in the Legion of Tarn in January 1816. Ten months later he resigned: 'une place ambulante finirait, avec une famille si nombreuse, par me ruiner'.[1] There were no necessary conditions for entry to the Corps, although it became fairly common for those seeking places to have a degree in law. This, on the evidence on Charles de Rémusat—a more serious student than Rastignac—could be attained with the minimum effort and attendance.[2] During the 1820s something like a regular cursus honorum was established, young men spending a certain period in a prefecture or in the Ministry of the Interior before entering the administration, but this was too limited in application to change conditions as a whole.[3] Broadly speaking, a man of good family and the proper connexions was assumed capable of taking up an administrative post without any special qualifications, learning his functions while in office. Few candidates had any scruples as to their fitness for a post: their attitude was well expressed by a former Hundred Days sub-prefect, applying for a post under the July Monarchy—'il y a toujours place pour la capacité dans cette Babel des cupidités qui rongent la Patrie'.[4] Nicollon des Abbayes displayed a totally unrepresentative humility when he wrote to Lainé refusing his sub-prefecture: '...J'ai l'honneur de faire observer à Votre Excellence, que mon éducation n'a point été dirigée vers les affaires de l'administration, j'ai été militaire toute ma vie...ce serait de ma part une présomption coupable...d'accepter des fonctions au-dessus de mes forces, [et] d'une importance aussi majeure.'[5]

The Corps recruited from those who had hoped to join another profession: but also from those who had been members of other professions. The motive varied. Entrants came from posts that

[1] AN doss. Brancas, 176(2). Thuisy, 174(7). Juigné, 164(8). Bertier: Bertier de Sauvigny, *Bulletin...de Normandie*, LIV, 196. P.-J.-Justin de Bonne: letter of 13 Nov. 1816 to Min. War (AAG, CG 384).
[2] *Mémoires*, I, 240.
[3] See above, pp. 133–5.
[4] Philpin to Min.Int. 25 June 1832 (AN doss. 170(14)).
[5] Nicollon des Abbayes to Min.Int. 20 Nov. 1816 (AN doss. Auvynet, 155(11)).

had been suppressed in 1814, as Mareste came from the inspector-
ate of navigation on the Rhine, or from temporary positions
created during the crisis of 1813–14: both Des Mazis and Théo-
dore de Vielcastel had been attached to the Napoleonic *commissaires extraordinaires*.[1] In other professions the fall of the
Empire had led to a reduction in the number of posts available
and to a consequent block in promotion. A transfer to the
prefectoral administration was easiest and most advantageous
when the candidate's patron had influence in its nominations.
André d'Arbelle, whom Talleyrand had used as a tame leader-
writer, and Saint-Genest left the diplomatic service for the
prefectoral corps when Talleyrand formed his ministry in July
1815.[2] Several members of the Ministry of Police joined the
Corps when Decazes became Minister of the Interior.[3] The army
presents something of a special case. Napoleon had found places
in the Corps, not only for retired officers like Lachaise or
Mengaud, but, as a matter of policy, for younger men who had
been too badly wounded to continue on active service.[4] Imbert
de Trémiolles had been seriously wounded at Iéna, Gaspard de
Contades had been left for dead at Essling, Corn wounded at
Friedland, Chambray had lost an arm at Talavera, Lantivy had
had one foot amputated as the result of frostbite on the retreat
from Moscow.[5] The Restoration army saw little active service,
living, as Vigny was to describe it, 'entre l'écho et le rêve des
batailles', but this apparent stagnation itself led a number of
former officers like Blacas-Carros, Giraud des Echerolles or the
young Kersaint to forsake the army for the administration,
and others joined the Corps after the suppression of the Maison
Militaire at the Second Restoration.[6]

[1] AN doss. Mareste, 167(6); Des Mazis, 158(19); Vielcastel, 176(11).
[2] AN doss. André d'Arbelle, 155(6); Talleyrand to Jaucourt 13 Oct. 1815
(*Correspondance du comte de Jaucourt...*, p. 33). Saint-Genest, 157(34), 173(3).
[3] See above, p. 89.
[4] AN doss. Lachaise, 166(2); Mengaud, 167(26). Vaublanc, *Mémoires*, III, 87.
[5] Imbert de Trémoilles: AAG, CG 1872. AN doss. Contades, 157(31). Corn:
AAG, CG 804. AN doss. Chambray, 157(14). AAG doss. Lantivy, communicated individually.
[6] Blacas-Carros: AAG, CG 328. Des Echerolles: AAG, CG 1610. Kersaint:
AAG, CG 1960. See above, pp. 40–1, 117.

The Corps was frequently a second option. The advantages it offered were similarly negative. There is one exception: to a greater degree than under the Empire, it offered the possibility for a member of the nobility to re-create or consolidate his local position. Throughout the Restoration, but particularly during Villèle's ministry, there are examples of men crowning a long career in local administration with a post as sub-prefect or secretary-general. Fresnoy became *conseiller de préfecture* in the Loir-et-Cher at the Second Restoration, secretary-general in September 1820. Duhamel-Fougeroux moved from the *conseil général* of the Loiret to the sub-prefecture of Pithiviers in 1823, Pontbriant spent seventeen years on the *conseil général* of the Vaucluse before becoming sub-prefect of Orange in the same year. Rochefort, who had been a member of the *conseil général* of the Loire since 1802, became sub-prefect of Saint-Etienne in 1827.[1] These examples throw some light on the sub-prefect's ambivalent position, as much local figure as government servant. All these sub-prefects had entered the administration when already over fifty years of age. They had little hope of promotion, and perhaps as little desire. Their sub-prefecture represented rather the culmination of a career in local administration than the start of a career in the government service.

For the majority of entrants, the Corps might seem to have had one initial advantage, that of sheer numbers. In April 1814 there were over 530 posts. Yet this advantage was more apparent than real. With the fall of the Empire a large number of trained administrators were thrown out of work. The extent of this glut of trained personnel can be guessed at from the ease with which Carnot recruited experienced functionaries during the Hundred Days.[2] It coincided with the irruption of devoted if often untrained royalists on to the labour market. Their scruples at serving the state had disappeared: but so had a large number of the posts previously available. A three-cornered struggle of some acerbity developed. Those in office fought to remain: their less

---

[1] AN doss. Fresnoy, 158(19). Duhamel-Fougeroux, 160(11), filed as F. de Denainvilliers. Pontbriant, 170(21). Rochefort, 172(12).

[2] See above, pp. 61–2.

fortunate colleagues fought to get back: and the intransigeant royalists fought to get in. As Germain wrote, with the self-righteousness of a man who had been given a prefecture two months before, 'si l'on met en France autant de zèle à bien remplir les places qu'à les obtenir, le roi peut se vanter d'être le monarque le mieux servi de l'Europe'.[1] The pressure continued on a diminished scale throughout the Restoration. The Hundred Days disqualified a large number of former administrators, but it led also to a considerable reduction in the number of posts: 537 in March 1815, there were 448 in March 1816, 449 in July 1830. The politically motivated movements of personnel during the Restoration made for a quicker turnover of personnel than had been the case under the Empire, but the preference ministers showed for administrators dismissed by their predecessors lessened the chances a newcomer might have had of entering the Corps. One result can be seen in the dwindling proportion of young men with posts in the prefectoral administration. In April 1814, $12\frac{1}{2}$ per cent of the personnel in office in France had been under thirty years of age, $46\frac{1}{2}$ per cent under forty. In July 1830 the figures were $4\frac{1}{2}$ and $23\frac{1}{2}$ per cent.

The real advantage the Corps possessed was that no formal training was required. Napoleon had made an attempt to enforce some standard of education. The decree of 26 December 1809 laid down that from January 1813 every candidate to the auditoriat would have to be a *licencié en droit* or *ès sciences*, and would also have to pass an oral examination.[2] A degree in law was of no great benefit to an administrator, while, whatever the emperor's intention, the members of the Council of State who conducted the oral examinations did not take them over-seriously. The Restoration did not indulge in this form of pious fraud.

Tradition, as well as training, is a form of preparation for an administration. If the prefectoral administration appears amateur rather than professional in recruitment as in action, it was partly because it lacked this tradition: unsurprisingly, since the Corps had only been founded in 1800. Generation after genera-

[1] Germain to Barante 31 Aug. 1814 (Barante, *Souvenirs*, II, 82).
[2] Durand, *Les auditeurs*, p. 32.

tion had not served in the Corps as they had served in the pre-revolutionary Parlements. But during the Restoration what might, without exaggeration, be called prefectoral dynasties began to emerge. Four Villeneuve-Bargemon brothers served as prefects, two Chabrols, two Delaitres. Louis-Jules de Chaulieu had a brother and son in the administration, Rogniat a son and a cousin; Coster, Indy, Martin de Puiseux and Walckenaer, among others, followed their fathers into the Corps.[1] There is no example of a prefect succeeding his father in the same department during the Restoration (although this occurred, once, during the Hundred Days), as had been the case with certain intendants towards the end of the Ancien Régime.[2] But, as witness the Cabrières, Cherrier and Michel de Roissy, this did happen with the subordinate personnel.[3] It would also be mistaken to consider the administration as having no ancestors. Even superficially there is a resemblance between the prefects and the intendants, and several members of the Restoration administration, for example Andrezel, Ferdinand de Bertier, Blair, Esmangard, Feydeau, and Mégret d'Etigny were descended from or related to former intendants[4]. Intendants had been chosen from the *maîtres-des-requêtes*, and these had frequently come from families with a tradition in the Parlements. Of the 117 nobles whom the Bourbons made prefect, eleven had a father or grandfather in the Parlements. A further six had both father and grandfather, like Curzay, son and grandson of presidents in the Chambre des Comptes of Brittany, or Blondel d'Aubers, whose father had been a councillor in the Parlement of Paris, and whose

---

[1] AN doss. Villeneuve-Bargemon, 176(13); Chabrol, 157(13); Delaitre, 158(9), and as Raymond Delaitre, 172(3); Des Rotours de Chaulieu, 157(20), 158(20), 172(3, 17); Rogniat, 172(14); Coster, 157(33); Indy, 163; Martin de Puiseux, 167(10); Walckenaer, 177(1).

[2] The Hundred Days: AN doss. Rougier de la Bergerie, 172(17). The intendants: P. Ardascheff, *Les intendants de province sous Louis XVI* (1909), p. 82.

[3] AN doss. Cabrières, 157(1); Cherrier, 157(21); Michel de Roissy, 172(13). See above, p. 82.

[4] AN doss. Andrezel, 158(2); *DBF*, II, cols. 982–3. Bertier, 156(19); Bluche, *L'origine*, p. 88. Blair, 156(25); Bluche, *L'origine*, p. 94. Esmangard, 159(2); Roton, *Marc d'or*, p. 391. Feydeau, 160(5); Chaix, XVIII, 121–3. Mégret d'Etigny, 158(21), 159(3), 167(16); *GA*, V, 32; Bluche, *L'origine*, pp. 307–8.

THE NOBILITY AND THE PREFECTORAL CORPS

grandfather *premier président* in that of Flanders. Finally, three Restoration prefects were descended from three generations of magistrates. Dalon was the son and grandson of councillors in the Parlement of Bordeaux, the great-grandson of a president. Choppin d'Arnouville was the son, grandson and great-grandson of councillors in the Grand Conseil of Paris.[1] The most distinguished was Brosses, bearer of a name which, as he boasted, 'loin d'avoir démerité de la Patrie, a quelques droits de son bienveillance'. He was the grandson and great-grandson of councillors in the Parlement of Burgundy, and son of the celebrated Président de Brosses.[2] Among the subordinate personnel of the Restoration administration were other descendants of families with a tradition in the magistrature: the Casamajor de Charitte, Coriolis, Du Plessis de Grenédan, Forget, Jacquelot de Boisrouvray, Pichard, and Sauzet de Fabrias.[3] If the members of the nobility who were maintained or re-employed in the Corps by the Bourbons are added, among the prefects alone Arbaud-Jouques came from a family with a background of high office in the Parlement. of Provence, the Du Bouchage had served in the Parlement of Dauphiné, the Du Hamel in that of Bordeaux. Three Parisian families are represented, the Rouillé d'Orfeuil, the Camus du Martroy, who had a tradition of service in the Cour des Aides, and the Nicolay, with a far longer tradition in the Cour des Comptes.[4]

[1] AN doss. Curzay, 156(38), 158(40); Chaix, xv, 291–3. Blondel d'Aubers, 155(9), 156(27); Chaix, iv, 385–6; Roton, *Marc d'or*, pp. 372–3. Dalon, 155(3), 158(1); Révérend, *Titres et confirmations de titres...1830–1908* (1909), p. 266. Choppin d'Arnouville, 157(24); Chaix, x, pp. 392–4.

[2] AN doss. Brosses, 156(46); his undated demand for removal from the list of émigrés, F7 4827; Chaix, vii, 203–4; Roton, *Marc d'or*, pp. 98–9.

[3] AN doss. Charitte, 157(17); Dufau de Maluquer, *Armorial*, i, 91–8. Coriolis, 157(32); Chaix, xi, 386–9. Du Plessis de Grenédan, 158(38); *ADLN* (1896), pp. 271–5. Forget, 160(10); Chaix, xviii, 360–5. Jacquelot, 164(1); N. J. du B[oisrouvray], *La maison de Jacquelot*. Pichard, 170(14); *GA*, v, 276. Sauzet de Fabrias, 160(1), 173(10); *GA*, vi, 182; Jourda de Vaux, *Nobiliaire du Velay*, vi, 182–3.

[4] AN doss. Arbaud-Jouques 155(6), 158(3); Chaix, i, 271–4. Du Bouchage no personal doss.; *GA*, iv, 216. Du Hamel, 158(34); *ADLN* (1851), pp. 272–8. Rouillé d'Orfeuil, 172(17); Bluche, *L'origine*, pp. 378–9; Révérend, *Restauration*, vi, 154–5. Du Martroy, 157(4), 158(35); Chaix, viii, 187–8. Nicolay, 158(3); Bluche, *L'origine*, pp. 326–7.

There is a danger of exaggerating both the extent to which it is meaningful to speak of a family's 'tradition', and the degree to which the prefectoral administration was heir to the Ancien Régime magistracy. The Nicolay might have a monopoly of presidencies in the Cour des Comptes, they also produced a Marshal of France. The Ferrand had a dual tradition, both military and in the magistracy, the prefect being the great-grandson of an inspector-general of infantry, the grandson of a brigadier, and the son of an officer who entered the Parlement of Paris only after his military career ended with the loss of a limb at Fontenoy. Similarly the baron de Montureux, lieutenant of infantry before the Revolution and prefect during the Restoration, was the son of a brigadier, but the grandson and great-grandson of *premier présidents* in the sovereign court of Lorraine.[1] Nor was the prefectoral corps exclusive heir to the magistracy of the Ancien Régime. Families with a long tradition in the magistracy, the Dupont des Loges, Farcy or La Forest d'Armaillé in Brittany, the Du Bois de Riocour in Lorraine, the Gilbert de Voisins in the Parlement of Paris, had members not in the administration but in the judiciary proper, the Royal Courts of the Restoration.[2] There are also families with one member in the prefectoral corps and another in the judiciary, the case of the Arthuys, Charitte and Malartic: another reminder of the danger of oversimplifying a tradition.[3] It seems, nevertheless, possible that members of families with a tradition in the magistrature found in the prefectoral administration an heir to the Parlements of the Ancien Régime. Molé's choice of career would seem to support this. On being made an auditor, Molé was attached to the Ministry of Justice. As Napoleon told him, it seemed an obvious posting since his family had been in the Parlement of Paris. Molé disagreed. There was nothing in common, he alleged, between the magistrature of the Ancien Régime

---

[1] AN doss. Ferrand, 160(5); *GA*, III, 370; Bluche, *L'origine*, pp. 173–5. Bourcier de Montureux, 167(29); *GA*, II, 222.

[2] *Almanach Royal* (1824–5); *GA*, II, 158, III, 243, 337, IV, 30, 152.

[3] AN doss. Arthuys, 155(8). Charitte, 157(17); Dufau de Maluquer, *Armorial*, I, 97. Malartic, 167(2); P.-L. Lainé, *Archives généalogiques et historiques...* (11 vols., 1818–50), IV, article M.

and that of the Empire. The link was with the administration; he asked to be, and was, attached to the Ministry of the Interior.[1]

The desire to enhance their local prestige: the difficulty of entering any other branch of service: the possible connexion between the magistrature of the Ancien Régime and the prefectoral administration; these were contributory reasons for the nobility entering the Corps, but not the most important. The most important, as the least tangible, was the nobility's tradition of service. In this context the particular branch of service their families had favoured is less important than the habit of serving. With this tradition the nobility had, in their own eyes, not only a right to the places but a duty to hold them. So Albert de Lezay-Marnésia believed, when he wrote to Vaublanc in December 1815:

Aujourd'hui que la monarchie française reprend ces honneurs avec l'ancienne race de ses Rois, qu'elle va se rasseoir sur ses antiques bases, il ne faut, s'il se peut, rien transporter dans cette ère de réparation qui commence, des ignobles allures, des ordures enfin de cette sale révolution qu'il faut croire enfin finie; chacun doit se revêtir de tout ce qu'il a de noble, se montrer avec tout ce qu'il a de dignité personnelle et soutenir ce qu'il en reçoit de ses fonctions. Comme une des causes principales des désordres de nos malheureux temps, et qui, plus que tout autre, contribue à les maintenir, est venue de l'avidité avec laquelle on a recherché les emplois moins pour l'honneur que pour les profits qu'ils donnent, et de ce que tout le monde s'est laissé emporter par ce dérèglement d'ambition intéressée hors de la place qui lui était marquée dans la société, un des plus sûrs moyens de retour à l'ordre est donc que chacun rentre et reste dans les convenances de son état, soit en modérant des prétentions qui seraient au-dessus du mérite qu'on a pour les soutenir, soit en ne se ravalant pas au-dessous de ce qu'on est.[2]

It is this attitude that gives the Restoration administration its characteristically amateur air. It was a service, not a profession. No technical qualifications were needed to enter the Corps: a man of good family offered a guarantee that mere experience could not rival. In petition after petition the applicants listed their family's genealogy and services, before mentioning their

[1] Molé, *Mémoires*, I, 50.
[2] Letter 27 Dec. 1815 to Min.Int. (AN doss. Helyot, 162(4)).

own administrative ability or experience, as Jean de Ruffray started his application for a sub-prefecture with the information that one of his ancestors had accompanied the king into captivity after the battle of Poitiers.[1]

What distinguishes the nobility of the Restoration from that of the later nineteenth century is the part it played in the service of the state, a part assumed both as privilege and duty. The importance of a social group cannot be measured by numbers alone, but even numerically the nobility provided two-fifths of the subordinate personnel nominated between 1814 and 1830, and nearly three-quarters of the prefects. The combination of the Monarchy and the apparatus of a modern state gave them an importance, and above all a link with reality, that they were never to possess again. That the nobility chose one branch of service rather than another is less important than the fact that they served, and served the king. The cult of the Bourbons was undoubtedly fed by royalist propaganda, and not always intelligently: the continued comparison of Louis XVIII and Henri IV, the quasi-religious exaltation surrounding the duc de Bordeaux—'l'enfant du miracle'—were errors of tactics as much as of taste. The cult was nevertheless based on a reality. Only a king could justify the nobility's existence, as he could claim their services. To the principle of service was added the possibility, at a time when the Revolution and Empire had fashioned a new France. The possibility might continue after 1830, but the principle was shattered. There were, of course, nobles whose convictions had led them into constitutional opposition during the Restoration, former prefects like Rambuteau or Saint-Aulaire who rallied to a more 'liberal' government; others, whose dismissal by the Bourbons and consequent unemployment might be presented, with a greater or lesser degree of plausibility, as the result of political convictions which the new government could hardly fail to honour.[2] Certain prefects rode the Revolution, Jessaint, because no government had enough powder to

[1] Petition of 20 Apr. 1826 (AN, 172(21)).
[2] AN doss. Rambuteau, 172(2); R+C, v, 78–9; Rambuteau, *Mémoires*, p. 218. Saint-Aulaire, 173(1); R+C, I, 225.

move such a rock, Albert de Lezay-Marnésia, Armand de Beaumont, who could cheerfully accept a new régime but not,
eighteen months later, the possibility that he might have to
arrest the duchesse de Berry.[1] Even such a modest measure of
survival was not uniformly appreciated. As the dust settled after
the Trois Glorieuses, there were those disillusioned by a Revolution which substituted the tricolour for the Fleur de Lys on the
prefecture but left the incumbent unchanged. 'Si ce departement
n'avait pas de journaux il ignorerait la Révolution qui s'est
operée à Paris...,' a correspondent wrote in September 1830
from the Ardennes, where Lascours remained in office, 'tant les
choses sont encore dans le même état qu'il y a six mois....'. Even
had there been changes, he speculated gloomily, they would
have been nugatory: 'on deplacera des hommes de la faction
jésuitique pour y placer des hommes de la congrégation'.[2]

The majority of the Corps, the great majority of the nobility,
resigned or were replaced. This might mean, as had been the
case of several prefects compromised in the Hundred Days, a
brusque change of career. Walckenaer, prefect of the Aisne in
1830, was a *conservateur adjoint* in the Bibliothèque Nationale ten
years later. Dieudonné de Vezins, sub-prefect from 1822 to May
1830, later became mayor of Algiers, while his brother Aimé,
who succeeded him as sub-prefect, resigned at the Revolution,
was subsequently ordained, and became bishop of Agen.[3] There
were other nobles who had served in the Corps before 1830, who
played an active part in the Legitimist opposition to Louis-
Philippe. Ferdinand de Bertier was one of the most important
figures in the planning of the duchesse de Berry's rising in which
Calvière, Frotier de Bagneaux and Emmanuel de Villeneuve-
Bargemon were assigned parts, and in which Bonchamps and
Ferrand were actively involved.[4] There were former prefects

---

[1] AN doss. Jessaint, 164(4); Lezay-Marnésia, 166(32); Beaumont to Min.Int.
6 June 1832 (156(11)).
[2] Letter 30 Sept. 1830 to Min.Int. (AN doss. Lascours, 166(13)).
[3] AN doss. Walckenaer 177(1); Révérend, *Restauration*, VI, 465. Vezins, 176(10).
[4] G. de Bertier de Sauvigny, *La conspiration des légitimistes et de la duchesse de
Berry contre Louis-Philippe 1830–32* (1950), partic. pp. 56–7, 63. Frotier:
R + C, I, 137. Bonchamps: *DBF*, VI, col. 940. Ferrand: Chaix, XVIII, 54.

like Balzac and Blin de Bourdon among the Legitimist opposition in the Chamber of Deputies, others wrote for Legitimist journals, Croze for the *Gazette de France*, Dufeugray for *L'Ami de la Verité*, Nonneville for *L'Orléanais*.[1] This activist fringe was a minority. The remainder of the Legitimist nobility retired to their tents, only briefly to re-emerge as a body on the political scene between 1848 and 1851, 1871 and 1877. The Lorgeril, for example, produced a deputy of the Manche in the *Chambre Introuvable*, a deputy of the Ille-et-Vilaine from 1828 to the July Revolution, and a deputy of Côtes-du-Nord, later a senator, in 1871. Louis de Sesmaisons was deputy for the Loire-Inférieure from 1815 to 1816, and 1820 to 1827, when he was made a peer. His brother then became deputy of the same department, until the Revolution of 1830: his nephew, a cavalry officer who resigned his commission rather than serve Louis-Philippe, was elected deputy at the start of the Second Republic, in 1848, once again in the Loire-Inférieure. Among the prefectoral personnel, Suleau, prefect from 1822 to April 1830 when he was made *directeur général de l'enregistrement*, returned to the Corps as prefect of Eure-et-Loir after eighteen years in the wilderness, in January 1849.[2] But in spite of these comebacks, the nobility never again controlled the machinery of state after 1830. Their participation was limited to posts at the lower level of local administration, as mayors or members of the local deliberative councils, and to a lesser degree service in an army which could be regarded as the nation's rather than the régime's. The mass of Legitimist nobility remained inactive, their cause too good to fight for. With one exception. After the formation of the Zouaves Pontificaux in 1860 to defend the Papacy, volunteers came from all over Catholic Europe, from Ireland as from Belgium, but particularly from France. The regimental roll of the Papal Zouaves, and the affiliated Volunteers of the West during the Franco-Prussian

[1] Balzac: R+C, I, 147. Blin de Bourdon: R+C, I, 348. Croze: Alboize, *M. le baron de Croze*, p. 4. Dufeugray: Mancel, *Biographie de M. Du Feugray*, p. 98. Nonneville: *Notice nécrologique sur M. le vicomte Tassin de Nonneville* (1834), pp. 7–8.

[2] Lorgeril: *ADLN* (1896), pp. 355–9. Sesmaisons: *ADLN* (1900), pp. 250–3. AN doss. Suleau, 173 (21).

War, reads like the *ban* and *arrière-ban* of the Legitimist nobility: the Du Puy-Montbrun from Dauphiné, the Gigord and Tournon-Simiane from the Vivarais, the Levezou de Vézins from Rouergue, the Flotte, Foresta and Villeneuve-Bargemon from Provence, the Limairac and Delbreil de Scorbiac from Languedoc, and from the great royalist fief of the west a Bessay, Cambourg, Jégou du Laz, Quatrebarbes, Quélen, Sainte-Marie.[1] All were members of families which had been represented in the Restoration prefectoral corps.

The year 1830 marked the start of the Legitimist syndrome. With the July Revolution the Legitimist nobility's control of state machinery disappeared: with the *révolution des mairies* of 1879–81 they lost control of local government, except in certain areas of the west: from the early 1880s economic decline threatened to supplement political: and in 1883 the last Bourbon of the elder line, the comte de Chambord, died. Between Versailles and Proust's 'noble Faubourg', between the Du Guénic and the Guermantes, the Restoration is an almost anomalous episode in the history of the French nobility, 'cette petite armée de bougres à beaux noms qui marchent sur toute l'épaisseur de l'histoire et des traditions'.

[1] *Matricule des Zouaves Pontificaux...* (2 vols., Lille, 1910), I, 23, 28, 46, 56–7, 66, 83, 109, 140, 211, 277; II, 88–9, 112, 223, 404.

# MINISTRIES AND MINISTERS OF THE INTERIOR, APRIL 1814– JULY 1830

| Ministry | Date | Minister of the Interior | Political tendency |
|---|---|---|---|
| Provisional government | 3 Jan. 1814 | Beugnot (Commissaire) | — |
| First Restoration | 13 May 1814 | Montesquiou | — |
| Talleyrand | 9 July 1815 | Pasquier | Centre Left |
| First Richelieu | 27 Sept. 1815 | Vaublanc | Right |
|  | 7 May 1816 | Lainé | Centre Right |
| Decazes | 29 Dec. 1818 | Decazes | Centre Left |
| Second Richelieu | 21 Feb. 1820 | Siméon | Centre Right |
| Villèle | 14 Dec. 1821 | Corbière | Right |
| Martignac | 4 Jan. 1828 | Martignac | Centre Right |
| Polignac | 8 Aug. 1829 | La Bourdonnaye ⎫ |  |
|  | 18 Oct. 1829 | Montbel ⎬ | Extreme Right |
|  | 19 May 1830 | Peyronnet ⎭ |  |

Sources: *BL*, 5th–8th series.

# THE MOVEMENT OF PREFECTORAL
# PERSONNEL BY MINISTRY, 1814–30

1. The first three columns of figures in the tables represent the number of individuals who were dismissed, transferred and newly nominated by each ministry. A member of the Corps might be displaced more than once during the same ministry: the figures given in parentheses represent the total number of dismissals, transfers or nominations. The sum total of these movements is given in the final column.

2. A post might be vacant when a ministry came into office: the ministry might have dismissed a functionary, but not given him a successor when it fell. There is therefore an occasional disparity between the number of dismissals and that of nominations.

3. The figures given for the Talleyrand ministry are based on a comparison between the members of the Corps in office on 15 March 1815, at the beginning of the Hundred Days, and those in office on 26 September, at the end of the Talleyrand ministry. They do not represent the total number of movements carried out between July and September.

## The prefects

| Ministry | Number dismissed | Number transferred | New nominations | Total movement |
|---|---|---|---|---|
| First Restoration† | 46 | 7 | 46 | 53 |
| Talleyrand | 38 | 31 | 38 | — |
| First Richelieu | | | | |
|   Vaublanc | 12 | 11 | 12 | 23 |
|   Lainé | 26 | 32(34) | 26 | 60 |
| Decazes | 19 | 13 | 19 | 32 |
| Second Richelieu | 9 | 21 | 9 | 30 |
| Villèle | 41(42) | 48(57) | 42 | 99 |
| Martignac | 19 | 35(36) | 19 | 55 |
| Polignac | 12 | 20 | 12 | 32 |

† Including the Provisional Government.

## The sub-prefects

| Ministry | Number dismissed | Number transferred | New nominations | Total movements |
|---|---|---|---|---|
| First Restoration | 106 | 16 | 145 | 161 |
| Talleyrand | 115 | 39 | 108 | — |
| First Richelieu | | | | |
|   Vaublanc (a) | 85 | 14 | 82(87) | 101 |
|      (b)† | 86(88) | — | — | 86(88) |
|   Lainé | 65 | 40(43) | 64 | 109 |
| Decazes | 57(58) | 16(17) | 60 | 77 |
| Second Richelieu | 52 | 43(47) | 52 | 99 |
| Villèle | 118 | 65(73) | 119 | 192 |
| Martignac | 30 | 21 | 29 | 51 |
| Polignac | 12 | 12 | 13 | 25 |

† In December 1815 the 85 sub-prefectures of the *arrondissement chef-lieu* were suppressed. 83 of these were occupied. At the same time the former department of Mont-Blanc (3 sub-prefectures) was handed over to Sardinia.

## The secretaries-general

| Ministry | Number dismissed | Number transferred | New nominations | Total movements |
|---|---|---|---|---|
| First Restoration | 23 | — | 23 | 23 |
| Talleyrand | 31 | 3 | 28 | — |
| First Richelieu | | | | |
|   Vaublanc | 22 | — | 22 | 22 |
|   Lainé (a) | 3 | — | 3 | 3 |
|      (b)† | 85 | — | — | 85 |
| Decazes | — | — | — | — |
| Second Richelieu | | | | |
|   (a)† | — | — | 85 | 85 |
|   (b) | 5 | — | 5 | 5 |
| Villèle | 43 | 11 | 43 | 54 |
| Martignac | 18 | 4 | 18 | 22 |
| Polignac | 13 | 4 | 13 | 17 |

† With the exception of the Seine, the secretaries-general were suppressed in April 1817 but restored in August 1820.

# APPENDIX III

# SOCIAL BACKGROUND OF MEMBERS OF THE PREFECTORAL CORPS, 1814–30

## A. PERCENTAGE OF NOBLES AMONG THE PERSONNEL IN OFFICE

| Date | Prefects | Sub-prefects | Secretaries-general | Total |
|---|---|---|---|---|
| 1 Apr. 1814 | 34·5 | 21·7 | 4·6 | 21 |
| 15 March 1815 | 66·6 | 29·0 | 9·3 | 32 |
| 27 Sept. 1815 | 70·1 | 37·3 | 10·3 | 38·3 |
| 7 May 1816 | 75·6 | 45·1 | 19·8 | 46·1 |
| 21 Feb. 1820 | 61·6 | 36·6 | — | 42·4 |
| 1 Jan. 1828 | 73·3 | 43 | 37·2 | 47·7 |
| 27 July 1830 | 67·4 | 40·1 | 37·2 | 44·8 |

## B. PERCENTAGE OF NOBLES AMONG THE PERSONNEL GIVEN OFFICE

| Ministry | Prefects | Sub-prefects | Secretaries-general | Total |
|---|---|---|---|---|
| First Restoration | 89·1 | 40·7 | 26 | 49·5 |
| Talleyrand | 65·8 | 44·4 | 10·7 | 43·7 |
| First Richelieu | | | | |
|    Vaublanc | 83·3 | 53·6 | 40·9 | 54·3 |
|    Lainé | 76·9 | 31·2 | † | 44·1 |
| Decazes | 31·6 | 20 | — | 22·8 |
| Second Richelieu | 66·6 | 44·2 | 24·4 | 33·8 |
| Villèle | 76·2 | 51·3 | 48·8 | 55·9 |
| Martignac | 78·9 | 27·6 | 22·2 | 40·9 |
| Polignac | 58·3 | 53·8 | 53·8 | 55·3 |

† Lainé's three new secretaries-general have not been included.

# AGES OF MEMBERS OF THE PREFECTORAL CORPS, 1814–30

## A. PERSONNEL IN OFFICE

### Prefects (*percentage*)

|  | 1 Apr. 1814 | 15 March 1815 | 27 Sept. 1815 | 7 May 1816 | 21 Feb. 1820 | 4 Jan. 1828 | 31 July 1830 |
|---|---|---|---|---|---|---|---|
| Under 30 | 5·6 | 2·3 | 5·7 | 2·3 | — | — | — |
| 30–39 | 34·5 | 31 | 37·9 | 36 | 30·2 | 9·3 | 6·9 |
| 40–49 | 32·2 | 41·4 | 42·5 | 46·5 | 47·6 | 43 | 43 |
| 50–59 | 19·5 | 17·2 | 10·3 | 8·1 | 18·6 | 36 | 36 |
| 60+ | 8 | 8 | 3·4 | 6·9 | 3·4 | 11·6 | 13·9 |
| Under 40 | 40·2 | 33·3 | 43·6 | 38·3 | 30·2 | 9·3 | 6·9 |
| Over 50 | 27·5 | 25·2 | 13·7 | 15·1 | 22 | 47·6 | 49·9 |
| Average age | 43·5 | 44·4 | 41·2 | 42·5 | 43·6 | 50·1 | 50·2 |

### Sub-prefects (*percentage*)

| Age | 17 Apr. 1814 | 15 March 1815 | 27 Sept. 1815 | 7 May 1816 | 21 Feb. 1820 | 4 Jan. 1828 | 31 July 1830 |
|---|---|---|---|---|---|---|---|
| Under 30 | 17·5 | 17·5 | 16·4 | 17·4 | 10·2 | 3·6 | 3·6 |
| 30–39 | 20 | 23·5 | 28·8 | 30·8 | 32·8 | 20·9 | 17·7 |
| 40–49 | 21·8 | 28 | 27·9 | 29·7 | 26·6 | 33·8 | 33·9 |
| 50–59 | 28·9 | 22 | 19 | 17·4 | 24·4 | 29·4 | 28·4 |
| 60+ | 11·6 | 8·7 | 7·8 | 4·4 | 5·8 | 12·1 | 16·2 |
| Under 40 | 37·5 | 41 | 45·2 | 48·3 | 43 | 24·6 | 21·4 |
| Over 50 | 40·6 | 30·8 | 26·8 | 21·9 | 30·2 | 41·5 | 44·6 |
| Average age | 44·3 | 39·7 | 42·1 | 40·8 | 42·7 | 47·3 | 48 |

## A. PERSONNEL IN OFFICE (*cont.*)

### Secretaries-general (*percentage*)

| Age | 1 Apr. 1814 | 15 March 1815 | 27 Sept. 1815 | 7 May 1816 | 4 Jan. 1828 | 31 July 1830 |
|---|---|---|---|---|---|---|
| Under 30 | 2·4 | 3·6 | 8 | 6·9 | 6·9 | 11·7 |
| 30–39 | 12 | 19·2 | 25·2 | 25·5 | 17·4 | 11·7 |
| 40–49 | 40·9 | 37·3 | 36·7 | 45·3 | 23·2 | 25·5 |
| 50–59 | 28·9 | 20·4 | 17·2 | 13·9 | 30·2 | 27 |
| 60+ | 15·6 | 19·2 | 12·6 | 8·1 | 22 | 23·5 |
| Under 40 | 14·4 | 22·8 | 33·3 | 32·5 | 24·4 | 23·5 |
| Over 50 | 44·5 | 39·7 | 29·8 | 22 | 52·3 | 50·5 |
| Average age | 49·1 | 48·3 | 45 | 44 | 48·8 | 48·8 |

## B. PERSONNEL GIVEN OFFICE

### Prefects

| Age | First Restoration | Talleyrand | Vaublanc | Lainé | Decazes | Second Richelieu | Villèle | Martignac | Polignac |
|---|---|---|---|---|---|---|---|---|---|
| Under 30 | 3 | 4 | — | 2 | — | — | 2 | — | — |
| 30–39 | 11 | 19 | 2 | 10 | 9 | 3 | 13 | 2 | 2 |
| 40–49 | 21 | 12 | 7 | 7 | 6 | 2 | 11 | 9 | 9 |
| 50–59 | 7 | 1 | 1 | 7 | 4 | 4 | 12 | 7 | 1 |
| 60+ | 4 | 2 | 2 | — | — | — | 4 | 1 | — |
| Percentage under 40 | 30·4 | 60·5 | 16·6 | 46·1 | 47·3 | 33·3 | 35·7 | 10·5 | 16·6 |
| Percentage over 50 | 23·9 | 7·8 | 25 | 26·9 | 21 | 44·4 | 38 | 42·1 | 8·3 |
| Average age | 44 | 41·1 | 46·8 | 42 | 41·4 | 45 | 45 | 47·4 | 43·5 |

## Sub-prefects

| Age | First Restoration | Talleyrand | Vaublanc | Lainé | Decazes | Second Richelieu | Villèle | Martignac | Polignac |
|---|---|---|---|---|---|---|---|---|---|
| Under 30 | 27 | 19 | 18 | 9 | 12 | 6 | 22 | 4 | 4 |
| 30–39 | 39 | 46 | 26 | 28 | 18 | 23 | 35 | 9 | 6 |
| 40–49 | 47 | 20 | 23 | 19 | 12 | 12 | 35 | 9 | 2 |
| 50–59 | 20 | 13 | 12 | 7 | 15 | 7 | 20 | 5 | — |
| 60+ | 8 | 4 | 1 | 1 | 3 | 3 | 3 | 2 | — |
| Age unknown | 4 | 6 | 2 | — | — | 1 | 4 | — | 1 |
| Percentage under 40 | 46·4 | 63·7 | 55 | 57·8 | 50 | 56·8 | 49·5 | 44·8 | 83·3 |
| Percentage over 50 | 19·7 | 16·6 | 16·2 | 12·5 | 30 | 19·6 | 20 | 24·1 | — |
| Average age | 40·7 | 38·3 | 38·4 | 38·3 | 41·5 | 39·9 | 40·5 | 41·3 | 32 |

## Secretaries-general

| Age | First Restoration | Talleyrand | Vaublanc | Second Richelieu | Villèle | Martignac | Polignac |
|---|---|---|---|---|---|---|---|
| Under 30 | 3 | 4 | 1 | 11 | 16 | 8 | 6 |
| 30–39 | 7 | 10 | 9 | 19 | 7 | 1 | 3 |
| 40–49 | 7 | 12 | 11 | 29 | 10 | 5 | 2 |
| 50–59 | 1 | 2 | 1 | 25 | 7 | 2 | 1 |
| 60+ | 5 | — | — | 5 | 3 | 2 | — |
| Age unknown | — | — | — | 1 | — | — | 1 |
| Percentage under 40 | 43·4 | 50 | 45·4 | 33·7 | 53·4 | 50 | 75 |
| Percentage over 50 | 26 | 7·1 | 4·5 | 33·7 | 23·2 | 22·2 | 8·3 |
| Average age | 44·5 | 39·4 | 40·8 | 44·2 | 39·2 | 38·7 | 32·9 |

Lainé's three new secretaries-general have not been included.

# EMIGRES GIVEN POSTS IN THE PREFECTORAL CORPS, 1 APRIL 1814–15 MARCH 1815

## I. SOURCES

### (a) Archives Nationales

The *fichier des émigrés* is a card index of émigrés, classified alphabetically, with a synopsis of their careers and references to the relevant documents in the Archives. An invaluable guide, the *fichier* suffers from two handicaps: based on material often deliberately inadequate or ambiguous, the alphabetical classification is often incorrect; and the *fichier* is as yet incomplete. There are three main sources for the documentary material:

(i) *Series BB¹, Ministry of Justice*

The most valuable, BB¹ 78–96, are reports by the *Commission des Emigrés*, set up under the Consulate to examine petitions from former suspected or certified émigrés for their removal from the lits.

(ii) *Series F7, Ministry of Police*

Lists, general information and dossiers of émigrés drawn up and classified by the Ministry.

(iii) *Series O3, Maison du Roi*

This includes registers of regiments in the armies of the emigration, miscellaneous documents dealing with the military personnel, and a series of registers of recommendations for pensions to be given to former émigrés, drawn up during the Restoration.

### (b) Archives administratives de la Guerre

(i) An incomparable—and uncatalogued—source, the registers produced by the commission of May 1814 dealing with former émigré officers: twenty-two volumes, complete with index, containing a précis of the claimant's services.

(ii) Individual military dossiers.

## 2. ESTABLISHMENT OF EMIGRE STATUS

The definition of an émigré has been taken to be his absence from France—except when organized or authorized by the government—for any part of the period between 1 July 1789 and March 1814. Inclusion on the various lists of émigrés drawn up by the government and by the local authorities has not been held to prove absence from France, any more than removal from the lists has been held to prove uninterrupted residence in France. The mistakes, reduplications and omissions in the lists were legion.[1] A man might be included simply because he had moved from one department to another, because he had joined the army—or because he was dead. Nicolay's father, Louis-Scipion-Guillaume, had been put on the list after his death in 1793. In spite of all their efforts the family could not obtain his removal during the Revolution. As late as 23 Floréal An VIII (13 May 1800) the commission held the matter to be insufficiently proved, and recommended its adjournment: although, as one member wrote, 'un très grand nombre de citoyens et d'administrateurs regardent la mort de Nicolay, arrivé le 13 Septembre 1793, comme un événement aussi notoire que la siège de Lyon'.[2]

The very inaccuracy of the lists made removal easier for a number of those inscribed. Quélen could argue that his inscription was invalid, since no Christian name was given, and his family had never possessed any property in the *arrondissement* in which they were listed. La Vieuville attempted to identify himself with the 'Baude ainé, Auguste dit Lavieuville', ex-officer in the Gardes Françaises, who had been removed from the list; although, as the Ministry of Justice pointed out, this identification was invalid: the Baude in question had only been removed from the list because he had been executed in 1794.[3] On the whole it was easier to be removed from the lists by providing the certificates of uninterrupted residence in France that the law required.

[1] See D. Greer, *The Incidence of the Emigration during the French Revolution* (1951), pp. 7–9.
[2] AN, BB¹ 91 plaque 7.
[3] Quélen: AN, F7 5031. La Vieuville: Min. Justice to Min. Police, 18 Germinal An X (8 Apr. 1802) (AN, BB¹ 71).

APPENDIX V

The necessary witnesses were not hard to find. Castelpers and Planard could prove their uninterrupted residence in France from 1791 to 1797 although they had been campaigning in the armies of the emigration at the time. Pons had allegedly been living quietly in the Ardèche when he was in fact a member of a regiment of Austrian hussars; Roullet de la Bouillerie had apparently spent in the Maine-et-Loire the time his military dossier shows him to have been either campaigning or living in England.[1] Barrême and Olivier de Maisonneuve were less fortunate. Olivier de Maisonneuve and his brother insisted that their absence in England was connected with their firm's legitimate business. The commission demurred. The firm had never had dealings with England before, it had never previously employed two agents in any country whatsoever, and why had the brothers suddenly left France without telling anyone? An awkward question to answer for a man who had served in various émigré formations from 1791 to 1804. Barrême produced a certificate showing that he had blonged to the 184th (later the 40th) demi-brigade from 1792 to 1796. The Minister of War alleged that Barrême's inscription of the register of the demi-brigade was fraudulent: thirty pages of the register, previously left blank, had been used for such entries. He was right. Barrême's military dossier shows that he had emigrated in 1791 and had campaigned during 1791-2 and 1794-6.[2]

As these examples indicate, proof of emigration is easiest in the case of military personnel. By no means all émigrés were, or had been, officers: it is therefore necessary to use the great, if ambiguous, mass of documentation available in the series F7, with the occasional possibility of checking it against the pension registers of the Restoration Maison du Roi (O3). In very few cases has information in the series F7 appeared sufficient to prove emigration without being confirmed from other sources.

[1] Castelpers: AN, BB¹ 85 plaque 4; O3 2571. Planard: F7 4901(1); AAG, Emigrés, 519(14). Pons: AN, BB¹ 92 plaque 8; AAG, CG 3128. Roullet de la Bouillerie: AN, F7 5608(3); AAG, Emigrés, 519(4).
[2] Olivier de Maisonneuve: AN, BB¹ 91 plaque 8; F7 5298; AAG, Emigrés, 519(1). Barrême: Report of Commission, 13 Prairial An VIII (2 June 1800) (AN, BB¹ 78 plaque 3); AAG, CG 164.

### 3. M. POUTHAS AND EMIGRATION

M. Pouthas has used only one source in establishing the number of émigrés given posts in the prefectoral administration by the Montesquiou ministry. This is a list of émigrés who had been given a post depending on the Ministry of the Interior during the First Restoration, which was drawn up during the Hundred Days at Napoleon's demand, and can be found in AN, F1cI 26. The total of those employed in the prefectoral corps is given as thirty-seven. Since the list was produced with an eye to propaganda purposes, to prove the Bourbons' penchant for former émigrés, M. Pouthas takes it as the maximum possible total. It is not. This is hardly surprising. The ministry's lists of personnel holding office in the Corps are themselves not infrequently inaccurate, and this particular list of émigrés was evidently produced at high speed. A corrected version is given below.

Table 1. *Emigrés given posts in the prefectoral corps,*
*1 April 1814–15 March 1815†*

|  | Prefects | Sub-prefects | Secretaries-general | Total |
|---|---|---|---|---|
| I. Proved émigrés |  |  |  |  |
| (a) Rallied to Empire | 8 | 10 | — | 18 |
| (b) Local administration only | 9 | 29 | 5 | 43 |
| Total | 17 | 39 | 5 | 61 |
| As percentage of new nominations | 36·9 | 26·8 | 21·7 | 28·5 |
| II. Possible émigrés | 2 | 9 | 1 | 12 |

† Includes members of the Corps who had formerly held office outside France.

Table 2. *Emigrés among Montesquiou's new prefects*

|  | Total nominations | Emigrés | Percentage of emigrés among nominations |
|---|---|---|---|
| Rallied to Empire | 20 | 4 | 20 |
| Local administration | 16 | 8 | 50 |
| Total | 36 | 12 | 33·3 |

# APPENDIX V

*Emigrés given positions, 1 April 1814–15 March 1815*

## A. PROVED EMIGRES

**RALLIED TO THE EMPIRE**

*Prefects*

| | | |
|---|---|---|
| 1. | Allonville | AN, 155(3) |
| 2. | Bouthillier-Chavigny | AN, 156(41); F1cI 26; AAG, Emigrés, 519(1) |
| 3. | Brosses | AN, 156(46); F1cI 26; F7 4827; *DBF*, VII, col. 435 |
| 4. | Goyon | AN, 161(16); BB¹ 72 plaque 13; BB¹ 86 plaque 2 |
| 5. | Milon de Mesne | AN, 167(24); F1cI 26; F7 3331; AAG, CG 2701 |
| †6. | Montlivault | Vitrolles, *Mémoires*, I, 47–8 |
| †7. | Riccé | AN, 172(8); AAG, doss. communicated individually |
| †8. | J.-J. Siméon | AN, 173(17); R+C, v, 319–20 |

*Sub-prefects*

| | | |
|---|---|---|
| 1. | Barbier de Landrevie | AN, 166(9); F1cI 26; O3 2571 |
| 2. | Bonald | AN, 156(30); F1cI 26; AAG, Emigrés, 519(4) |
| 3. | Boulancy | AN, 156(37); F1cI 26; F7 5614 |
| 4. | Foresta | AN, 160(10); Bousquet, *Foresta*, p. 2 |
| 5. | Hardy de Lévaré | AN, 166(31); F1cI 26; AAG, Emigrés, 519(4) |
| 6. | F.-F. Houdetot | AN, 162(7); O3 2565 |
| 7. | Huot de Neuvier | AN, 162(8); F1cI 26; O3* 745 |
| 8. | Kerespertz | AN, 165; O3 2565 |
| 9. | Meynier de la Salle | AN, 158(11), 166(13); AAG, Emigrés, 519(3) |
| 10. | Prudhomme | AN, 170(26); F1cI 26; O3 2560 |

*Secretaries-general* – none.

**LOCAL ADMINISTRATION ONLY**

*Prefects*

| | | |
|---|---|---|
| 1. | Floirac | AN, 160(8); F1cI 26; O3 2561 |
| 2. | Frondeville | AN, 160(15); Henri de Frondeville, *Notice biographique sur le président de Frondeville...* (1926), pp. 36–40 |
| 3. | Guer | AN, 167(8); BB¹ 90 plaque 4; F7* 105 |
| 4. | Montagut | AN, 167(26); F7* 105; Woelmont, I, 390 |
| 5. | Montureux | AN, 167(29); F1cI 26; Grouvel, *Corps de Troupe*, I, 158 |
| 6. | Saint-Luc | AN, 173(4); F1cI 26; F7 5790 |
| †7. | Scey | AN, 173(11); F1cI 26; AAG, Emigrés, 519(11) |
| 8. | Terray | AN, 174(3); F7 4890(3); F.Descostes, *Les émigrés en Savoie...* (1903), pp. 534–5 |
| 9. | Tocqueville | AN, 174(8); F1cI 26 |

† Appointed by Beugnot.

*Sub-prefects*

1.  L.-J.-B.-M. Asselin — AN, 155(8); F7* 106; F7 3331; F7 5082; O3 2652
2.  Besse de Fromental — AN, 156(20); F1cI 26; F7 5032; O3 2561
3.  Béville — AN, 156(22); O3 2571
4.  Castelpers — AN, 157(10); BB1 85 plaque 4; F1cI 26; F7 5235; O3 2571
5.  Chamisso — AN, 157(15); F1cI 26; O3* 2572
6.  Charitte — AN, 157(17); F1cI 26; AAG, Emigrés, 519(7)
7.  Cheux de Saint-Clair — AN, 158(6); O3 761; AAG, Emigrés, 519(2)
8.  Du Blaisel — AN, 158(28); O3* 2595
9.  Espinasse — AN, 159(2); F1cI 26; AAG, Emigrés, 519(6)
10. Girod de Novillars — AN, 168(4); F1cI 26; AAG, CG 1612
11. Guillin de Pougelon — AN, 161(24); F1cI 26; O3 2565
12. Jacquier de Terrebasse — AN, 164(1), 174(3); Descostes, *Savoie*, pp. 512–13
13. Lavergne-Cerval — AN, 158(6); F7 5040
14. Léotard — AN, 166(26); AAG, CG 2307
15. Lestrade — AN, 166(31); F1cI 26; AAG, Emigrés, 519(8)
16. Martillat — AN, 167(9); F1cI 26; O3* 2566
17. Maugin de la Pastandry — AN, 167(12); F1cI 26; AAG, Emigrés, 519(10)
18. Pardeilhan — AN, 170(2); F1cI 26; O3 2560
19. Planard — AN, 170(17); F7 4901(1); O3* 767; AAG, Emigrés, 519(14)
20. V.-A. Pons — AN, 170(19); BB1 92 plaque 8; F7 4850(3); AAG, CG 3128
21. Puységur — AN, 170(26); F1cI 26; AAG, Emigrés, 519(3)
22. Quélen — AN, 171; F1cI 26; F7 5031; O3 2560
23. Regnon de Chaligny — AN, 172(4); AAG, CG 3266
24. Reinach — AN, 172(5); AAG, Emigrés, 519(3)
25. F.-B.-E. Robinet de Plas — AN 158(16); F7 3052(1); AAG, Emigrés, 519(1); F1cI 26 applies to his brother François
26. Roesch — AN, 172(13); Leuilliot, *La première Restauration*, p. 101
27. Roullet de la Boillerie — AN, 172(18); F1cI 26; F7 5608(3); AAG, Emigrés, 519(4)
28. Saporta — AN, 173(8); F1cI 26; F7 5766; O3* 748
29. Thieriet — AN, 174(6); F7 5785(3)

*Secretaries-general*

1.  J.-P. André — AN, 155(4); *DBF*, II, col. 929
2.  L.-I.-J. Legrand — AN, doss. in 170(9) Polluche; F1bII Finistère (6); F1cI 26; F7 5096
3.  Olivier de Maisonneuve — AN, 167(2), 169(1); BB1 91 plaque 8; AAG, Emigrés, 519(1)
4.  A.-J. Roy — AN, 172(20); F7 4991(2); O3* 772
5.  Teynier du Pradellet — AN, F1cI 26; AAG, Emigrés, 519(5)

# APPENDIX V

## B. POSSIBLE EMIGRES

### Prefects

1. Carrère de Loubère     AN, F1cI 26
2. Séguier     AN, F7* 116(1); F7 5651(5)

### Sub-prefects

1. Bezanson     AN, 156(22); F7 5790
2. Bruys d'Ouilly     AN, F1cI 26
3. Dandouins     AN, 158(2)
4. David des Etangs     AN, 158(18)
5. Gigord     AN, 161(11); Gigord, *Villeneuve-de-Berg*, p. 242
6. Lamorre     AN, 166(8)
7. J.-B. de Lesseps     AN, 166(30)
8. Mathieu de Moulon     AN, 167(32)
9. Miegeville     AN, 167(23); F7* 678; F7 5115

### Secretaries-general

1. J.-E.-J.-E. de Gacon     AN, 161(1); F1cI 26

# BIBLIOGRAPHY

## I. THE ADMINISTRATIVE PERSONNEL

The necessary prelude to any study of the prefectoral personnel during the Restoration must be the establishment of a base-list of those who held office. It is impossible to establish such a list with any rapidity. The registers of personnel which can be found in the Archives Nationales, F1bI* 143–149(1), were discontinued after the early 1820s, and are frequently incomplete even for the earlier period. The most convenient source is the *Almanach Royal*, but unfortunately no *Almanach* was published in 1814, that for 1815 was obsolete before it appeared, and the publication of the *Almanach* for 1816 was delayed. As a result, the *Almanach* is useless for the fifteen months that saw both rapid and massive changes. It can be supplemented from the *Bulletin des Lois*, which would in turn be of greater value if the material was more accessible, and if the series possessed a more satisfactory index. In both the *Almanach* and the *Bulletin des Lois* the spelling and presentation of the administrators' names has an element of complaisant fantasy which may hamper identification.

The personal dossiers of members of the Corps are to be found in the 384 cartons in the series F1bI 155(1)–180 in the Archives Nationales. They are classified alphabetically by administrator, a system whose logic could better be appreciated if those who filed the documents had been able to decide which was the relevant part of an administrator's name, and use it consistently. Certain variations in classification are so common that they can themselves be classified:

(*a*) Members of the Corps whose names are preceded by the particule, whether d' or de (or who could practise the fortunate caesura in order to preface them with the particule), and those whose names are preceded by du or la, may have been given two dossiers. Examples are Cazes and Decazes, Arros and Darros, Bourblanc and Du Bourblanc, Corbière and La Corbière.

(*b*) Where the surname includes a *nom de terre* or is otherwise complex, there may be two dossiers. Examples are Aubers and Blondel d'Aubers, Bellisle and Pépin de Bellisle, Guer and Marnière de Guer, Saint-Genest and Courbon de Saint-Genest.

(*c*) A variant of the above occurs when a Christian name is taken to be part of a surname, and the dossier filed alternately under, e.g.

221

Lestrade and Odon de Lestrade, Delaitre and Raymond Delaitre, D.-S. Bernard and Samuel Bernard. This is more inconvenient when the misclassification is more systematic. There is no dossier Brancas: it is classified under Woldemar de Brancas.

(*d*) A combination of all three principles listed above may produce a multiplicity of dossiers. F.-B.-E. Robinet de Plas is separately classified under Robinet, Deplas and Plas: Des Rotours de Chaulieu under Des Rotours, Rotours and Chaulieu: Mégret d'Etigny under Mégret, Détigny and Etigny.

The vagaries of the classification indicate the advantage, not to say the necessity, of seeing all the dossiers. An administrator's dossier, or a part of it, may be included in that of his successor or predecessor: a ministerial note on the administrative personnel of a department may be in any one of the dossiers concerned.

The information in any dossier falls into three broad categories. There is the form completed by each official, at least in theory, on taking up an administrative post. The form was divided into several columns, and the data demanded included the administrator's name and Christian names, his date and place of birth, his gross (private) income and details of his previous career. In addition to this form, there may be copies of the ordinance appointing the administrator to his post, and a *procès-verbal* of his installation. Lastly, there are miscellaneous documents of differing interest and in varying quantities: letters demanding promotion, decoration, an indemnity or a transfer, a sub-prefect's notes on his *arrondissement*, a prefect's on his department and subordinates. In many cases the dossiers also include drafts of the minister's replies.

As outlined above, the dossiers can vary very greatly in value. Certain are missing altogether. The reason may not be hard to surmise in Vaublanc's case, as he subsequently became Minister of the Interior. There are others which seem simply to have disappeared: those of the two Du Bouchage, Combe-Sieyès, or Roussy. A large number of the dossiers which do exist contain little more than the dates at which an administrator was given a post, and lack details of his previous career, even of his full name and age. There are various other sources which may supplement the dossiers. For those administrators formerly in the police or judiciary, the series F7 and BB¹: for those who had emigrated, the series F7 or O3. A considerable number of administrators had served at one time or another in the army: it is for this reason that so much use has been made of the archives in the Château de Vincennes. The relevance of the military dossiers for emigration has already been indicated. They also supply a necessary confirmation of the age and parentage of those concerned (frequently including copies of their birth certificates), as well as details of their careers. Some of these dossiers cannot be found—experience in the Archives Nationales would indicate the unwisdom of assuming that they do not therefore exist—and in these cases the registers of regiments during the Ancien Régime have been used. In contradistinction to the majority of sources mentioned, these are both accessible and well classified.

A subsidiary source for the details of an administrator's previous career can be found in the departmental cartons, series F1bII in the Archives Nationales. These contain lists of mayors, of municipal councillors, of members of the *conseils d'arrondissement* and *conseils généraux*. The real utility of the series lies elsewhere. They are an indispensable source for the administrative history of the Hundred Days, as they contain the lists of provisional appointments made by the *commissaires*, and form a pendant to the cartons F1a 553–556(2) dealing with these missions.

The printed sources are disappointing, both for studies of individual prefects and for accounts of the administration as seen on a departmental level. In the fifty years since the publication of the abbé Moulard's study of Camille de Tournon as prefect of the Gironde, no comparable work on any other prefect has appeared. Local administrative history is not much better served: M. Leuilliot's exhaustive history of Alsace during the Restoration being a notable exception. To a certain degree these lacunae can be filled from the memoirs left by the administrators themselves, although their main value is in the insight they provide into the workings of the patronage system. Among the collective biographies, the major merit of Robert and Cougny's *Dictionnaire des parlementaires* is that it was finished. Erroneous accounts of the administrators' careers abound, while the information on their parliamentary careers is often spread somewhat too thinly. The utility of the *Dictionnaire de biographie française* (1932– ) is necessarily limited to the four letters of the alphabet with which it has dealt so far. At least in the early volumes its coverage of administrators was generous, but there are more errors than are excusable in a work of this nature. Among others, the biographies of L.-H. Affre, Agrain des Hubas, Aubernon, Bacot de Romand, Chevalier de Caunan and J.-C. Cherrier are incorrect.[1] It is only lacunae

[1] *DBF*, I, cols. 670–1, 801; IV, cols. 2–3, 1114–15; VIII, cols. 107, 1029, 1062–3.

and errors of this kind, whether in the dossiers or in collective bio-graphies, that can justify reference to Faure or Lamothe-Langon.

## 2. THE SOCIAL BACKGROUND OF THE CORPS

A summary of much of the genealogical material available can be found in volume VI of the *Grand armorial*; critical bibliographies of much of that used can be found in Jougla de Morenas, *Le second ordre*, and Bluche, *L'origine des magistrats du parlement de Paris au XVIII<sup>e</sup> siècle*. A large number of the Corps were of bourgeois extraction, but had been ennobled by Napoleon or during the Restoration. Révérend's eleven volumes listing the ennoblements, confirmations and peerages of the nineteenth century cover these cases adequately. For members of the old nobility documentation is often harder to find. The *Grand armorial*, limited to those families extant at the time of publication (1934–52), is still more limited by pressure of space. By far the best guide is Chaix d'Est-Ange's *Dictionnaire*, a remarkable work that unfortunately ends at volume 20 and the letters GA. It can be supplemented by Woelmont de Brumagne's *Notices généalo-giques*, and by the articles in the *Annuaire de la noblesse* (1843–1911). In view of Dr Thomson's strictures on the *Annuaire* during the inter-war years, its utility should be stressed, particularly during the years 1892–1911 when it was edited by Révérend.[1]

There are numerous genealogies of specific provinces or depart-ments, of various groups within the nobility, and of individual families. Those more widely used in the present study have been Frotier de la Messelière's series on Breton families, Meller on those of Bordeaux and the Gironde, and the comte de Roton's collection of documents, *Les arrêts du grand conseil portant dispense du marc d'or*. Establishing the social background of the prefectoral personnel is very different from understanding it. The memoirs and biographies listed in the bibliography are those directly concerning the prefectoral career, politics and the prefectoral movements, and the mechanics of patronage, but no understanding of the Restoration would be complete without recourse to a mass of material not immediately relevant to the Corps, from Rodolphe Apponyi's Memoirs to General Fantin des Odoards's Journal, and in particular to the works of Balzac and Stendhal. The bibliography appended is therefore necessarily

---

[1] David Thomson, *Democracy in France. The Third and Fourth Republics* (2nd ed. London, 1952), p. 65.

incomplete. The material has been arranged under the following headings:

A. Unpublished sources: I. Archives Nationales. II. Archives Administratives de la Guerre (Château de Vincennes). III. Personal communications from departmental archivists.

B. Printed material: 1. General history. 2. Local history. 3. Local government and the prefectoral administration. 4. Collective biographies. 5. Individual biographies; memoirs; letters. 6. The nobility: general. 7. Collective and corporate genealogies. 8. Regional genealogies. 9. Studies of individual families. 10. Emigration. 11. Miscellaneous.

## A. UNPUBLISHED SOURCES

### I. ARCHIVES NATIONALES

(i) Series AF III, AF IV.   Imperial Secretariat of State

AF III 51 (A).   Notes on counter-revolutionary manœuvres by émigrés in Germany and Switzerland.

AF III 147.   Police reports to the Directory on émigrés, Brumaire –5ᵉ jour complementaire, An IV.

AF IV 8, 438, 457, 755, 758, 859(6), 859(10), 859(11), 859(12). Imperial decrees.

AF IV 1334, 1335.   Auditors.

(ii) Series BB¹, BB⁶.   Ministry of Justice

BB¹ 71, 73 (2).   Eliminations from the list of émigrés. Correspondence and various other material, arranged alphabetically by name of émigré, An VIII–XI.

BB¹ 75.   Correspondence of division of Ministry dealing with émigrés, An VIII–XI.

BB¹ 78(3), 79(2), 79(9), 80(2), 81(2), 83(2), 83(5), 84(7), 84(8), 85(1), 85(4), 86(2), 87(7), 88(4), 89(3), 89(5), 90(4), 91(7), 91(8), 93(9), 95(1), 96(1).   Decisions given by the Commission des Emigrés on demands for elimination from the lists, arranged alphabetically by name of émigré, An VIII– .

BB⁶ 32, 33.   Nominations of magistrates to the tribunaux de première instance, 1815–18.

BB⁶ 60.   Nominations to places in the Imperial and Royal courts, 1813–18.

BB⁶ 68, 77. Nominations to the tribunaux de première instance, 1819.

BB⁶ 729. Personnel of the Council of State, 1814–44.

BB⁶ 733. Demands for places as maîtres-des-requêtes, 1823–30.

(iii) Series F¹. Ministry of the Interior

F1a 32, 34, 36. Circulars and instructions.

F1a* 88, 95 (1), 95 (2), 95 (4), 96 (2), 98 (4), 99 (1), 103 (2), 106 (2), 107 (5), 108 (1), 110 (5). Laws, ordinances and decrees.

F1a 251. Register of petitions exchanged by the Ministry of the Interior and the Maison du Roi, 1814–17.

F1a 553–556(2) [5 cartons]. The Commissaires Extraordinaires during the Hundred Days, classified by Military Division.

F1bI 82. Members of the prefectoral administration: salaries, expenses, indemnities, pensions, 1793–1856.

F1bI 83(1)–87(3) [16 cartons]. Administrative expenses. Classified by departments, c. 1813–30 at least.

F1bI* 143–149(1) [7 registers]. Lists of members of the prefectoral administration, classified by departments, An VIII–c. 1822.

F1bI 150–154(1–2) [3 cartons]. Miscellaneous information about members of the prefectoral administration.

F1bI 155–180 [384 cartons]. Personal dossiers of members of the prefectoral administration, arranged alphabetically, 1800–c. 1855.

F1bI 287–290 [2 cartons]. Members of the prefectoral administration, miscellaneous information about pensions.

F1bI 687–689 [3 cartons]. Administrative personnel. Correspondence of prefects with the Ministry of the Interior, 1810–17.

F1bII. Departmental series: Ain (2, 4), Aisne (2, 4), Allier (4), Basses-Alpes (2, 3), Hautes-Alpes (2), Alpes-Maritimes (2), Ardèche (2), Ardennes (2, 4), Ariège (3, 4), Aube (2, 3), Aude (2, 3), Aveyron (4), Bouches-du-Rhône (2, 3), Calvados (3, 5), Cantal (2, 3), Charente (3, 4), Charente-Inf. (2, 3), Cher (4, 5), Corrèze (2, 4), Corse (3, 4, 5), Côte d'Or (5), Côtes-du-Nord (5), Creuse (4, 5), Dordogne (5, 6, 7), Doubs (5, 7), Drôme (4, 5), Escaut (3), Eure (5, 6), Eure-et-Loir (4, 5), Finistère (6, 7), Gard (3, 4), Haute-Garonne (6, 7), Gers (5, 6, 7), Gironde (4, 5, 6), Hérault (5, 6), Ille-et-Vilaine (3, 4), Indre (4), Indre-et-Loire (4), Isère (3, 4, 5), Jura (4, 5), Landes (3, 4, 5), Loir-et-Cher (4, 5), Loire (3, 4), Haute-Loire

(3), Loire-Inf. (4), Loiret (2, 4), Lot (4), Lot-et-Garonne (4, 5), Lozère (3), Maine-et-Loire (2, 5, 6), Manche (5), Marengo (2), Marne (3), Haute-Marne (4), Mayenne (3, 4), Meurthe (5, 7), Meuse (3, 4, 6), Mont-Blanc (3), Morbihan (4, 6), Moselle (5), Nièvre (4), Nord (6, 7, 8), Oise (3), Orne (7), Pas-de-Calais (6, 7), Puy-de-Dôme (4), Basses-Pyrénées (4), Hautes-Pyrénées (3, 5, 6, 7), Pyrénées-Orientales (3), Bas-Rhin (4, 5), Haut-Rhin (5), Rhône (4), Haute-Saône (7), Saône-et-Loire (3, 5), Sarre (3), Sarthe (3, 4, 5), Seine (5, 9), Seine-et-Marne (3, 6), Seine-et-Oise (4, 5), Seine-Inf. (5, 7), Deux-Sèvres (3), Somme (5), Tarn (4, 5), Tarn-et-Garonne (2), Var (2, 3, 4, 5), Vaucluse (3, 4, 5), Vendée (2, 3, 4), Vienne (3, 4, 6), Haute-Vienne (3, 4), Vosges (4, 6), Yonne (4).

F1cI 26. List of émigrés given posts in the prefectoral administration during the First Restoration.

F1cIII [elections and public opinion]. Allier (3), Basses-Alpes (4), Hautes-Alpes (3), Ardèche (4), Ardennes (4), Ariège (3, 4), Aube (7), Aude (3, 4), Aveyron (5), Bouches-du-Rhône (3), Calvados (5), Cantal (4), Charente (5), Charente-Inférieure (6), Cher (4), Corse (4), Côte-d'Or (5), Côtes-du-Nord (6), Creuse (4), Dordogne (4, 5), Doubs (4), Drôme (5), Eure (5), Eure-et-Loir (5), Finistère (8), Gard (4, 5), Haute-Garonne (6, 7), Gers (6), Gironde (3, 4), Hérault (6), Ille-et-Vilaine (4, 5), Indre (3), Indre-et-Loire (4), Isère (4, 5), Jura (4, 5), Landes (4), Loir-et-Cher (3), Loire (3, 4), Haute-Loire (2, 3), Loire-Inférieure (3, 4), Loiret (3), Lot (4, 5), Lozère (4), Marne-et-Loire (4), Manche (4), Mayenne (4), Meurthe (5), Meuse (6), Nord (5), Oise (4), Orne (5, 6), Puy-de-Dôme (4), Basses-Pyrénées (5), Hautes-Pyrénées (4), Rhône (3, 4), Saône-et-Loire (4, 5), Haute-Saône (4), Seine (8), Seine-et-Oise (6, 7), Seine-Inférieure (4, 5), Deux-Sèvres (4), Somme (4), Tarn-et-Garonne (2, 3), Var (3, 4), Vaucluse (4), Vienne (4), Vosges (6), Yonne (4).

F1d1* 1-4 [registers]. Requests for places in the prefectoral administration during the First Restoration.

F1d1* 8. Requests for places, 1815.

F1d1 31. Miscellaneous requests for places.

F1e 65. Administrative personnel in Illyria, 1809–13.

F1e 77. Administrative personnel in Piedmont, An IX–1813.

## (iv) Miscellaneous, series F

F14* 2139.  Tableau of the personnel of the Ponts-et-Chaussées, An IX–1832.

F14* 2140.  Register of engineers in the P-et-C, 1777–1846.

F21 1011.  Administration of theatres, subsidies, grants, etc. (doss. Dusaulchoy for Mique during the Revolution).

## (v) Series F7.  Ministry of Police

F7* 105, 106, 116(1).  Bureau des émigrés. Lists of émigrés and of amnestied émigrés, An II–1810.

F7* 676.  Surveillance of émigrés, Ans VI–X.

F7 3052(1).  Petitions to the First Consul for removal from the lists of émigrés.

F7 3331, 3334.  Laws, decrees, arrêtés and circulars concerning émigrés, 1791–1815.

F7 4336.  Lists of émigrés maintained, or excepted from measures of amnesty.

F7 [departmental series].  Dossiers of émigrés, arranged alphabetically by department. 4827, 4850(3), 4853, 4890(3), 4895, 4901(1), 4919, 4944, 4957, 4967, 4973, 4979(1), 4991(1), 4991(2), 5007, 5031(1), 5032, 5033, 5035, 5038, 5040, 5051, 5075, 5082, 5091, 5096, 5106(2), 5112, 5115, 5142, 5150, 5151, 5156, 5158, 5221, 5227, 5235, 5243, 5283, 5290(3), 5294, 5298, 5316, 5319, 5330(1), 5332, 5393, 5437, 5446, 5487, 5490, 5581, 5593, 5606, 5608(3), 5614, 5636, 5645, 5651(4), 5651(5), 5704, 5706, 5712, 5747, 5766, 5774(1), 5785(3).

F7 5790.  Emigrés removed from the lists, An II–XI.

F7 7027–7030 [4 cartons].  The Royal Commissaires Extraordinaires in 1814. Classified by Military Division.

F7 7674.  Confirmation of names inscribed on the lists of émigrés.

F7 9780.  Commissaires généraux and spéciaux of police: nominations.

F7 9781, 9784.  Dossiers.

F7 9854.  Dossiers of Commissaires of police, An XIII–1847 (Isère-Landes).

## (vi) Series O3.  Maison du Roi (Restoration)

O3* 745, 748, 752, 754, 756, 758, 759, 760, 761, 762, 763, 767, 768, 769, 772, 775, 776, 777.  Reports of the Commission studying pensions for former émigrés.

O3 895.  Lists of personnel, Maison du Roi. Requests for places.

O3 2243.  Register of the personnel of the Chevaux-légers at the suppression of the Corps (December 1815). The Maison Militaire at Ghent during the Hundred Days.

O3 2249.  Register of the personnel of the Maison Militaire, 1816–30.

O3 2560, 2561.  Armies of the emigration. Requests for promotion, various other material.

O3 2565.  Lists of those made Chevaliers de Saint-Louis in emigration.

O3 2566.  Armies of the emigration. Promotions.

O3 2571.  Lists of personnel.

O3 2572.  Register of the personnel, Condé's army.

O3 2595.  Proposals for pensions made by the bureau des émigrés, 1815–16.

O3 2600, 2624.  Finances of the Maison du Roi in emigration (including some details of personnel involved in the financial administration).

## II. ARCHIVES ADMINISTRATIVES DE LA GUERRE (CHATEAU DE VINCENNES)

(i)  Dossiers communicated individually: Agrain des Hubas, Aucapitaine, Audebard de Ferussac, Carrère de Loubère,[1] Cazaux, Coucy, F.-J. Dalmas, Du Boishamon, Du Mesnil, Lantivy, Nicollon des Abbayes,[1] Revel, Riccé, Saubert de Larcy, Sido,[1] Tocqueville, Ulliac,[1] Vignolle.

(ii)  Classement général of officers, Ancien Régime: Carton 24 (L.-M. de Bonne), 151 (Lozéran de Fressac). 1791–1847: Carton 164 (Barrême), 202 (Beaucorps), 209 (Beaumont), 281 (Berthot), 328 (Blacas-Carros), 350 (Blouquier de Trélan père), 384 (Félix de Bonne), 592 (Louis de Carbonnières), 604 (Carrère), 634 (Cellerier, Cellès), 648 (Salonnier de Chaligny), 712 (Cherrier), 729 (Chomel Saint-Ange), 751 (Clerget de Saint-Léger), 760 (Coetlosquet), 804 (Corn), 1032 (Desjoberts), 1149 (Ducasse de Horgues), 1316 (Fabre), 1610 (Giraud des Echerolles), 1612 (Girod de Novillars), 1642 (Giresse la Beyrie), 1720 (Guesnet), 1770 (Villot de la Tour), 1872 (Imbert de Saint-Paul, Imbert de Trémiolles), 1960 (Kersaint fils), 1997 (Lachadenède), 2005 (La Corbière), 2090 (Langle), 2204 (Le Caron de Fleury), 2251 (Le François de Drionville), 2288 (Le Melorel

[1] Dossier for pension.

de la Haichois), 2307 (Léotard), 2324 (Le Roux du Minihy), 2340 (Lespinasse de Peybèyre), 2533 (Marliave), 2590 (Mathieu de Moulon), 2701 (Milon de Mesne), 2790 (Mortemart de Boisse), 2823 (Musnier de la Converserie), 3128 (Auguste de Pons), 3142 (Potier), 3244 (Ravenel de Boisteilleul), 3266 (Regnon de Chaligny), 3396 (Ropert), 3613 (Sinard de Chevalier), 3739 (Trenqualye), 3820 (Urre), 3827 (Bluget de Valdenuit).

### (iii) Series X

X$^{AD}$ 26, 29.  Maison du Roi. Register of nominations and commissions 1814–30.

X$^{AE}$ 4.  Garde Royale, 1815–30.

X$^b$ 93.  Infantry, régiments de la filiation. Quercy 1705–76. Rohan-Soubise, 1776–90. Personnel.

X$^b$ 260.  Demi-brigades of the line, An IV to Ans XI/XII. 39th demi-brigade, personnel.

X$^c$ 195.  Light cavalry. 6th regiment chasseurs à cheval, 1791–1815. Personnel.

### (iv) Registers of non-commissioned personnel

Y7 c 22.  Dragoons, 1763–86; dragons de Lorraine, 1776–86.

### (v) Registers of officers, Ancien Régime

(a) YB 27.  Gardes Françaises, 1786–9.

YB 75.  Gendarmerie d'ordonnance, 1788–c. 1791.

YB 107.  Collective register of cavalry and dragoon officers, 1788–91.

(b) Registers of infantry officers by regiments: YB 169 (Aquitaine 1763), 181 (Bourbon 1763), 269 (Agenais 1776), 292 (Bourbonnais 1776), 335 (Picardie 1776), 341 (Roi 1776), 343 (Royal-Auvergne 1776), 370 (Austrasie 1788), 374 (La Marine 1788), 375 (Auxerrois 1788), 376 (Bourbonnais 1788), 378 (Béarn 1788), 379 (Agenois 1788), 384 (Guyenne 1788), 393 (Perche 1788), 395 (Bassigny 1788), 398 (Aquitaine 1788), 408 (Royal-Vaisseaux 1788), 410 (La Couronne 1788), 411 (Bretagne 1788), 422 (Bourbon 1788), 426 (Bourgogne 1788), 432 (Beauce 1788), 447 (Saintonge 1788), 465 (Royal Deux-Ponts 1788), 479 (Chasseurs royaux de Dauphiné, 2$^e$ léger, 1788).

(c)  Register of cavalry officers by regiments: YB 575 (Royal-Etranger 1776), 580 (Royal-Piémont 1776), 625 (Dragoons: Colonel Général 1776), 635 (Mestre de Camp Général 1776), 636 (Monsieur 1776).
(d)  YB 668, 670.  Artillery, registers of lieutenants, 1768–91.
(e)  YB 685.  Engineers: Officers, 1700–93.
(f)  YB 833.  Commissions in the infantry, 1788–91.
     YB 846.  Commissions in the cavalry, 1788–92.

(vi)  Reports of the commission set up by the ordinance of 31 May 1814 to examine the claims of émigré officers (uncatalogued)
519(1–4).  Promotion.
    (5–8).  Infantry.
    (9–11).  Cavalry.
    (12–19).  Retirement and pensions (including index 519(13)).
    (20).  Engineers.
    (21–22).  Artillery.

(viii) Miscellaneous

List of officers in the 18th dragoons, vol. III, An XII–1814.

III. PERSONAL COMMUNICATIONS FROM DEPARTMENTAL ARCHIVISTS

Personal communications from the archivists of the Basses-Alpes, Hautes-Alpes, Aude, Aveyron, Côtes-du-Nord, Doubs, Drôme, Indre, Loire-Atlantique, Hautes-Pyrénées, Pyrénées-Orientales, Seine-et-Oise, Deux-Sèvres, Somme, Vienne, Vosges.

B. PRINTED MATERIAL[1]

1. GENERAL HISTORY

Bastid, P.  *Les institutions politiques de la monarchie parlementaire française (1814–1848)* (1954).
Beau de Loménie, E.  *Les responsabilitiés des dynasties bourgeoises*, I, *De Bonaparte à Mac-Mahon* (4 vols., 1943–63).
Bennaerts, L.  *Les Commissaires extraordinaires de Napoléon Ier en 1814, d'après leur correspondance inédite* (1915).
Bertier de Sauvigny, G. de.  *La Restauration* (1st ed., 1955).
—— *La conspiration des légitimistes et de la duchesse de Berry contre Louis-Philippe (1830–32)* (1950).

[1] All books published in Paris, unless otherwise stated.

Charléty, S. *La Restauration* (1921). Vol. IV of *l'Histoire de la France contemporaine*, ed. Lavisse.

Daudet, E. *Louis XVIII et le duc Decazes (1815–1820)* (1899).

Duvergier de Hauranne. *Histoire du gouvernement parlementaire en France* (10 vols., 1857–72).

Houssaye, H. *1815. La première Restauration—le retour de l'île d'Elbe—les Cent Jours* (28th ed., 1899).

—— *1815. La seconde abdication—la Terreur blanche* (44th ed., 1909).

Lefebvre de Behaine, Comte. *Le comte d'Artois sur la route de Paris* (1921).

Le Gallo, Ch. *Les Cent Jours, essai sur l'histoire intérieure de la France depuis le retour de l'île d'Elbe jusqu'à la nouvelle de Waterloo* (1924).

Mater, A. 'Le groupement régional des partis politiques à la fin de la Restauration 1824–30', *La Révolution française*, XLII (Jan.–June 1902), 406–63.

Mazoyer, L. 'Catégories d'âge et groupes sociaux. Les jeunes générations françaises de 1830', *Annales d'histoire économique et sociale*, X (Sept. 1938), 385–423.

## 2. LOCAL HISTORY

Alleaume, Ch. 'Les Cent Jours dans le Var', *Mémoires de la Société d'études scientifiques et archéologiques de Draguignan*, XLIX (1938).

Boissonnet, J.-B. *La Bourbonnais sous la seconde Restauration. L'esprit public* (Moulins, 1924).

Borrey, Capt. F. *La Franche-Comté en 1814* (1912).

Bruchet, M. 'L'invasion et l'occupation du département du Nord par les Alliés 1814–18', *Revue du Nord*, VI (Nov. 1920), 261–99; VII (Feb. 1921), 30–61.

Contamine, H. *Metz et la Moselle de 1814 à 1870*, I, *La vie sociale, économique et politique* (2 vols., Nancy, 1932).

Fizaine, S. *La vie politique dans la Côte-d'Or sous Louis XVIII* (1931).

Gaffarel, P. 'La première Restauration à Marseille', *Annales des Facultés de droit et des lettres d'Aix*, I, no. I (Jan.–March 1905), 15–93.

—— 'Les Cent Jours à Marseille 1815', *Annales...d'Aix*, II, no. II (July–Sept. 1906), 153–219.

Hauteclocque, comte G. de. 'Les Cent Jours dans le Pas-de-Calais

(20 Mars–8 Juillet 1815)', *Mémoires de l'Académie des sciences, lettres et arts d'Arras*, XXXVI (1905), 29–185.

—— 'La seconde Restauration dans le Pas-de-Calais (1815–1830)', *Mémoires de l'Académie...d'Arras*, XXXVII (1906), 255–475.

Joxe, R. 'Le comité royal provisoire de Marseille (25 Juin–10 Juillet 1815)', *Annales historiques de la Révolution française*, XVI (1939), 38–5415.

Leuilliot, P. *La première Restauration et les Cent Jours en Alsace* (1958).

—— *L'Alsace au début du XIX^e siècle* (3 vols., 1959–60), I, *La vie politique*.

Loubet, J. 'Le gouvernement toulousain du duc d'Angoulême après les Cent Jours', *La Révolution française*, LXIV (Feb.–Apr. 1913), 149–65, 337–66.

Perrin, R. *L'esprit public dans le département de la Meurthe de 1814 à 1816* (Nancy, 1913).

Regné, J. 'Les Autrichiens dans l'Ardèche en 1814 et 1815', *Revue historique de la Révolution française et de l'Empire*, XIII (Apr.–Sept. 1918), 177–213, 397–438.

Richard, G. 'Nancy à la fin de l'Empire. L'entrée des Alliés en 1814', *Le Pays lorrain* (1954), no. 1, pp. 10–24.

—— 'Nancy sous la première occupation alliée (14 janvier au 30 avril 1814)', *Le Pays lorrain* (1954), no. 2, pp. 50–66.

—— 'Nancy sous la première Restauration', *Le Pays lorrain* (1955), no. 4, pp. 125–42.

—— 'Les Cent Jours à Nancy', *Le Pays lorrain* (1957), no. 3, pp. 81–96.

Rocal, G. *De Brumaire à Waterloo en Périgord* (2 vols., 1941–?), vol. 1 only.

Vidalenc, J. *Le département de l'Eure sous la monarchie constitutionnelle 1814–1848* (1952).

### 3. LOCAL GOVERNMENT AND THE PREFECTORAL ADMINISTRATION

'Un rapport du préfet Chazal au ministre de l'Intérieur au sujet de la famille Barrère-Dambarrère (23 Fév. 1811)', *Bulletin de la Société académique des Hautes-Pyrénées* (1956–7), pp. 38–40.

Antoine, A. *La sous-préfecture d'Auxerre 1811–1816* (Auxerre, 1908).

Ardascheff, P. *Les intendants de province sous Louis XVI* (tr. L. Jousserandot, 1909).

Aulard, A. 'La centralisation napoléonienne. Les préfets', *Etudes et leçons sur la Révolution française*, 7th ser. (1913), pp. 113–95.

Chapman, B. *The Prefects and Provincial France* (London, 1955).

Durand, Ch. *Les auditeurs au Conseil d'Etat de 1803 à 1814* (Aix-en-Provence, 1958).

Durand, R. *L'administration des Côtes-du-Nord sous le Consulat et l'Empire* (2 vols., 1925).

Godechot, J. *Les institutions de la France sous la Révolution et l'Empire* (1951).

Henry, Pierre (alias Pierre-Henry). *Histoire des préfets, cent cinquante ans de l'administration provinciale* (1950).

Pouthas, Ch. 'La réorganisation du Ministère de l'Intérieur et la reconstitution de l'administration préfectorale par Guizot en 1830', *Revue de l'histoire moderne et contemporaine*, IX (Oct.–Dec. 1962), 241–63.

#### 4. COLLECTIVE BIOGRAPHIES

*Notes biographiques sur les membres des assemblées municipales parisiennes et des conseils généraux de la Seine de 1800 à nos jours.* I, *1800–71* (1958).

Balteau, J., Barroux, M., Prevost, M., and Roman d'Amat, J.-C. *Dictionnaire de biographie française* (1932, 9 vols. and 4 fascicules to date).

Barrau, F. de. *Galerie des préfets de l'Aveyron* (Rodez, 1905).

Bertrand, J. 'Notes inédites sur les premiers sous-préfets de Vitry-le-François', *Almanach Matot-Braine, des trois departements de la Marne, de l'Aisne et des Ardennes*, LXVII (1924), 390–494.

Brissot-Thivars. *Le guide electoral ou Biographie legislative de tous les députés depuis 1814 jusques et y compris 1818 à 1819* (2 vols., 1819–20), vol. II only.

Capeille, abbé J. *Dictionnaire de biographies roussillonnaises* (Perpignan, 1910).

Dourille, J. *Biographie des députés de la nouvelle chambre septennale* (1829).

Faure, H. *Galerie administrative ou Biographie des préfets depuis l'organisation des préfectures jusqu'à ce jour* (2 vols. in 1, Aurillac, 1839).

Imhoff, A. *L'administration de Thionville et ses sous-préfets (1800–1870)* (Metz, 1924).

Lagarde, M.-A. *Nouvelle biographie pittoresque des députés de la Chambre septennale* (1826).

Lamothe-Langon, E.-L. *Biographie des préfets des 86 departements de la France. Par un sous-préfet* (3rd ed., 1826).

Le Bihan, A. 'Les préfets du Finistère', *Bulletin de la Société archéologique du Finistère*, LXXXV (1959), 189–205.

Martineau, H. *Petit Dictionnaire Stendhalien* (1948).

Régnier, J. *Les préfets de Consulat et de l'Empire* (1907).

Robert, A. and Cougny, G. *Dictionnaires des parlementaires français de 1789 à 1889* (5 vols., 1889–90).

Rougeron, G. *Les administrateurs du département de l'Allier, An VIII–1950* (Montluçon, 1956).

Salvarelli, J. *Les administrateurs du département du Var 1790–1897* (Draguignan, 1897).

Savant, J. *Les préfets de Napoléon* (1958).

5. INDIVIDUAL BIOGRAPHIES: MEMOIRS: LETTERS

'Notice biographique sur M. le comte de Vendeuvre', *Annuaire des cinq départements de l'ancienne Normandie* (1864), pp. 691–702.

Alboize. *M. le baron de Croze, ancien préfet* (no date or place of publication given).

Babaud-Landrevie, L. *Etudes historiques et administratives* (2 vols., Confolens, 1863), vol. 1 only.

Badiche, abbé. *Notice historique sur M. le comte de la Villegontier* (extract from the *Biographie universelle*, vol. LXXV, 1862).

Barante, P. de. *Souvenirs du baron de Barante* (8 vols., 1890–1901).

Bart, P. 'Un préfet des Cent Jours, Harel', *Feuilles d'histoire*, XIII, nos. 1–2 (Jan.–Feb. 1915), 41–52, 106–18.

Barthelémy, C.-H.-F. *Souvenirs d'un ancien préfet* (1886).

Bertier de Sauvigny, G. de. *Le comte Ferdinand de Bertier (1782–1864) et l'énigme de la Congrégation* (1948).

—— 'Ferdinand de Bertier, préfet du Calvados', *Bulletin de la Société des antiquaires de Normandie*, LIV (1957–8), 193–261; LV (1959–60), 191–260.

Beugnot, J.-C. *Mémoires du comte Beugnot, ancien ministre (1783–1815)* (3rd ed., 1889).

Blic, E. de. *Hervé Clérel, comte de Tocqueville* (Dijon, 1951).

Bousquet, C. *Marie-Joseph marquis de Foresta* (Marseille, 1858).

Broglie, Victor de. *Souvenirs 1785–1870 du feu duc de Broglie* (4 vols., 2nd ed., 1886).

Carnot, H.  *Correspondance inédite de Carnot avec Napoléon pendant les Cent Jours* (1819).

Chapuisat, E.  'La restauration de la république de Genève et le préfet Capelle', *La Révolution française*, LXXII (Feb.–March 1912), 132–47, 214–38.

Chateaubriand, vicomte de.  *Mémoires d'Outre-Tombe*, ed. M. Levaillant and G. Moulinier (3 vols., no date).

Conny, J-E. de.  *Un homme. Cent ans de révolutions* (Moulins, 1889).

Frénilly, baron de.  *Souvenirs du baron de Frénilly pair de France 1768–1828* (new ed., 1909).

Frondeville, H. de.  *Notice biographique sur le président de Frondeville 1757–1816* (Joigny, 1926).

Gaulandeau, H.  'Le comte Armand de Beaumont, sous-préfet de Vendôme de 1815 à 1824', *Bulletin de la Société archéologique, scientifique et littéraire du Vendômois*, 1960 (1959), pp. 22–38.

Haussez, baron d'.  *Mémoires du baron d'Haussez, dernier ministre de la marine sous la Restauration* (2 vols., 1896–7).

Jaucourt, comte de.  *Correspondance du comte de Jaucourt, ministre des affaires étrangères, avec le prince de Talleyrand pendant le Congrès de Vienne* (1905).

La Rochefoucauld, Sosthènes de.  *Mémoires de M. le vicomte de Larochefoucauld, aide-de-camp du feu Roi Charles X, 1814 à 1837* (5 vols., 1837).

Leuilliot, P.  'Le dernier préfet du Haut-Rhin sous la Restauration: le baron Locard', *Revue d'histoire moderne*, IV (1929), 416–30.

Lezay-Marnésia, Albert de.  *Mes souvenirs. A mes enfants* (Blois, 1851).

Mancel, G.  *Biographie de M. du Feugray* (Mémoires de l'Académie impériale des sciences, arts et belles-lettres de Caen, 1861), pp. 92–104.

Marboutin, J.-R.  'M. des Echerolles, sous-préfet de Saint-Gaudens', *Revue de Comminges*, XLI (1927), 101–8.

Molé, comte.  *Le comte Molé 1781–1855. Sa vie—ses mémoires* (6 vols., 1922–30).

Moulard, abbé J.  *Le comte Camille de Tournon préfet de la Gironde 1815–1822* (1914).

——*Le comte Camille de Tournon…1778–1833* (3 vols., 1927–32).

Napoléon I^er.  *Correspondance de Napoléon I^er* (32 vols., 1858–70), vol. XXVIII (1815) only.

Pasquier, duc.  *Histoire de mon temps. Mémoires du chancelier Pasquier* (6 vols., 5th ed., 1894–5).

Pietresson de Saint-Aubin, P. 'M. de Wildermeth, ancien agent secret des Bourbons, secrétaire-général du Nord'. *Revue du Nord*, XXI (May 1935), 89–98.

Plancy, comte de. *Souvenirs du comte de Plancy 1798–1816* (2nd ed., 1904).

Pouthas, Ch. *Guizot pendant la Restauration. Préparation de l'homme d'état (1814–1830)* (1923).

Puymaigre, comte de. *Souvenirs sur l'émigration, l'Empire et la Restauration* (1884).

Rambuteau, comte de. *Mémoires du comte de Rambuteau* (1905).

Reinhard, M. *Le grand Carnot* (2 vols., 1950–2).

Rémusat, Ch. de. *Correspondance de M. de Rémusat pendant les premières années de la Restauration* (6 vols., 1883–6).

—— *Mémoires de ma vie*, ed. Ch. Pouthas (4 vols., 1958–62), vols. I–II only.

Salaberry, comte de. *Souvenirs politiques du comte de Salaberry sur la Restauration 1821–30* (2 vols., 1900).

Sers, Jean-André. *Souvenirs d'un préfet de la Monarchie. Mémoires du baron Sers, 1786–1862* (1906).

Soudeval, Ch. Mourain de. *Notice sur le baron Angellier de la Bourdaiserie* (Tours, 1857).

Vaublanc, comte Viennot de. *Mémoires sur la Révolution de France, et recherches sur les causes qui ont amené la Révolution de 1789 et celles qui l'ont suivie* (4 vols., 1833).

Villèle, comte de. *Mémoires et correspondance du comte de Villèle* (5 vols., 1888–90).

Villeneuve-Bargemon, Emmanuel de. 'Mémoires de Ferdinand-Emmanuel marquis de Villeneuve-Bargemon (1777–1802)', *Carnets de la Sabretache*, no. 284 (July–Aug. 1923), pp. 265–391.

Villeneuve-Bargemon, Joseph de. *Souvenirs de soixante ans* (1870).

Villepelet, R. 'Le comte de Saint-Aulaire, préfet de la Haute-Garonne (1814–1815)', *Revue historique*, CLX (1929), 303–18.

Vitrolles, baron de. *Mémoires et relations politiques du baron de Vitrolles* (3 vols., 1884).

## 6. THE NOBILITY: GENERAL

Batjin, N. *Histoire complète de la noblesse de France, depuis 1789 jusqu'à vers l'année 1862* (1862).

Becarud, J. 'La noblesse dans les chambres', *Revue internationale d'histoire politique*, no. 11 (1953), pp. 189–205.

Bloch, Marc, and Febre, Lucien. 'Les noblesses. 1. Reconnaissance générale du terrain', *Annales d'histoire économique et sociale*, VIII (1936), 238–42.

Du Puy de Clinchamps, Ph. *La noblesse* (Coll. Que sais-je? No date given.)

Egret, J. 'L'aristocratie parlementaire française à la fin de l'Ancien Régime', *Revue historique*, CCVIII (1952), 1–14.

Ford, F. *Robe and Sword. The regrouping of the French aristocracy after Louis XIV* (Harvard Historical Studies LXIV, Cambridge, Mass., 1953).

[Jougla de Morenas, H.] *Le second ordre* (1947).

McManners, J. *The French Nobility* (*The European Nobility in the Eighteenth Century*, ed. A. Goodwin, London 1953, pp. 22–42).

Marsay, vicomte de. *De l'âge des privilèges au temps de vanités* (1932).

Neufbourg, comte de. 'Les noblesses. 2. Projet d'une enquête sur la noblesse française', *Annales d'histoire économique et sociale*, VIII (1936), 243–55.

Pradel de Lamasc, M. de. *Les marchands de merlettes ou verité passe honneurs* (1946).

Reinhard, M. 'Elite et noblesse dans la seconde moitié du XVIIIᵉ siècle', *Revue d'histoire moderne et contemporaine*, III (1956), 5–37.

Soutade-Rouger, Mme. 'Les notables en France sous la Restauration (1815–1830)', *Revue d'histoire économique et sociale*, XXXVIII (1960), 98–110.


7. COLLECTIVE AND CORPORATE GENEALOGIES

*Annuaire de la noblesse 1843–1911* (ed. Borel d'Hauterive *1843–91*, ed. vicomte Révérend *1892–1911*).

Bluche, J.-F. *L'origine des magistrats du parlement de Paris au XVIIIᵉ siecle* (1956).

—— *Les magistrats du parlement de Paris au XVIIIᵉ siecle (1715–1771)* (1960).

—— *Les honneurs de la cour* (Les cahiers nobles, nos. 10–11, 2 vols., 1957).

Boisgelin, marquis de (ed.). *Chronologie des officiers des cours souveraines de Provence par B. de Clapiers-Collongues* (Aix-en-Provence, 1904).

Bourée, A. *La chancellerie près le parlement de Bourgogne de 1476 à 1790* (Dijon, 1927).

C. d'E.-A. (Chaix d'Est-Ange). *Dictionnaire des familles françaises anciennes ou notables à la fin du XIXᵉ siecle* (20 vols., A-GA, Evreux, 1903–29).

Charondas (pseudonym). *Un juge d'armes au Jockey-Club* (Les cahiers nobles, no. 2, 1954).

—— *Le cahier noir* (Les cahiers nobles, nos. 8–9, 2 vols., 1957).

Coustant d'Yanville, comte. *Essais historiques et chronologiques sur la chambre des comptes de Paris* (1866–75).

Frondeville, H. de. *Les présidents du parlement de Normandie (1499–1790)* (Rouen, 1953).

Gentil de Rosmorduc, baron A.-N. *Preuves de noblesses des demoiselles bretonnes admises à la maison royale de Saint-Louis à Saint-Cyr depuis... 1686 jusqu'à... 1793* (Versailles, 1891).

*Grand Armorial de France* (first three vols. signed Henri Jougla de Morenas, remainder anonymous; 7 vols., 1934–52).

Lainé, P.-L. *Archives généalogiques et historiques de la noblesse de France* (11 vols., 1828–50).

Longeaux, C.-P. de. *La chambre des comptes du duché de Bar*, ed. by the baron de Dumast (Bar-le-Duc, 1907).

Mahuet, comte A. de. *Biographie de la cour souveraine de Lorraine et Barrois et du parlement de Nancy* (Nancy, 1911).

—— *Biographie de la chambre des comptes de Lorraine* (Nancy, 1914).

Révérend, vicomte Albert. *Armorial du premier Empire, titres, majorats et armoires concédés par Napoléon I* (4 vols., 1894–7).

—— *Les familles titrées et anoblies au XIXᵉ siecle; titres, anoblissements et pairies de la Restauration* (6 vols., 1901–6).

—— *Titres et confirmation de titres... 1830–1908* (1909).

Roton, comte R. de. *Les arrêts du grand conseil portant dispense du marc d'or de noblesse...* (1951).

Saint-Allais, N. Viton de. *Nobiliaire universel de France...* (21 vols., printed 1872–7).

Villain, J. *La France moderne. Grand dictionnaire généalogique, historique et biographique* (3 vols., 1908–13).

Warren, Raoul de. *Les pairs de France au XIXᵉ siecle* (Les cahiers nobles, nos. 20–21, 2 vols., 1959).

Woelmont de Brumagne, baron de. *Notices généalogiques* (9 vols., 1923–35).

## 8. REGIONAL GENEALOGIES

Angot, abbé A. *Dictionnaire historique, topographique et biographique de la Mayenne* (4 vols., Laval, 1900).

Arcelin, A. *Indicateur héraldique et généalogique du Mâconnais* (Mâcon, 1865).

Barrau, H. de. *Documents historiques et généalogiques sur les familles et les hommes remarquables du Rouergue...* (4 vols., Rodez, 1853–60).

Baux, J. *Nobiliaire du département de l'Ain (XVIIe et XVIIIe siecles)* (2 vols., Bourg-en-Bresse, 1862–4).

Beauchet-Filleau, Henri and Chergé, Ch. de. *Dictionnaire historique et généalogique des familles du Poitou* (2nd ed., Poitiers 1891–1915, 3 vols. and 4 fascicules A–G).

Benoit d'Entrevaux, F. *Armorial du Vivarais* (Privas, 1908).

Bouillet, J.-B. *Nobiliaire d'Auvergne* (7 vols., Clermont-Ferrand, 1846–53).

Bremond, Alphonse. *Nobiliaire toulousain* (2 vols., Toulouse, 1863).

Cabannes de Cauna, baron. *Armorial de Landes* (3 vols., Bordeaux, 1863–9).

Carré de Busserolle. *Archives des familles nobles de la Touraine, de l'Anjou, du Maine et du Poitou* (2 vols., Tours, 1889–90).

Champeval, J.-B. *Dictionnaire des familles nobles et notables de la Corrèze* (Tulle, 1911).

Clavière, R. de. *Les assemblées des trois ordres de la sénéchaussée de Beaujolais en 1789* (1935).

Colonna de Cesari Rocca, comte. *Armorial Corse* (1892).

Denis de Péage, P. *Notes généalogiques sur quelques familles d'Artois et de Flandre* (2 vols., Lille, 1951).

Dufau de Maluquer, A. de. *Armorial de Béarn, 1696–1701, extrait du recueil officiel dressé par ordre de Louis XIV* (2 vols., 1889–93).

Du Guerny, Y[annig. Y. R. Chassin]. *Recueil de filiations bas-poitevines* (Montauban, 1961).

Froidefond de Boulazac, A. de. *Armorial de la noblesse de Périgord* (2 vols., Périgeux, 1891).

Frotier de la Messelière, vicomte H. *Filiations bretonnes, 1650 à 1912* (6 vols., Saint-Brieuc, 1914–24).

Gigord, R. de. *La noblesse de la sénéchaussée de Villenauve-de-Berg, en 1789* (Lyon, 1894).

Gourdon de Genouillac, H. and Piolenc, marquis de. *Nobiliaire du département des Bouches-du-Rhône* (1863).

Icard, Dr Severin, and others. *Armorial de la Provence* (Mâcon, 1932).

Jourda de Vaux, vicomte G. de. *Nobiliaire du Velay et de l'ancien diocèse du Puy* (7 vols., Lyon, 1924–31).

Jouvencel, H. de. *L'assemblée de la noblesse de la sénéchaussée de Lyon en 1789* (Lyon, 1907).

—— *L'assemblée de la noblesse du bailliage de Forez en 1789* (Lyon, 1911).

La Morinerie, baron L. de. *La noblesse de Saintonge et d'Aunis convoquée pour les Etats Généraux de 1789* (1861).

La Roque, Louis de. *Armorial de la noblesse de Languedoc* (2 vols., 1860–3).

Le Clert, L. *Armorial historique de l'Aube* (Troyes, 1911).

Lepage, H. and Germain, L. *Complément au nobiliaire de Lorraine de Dom Pelletier...* (Nancy, 1885).

Lescure, vicomte M. de. *Armorial du Gévaudan* (Lyon, 1929).

Linière, R. de. *Armorial de la Sarthe* (2nd series). *Notices généalogiques sur les familles résidantes ou possessionnées dans la région sarthoise au cours des XVIIe et XVIIIe siècles* (2 vols., Le Mans, 1948).

Louvencourt, comte A. de. *Notices sur les familles nobles existant actuellement dans le département de la Somme* (Abbeville, 1909).

Lurion, R. de. *Nobiliaire de Franche-Comté* (Besançon, 1890).

Magny E. Drigon, comte de. *Nobiliaire de Normandie* (2 vols., 1863–4).

Maransange, H. Petitjean de. *Dictionnaire historique, généalogique et héraldique des anciennes familles du Berry* (2 vols., Bourges, 1926).

Meller, P. *Les anciennes familles de la Gironde* (3 vols. in 2, Bordeaux, 1895–6).

—— *Armorial du Bordelais, sénéchaussées de Bordeaux, Bazas et Libourne* (3 vols., 1906).

—— *Etat civil des familles bordelaises avant la Révolution* (Bordeaux, 1909).

Nadaud, abbé J. *Nobiliaire du diocèse et de la généralité de Limoges* (4 vols., Limoges, 1856–80).

Poidebard, W. *Notes héraldiques et généalogiques concernant les pays de Lyonnais, Forez et Beaujolais* (Lyon, 1896).

Poirier, abbé F.-J. *Metz, documents généalogiques...1561–1792* (1899).

—— *Metz et pays messin. Documents généalogiques...* (1930).

Poitier de Courcy, Pol. *Nobiliaire et armorial de Bretagne* (3 vols., 3rd ed., Rennes, 1890).

Révérend du Mesnil, Edmond. *Armorial historique de Bresse, Bugey, Dombes, Pays de Gex, Valromey et Franc-Lyonnais* (2 vols. in 1, Lyon, 1872–4).

Ribier, docteur de. *Preuves de la noblesse d'Auvergne. Preuves de noblesse des gentilshommes d'Auvergne admis dans les Ecoles Royales militaires* (Riom, 1909).

—— *Preuves de la noblesse d'Auvergne. Les anoblis et les confirmations de noblesse en Auvergne 1643–1771* (1927).

Saint-Venant, R. Barré de. *Dictionnaire topographique, historique, biographique, généalogique et héraldique du Vendômois* (4 vols., Blois, 1912–17).

Soultrait, comte G. de. *Armorial de l'ancien duché de Nivernais* (1847).

Tardieu, Ambroise. *Dictionnaire des anciennes familles de l'Auvergne* (Moulins, 1884).

—— *Grand dictionnaire historique, généalogique et biographique de la Haute-Marche, département de la Creuse* (Herment, Puy-de-Dôme, 1894).

Villenaut, A. de. *Nobiliaire de Nivernais* (Nevers, 1900).

## 9. STUDIES OF INDIVIDUAL FAMILIES

Albrier, A. *La famille Varenne de Fenille, d'après des documents authentiques...* (Lyon, 1872).

Beaumont, comte Charles de. *La maison Bonnin de la Bonninière de Beaumont* (Vendôme, 1907).

Beaumont, Léon de. *Origines, services et alliances de la maison de Bremond d'Ars* (Jonzac, 1861).

B[oisrouvray], N. J. du. *La maison de Jacquelot. Anjou–Bretagne 1500–1959. Documents généalogiques et souvenirs* (1950).

Bombal, E. *Notes et documents pour servir à l'histoire de la maison de Saint-Chamans* (1885).

Diné, H. *Une famille de trésoriers et gens de robe sous l'Ancien Régime et la Révolution. Les Boula* (1957).

Du Guerny, Y[annig. Y. R. Chassin]. *Généalogie de la famille de Roujoux (Ardennes, Bretagne, Poitou)* (La Roche-sur-Yon, 1960).

Lestrange, comte H. de. *La maison de Lestrange* (1912).

M.-B. *Les Bédée et l'ascendance maternelle de Chateaubriand* (Vannes, 1936).

Montrichard, comte Roland de. *Trois siècles de parentés, 1640–1940* (1953).

Sarrazin, comte P. de. *Notice historique et généalogique sur la maison de Tinseau* (Compiègne, 1955).

Simon, chanoine G.-A. *Histoire généalogique des Clérel…comtes de Tocqueville* (Caen, 1954).

## 10. EMIGRATION

Beauchet-Filleau, H. *Tableau des émigrés du Poitou aux armées des princes et de Condé* (Poitiers, 1845).

Descostes, F. 'Les émigrés en Savoie à Aoste et dans le pays de Vaud 1790–1800', *Mémoires de l'Académie des sciences, belles-lettres et arts de Savoie*, 4th ser., X (1903).

Dubois, Jean. 'Liste des émigrés…du département de la Meuse', *Mémoires de la Société des lettres, sciences et arts de Bar-le-Duc*, 4th ser., VIII (1910).

Gain, A. *La Restauration et les biens des émigrés* (2 vols., Nancy, 1929).

Greer, D. *The Incidence of the Emigration during the French Revolution* (Harvard Historical Monographs, XXIV, Cambridge, Mass., 1951.)

Grouvel, vicomte. *Les Corps de Troupe de l'émigration française 1789–1815. I. Service de Grande-Bretagne et des Pays-Bas* (1957).

Honoré, L. 'L'émigration dans le Var 1789–1825', *Mémoires de la Société d'études scientifiques et archéologiques de Draguignan*, XII (1923).

Le Verdier, P. *Les émigrés normands à Coblentz…5 novembre–23 decembre 1791* (Caen, 1931).

Montarlot, P. 'Les émigrés de Saône-et-Loire', *Mémoires de la Société éduenne*, XLIV (1920–3), XLV (1924–7).

Sainte-Colombe, comte de. *Catalogue des émigrés français à Fribourg, en Suisse, de 1789 à 1798* (Lyon, 1884).

Sangnier, G. *Les émigrés du Pas-de-Calais pendant la Révolution* (Blangermont, Pas-de-Calais, no date).

Vidalenc, J. *Les émigrés français 1789–1825* (Publications de la Faculté des lettres et sciences humaines de l'Université de Caen, 1963).

BIBLIOGRAPHY

## II. MISCELLANEOUS

*Almanach Impérial, Almanach Royal.*
Archives parlementaires de 1787 à 1860 (2nd ser., 1800–60).
*Bulletin des Lois.*
*Recueil des lettres, circulaires, discours et autres actes publics émanés du
   ministère de l'Intérieur* (20 vols., Paris, Thermidor An V–1820).

# INDEX

*Entries in capitals, and dates of birth and death where known, are given only for prefects who held office between April 1814 and July 1830 (including the Hundred Days). Christian names in italic type are those normally used. Reference is to the text alone and complex family names are listed under the shortened form current during the Restoration (and used throughout the text).*

Assemblies
  Ancients, 50, 109
  Chambre Introuvable, 36, 38, 67, 71, 76, 94, 95, 149, 205
  Convention, 15, 40, 47, 50, 60–2, 65, 76, 107–8, 109–10, 121
  Corps Législatif, 94, 146
  Five Hundred, 7, 108, 109, 121, 146
  Legislative Assembly, 7, 42
  States General, 27, 50, 103
  Tribune, 50, 108
  *see also* Chamber of Deputies, Chamber of Peers
Aube, dept., 105, 119, 148
AUBERJON, Jean-Antoine-Paul-*Serge* d' (1772–1832), 38, 144
Aubert de Vitry, François-Jean-Philibert, 17
Aucapitaine, Pierre, 183
  family, 183
Auch (Gers), 106
Aude, dept., 38, 56, 57, 106, 189, 190
AUDERIC, François-Marie-Gabriel d' (1786–1848), 148, 153, 189
Auditors, auditoriat, 13, 35, 41, 50, 61, 76, 77, 100, 102, 107, 121, 125, 132–3, 192–3
Augier de Crémiers, Jean, 84
  family, 84–5
Autun (Saône-et-Loire), 27
Avallon (Yonne), 104, 172
Avaray, duc d', 92
Avesnes (Nord), 104, 109, 111
Aveyron, dept., 58
Avignon (Vaucluse), 44, 111
Avranches (Manche), 82

Babut, Jean, 89
Bagnères (Hautes-Pyrénées), 41
Bain, Marc-Antoine, 111, 116
Balahu de Noiron, family, 7
Balzac, Honoré de, 4, 6, 11, 12, 86, 134, 188
BALZAC, Marie-Auguste de (1788–1880), 111, 205
BARANTE, Amable-Guillaume-*Prosper* BRUGIERE DE (1782–1866), 16, 39, 56, 58, 64, 68, 72, 73, 112, 164, 193

Barbezieux (Charente), 90, 101
Bardonnenche, Antoine-Joachim-Claude-Ferdinand de, 89, 121–2
Barrère, Bertrand, 93
  Dembarrère, family, 93
Barrès, Maurice, 17
BARRIN, Joseph-Prosper-Hippolyte de (1779–?), 41
Barruel-Beauvert, 54
Barthélemy, Claude-Hyacinthe-Félix, 40, 143
  marquis de, 142–3
Bascle de Lagrèze, Paul-Gabriel [-Gratien], 96–7
Bassano (Maret), duc de, 58
Basses-Alpes, Basses-Pyrénées, *see* Alpes (Basses-), etc.
BASSET DE CHATEAUBOURG, Anne-Léonard-*Camille* (1781–1852), 18, 50
BASTARD D'ESTANG, Jean-Marie-Hyacinthe-*Armand* (1786–1857), 36, 37, 189
Bastia (Corsica), 85, 166
Baugé (Maine-et-Loire), 112
Bayeux (Calvados), 172
Bayne, René-Louis-Marie de, 122
Bayonne (Basses-Pyrénées), 34, 99
Bazas (Gironde), 174
Beau de Loménie, Emmanuel, 7, 188
Beaucorps, Henri-Charles-Marie de, 190
BEAUMONT, Armand [BONNIN] DE LA BONNINIERE DE (1782–1859), 134, 171
  family, 184
BEAUMONT, Christophe-*Armand*-Paul-Alexandre de [Armand de Beaumont] (1770–1841), 138, 190, 204
Beaumont, Joseph-Gabriel-Marie de, 169
Beaune (Côte-d'Or), 123
Beauvais (Oise), 35
Becquey, Charles, 90
  deputy, 90
Bedoch, comte, 106
Bejarry, *Amédée*-Paul-François de, 15
Belfort (Haut-Rhin), 108
Belgium, 61, 102, 205

INDEX

CAVAIGNAC, Jean-Baptiste (1762–
1829), 62
Cazaux, Jean-Raymond, 108
Cellès, François-*Xavier*-Charles-
Joseph-Julien [de], 85, 117
Céret (Pyrénées-Orientales), 174
Chabanon, Antoine-Dominique, 121,
126
CHABROL-CROUSOL, Christophe-
André-Jean de (1771–1836), 34,
51, 137, 191
CHABROL DE VOLVIC, Gilbert-Joseph-
Gaspard de (1773–1843), 143
family, 199
CHAILLOU [DES BARRES], Claude-
Etienne (1784–1857), 144
Chaix, Jean-François-Marie-
Barthélemy, 17
Chalon-sur-Saône (Saône-et-Loire),
174
Chamber of Deputies, deputies, 15, 16,
36, 37–9, 50, 64, 71, 77, 94–7, 99,
122, 131, 144, 205; *see also*
Assemblies
Chamber of Peers, peers, 4–5, 7, 8, 16,
95, 131, 143, 165
Chambord, comte de, 203, 206
Chambray, Edouard-Georges de, 196
Champagne, 93, 180
Chantreau, Charles-Frédéric-Auguste
de, 98
Charente, dept., 28, 41, 91, 101, 103,
147, 148
Charente-Inférieure, dept., 15, 42, 65,
91, 150, 153
Charles X, 17, 18, 32, 41, 42, 47, 48, 73,
90, 102
Charolles (Saône-et-Loire), 107, 172
Charrier, François, 100
Charritte, Louis-Honoré-François-
Marie-Romain de Casamajor de,
188, 190
family, 188–9, 200, 201
CHASSEPOT DE CHAPELAINE, Aimé-
Jean-François (1770–1848), 50,
65, 96–7
Chasset, comte, 106
Chassoux, Antoine, 166

Chastenet de Puységur, *see* Puységur
Chateaubriand, vicomte de, 64, 71, 89,
193
family, 187
Châteaubriant (Loire-Inférieure), 171
Châteaulin (Finistère), 91, 123
Châteauneuf (Ille-et-Vilaine), 161
Château-Salins (Moselle), 81, 133,
172
Chaudruc de Crazannes, Jean-César-
Marie-Alexandre, 100
CHAULIEU, Louis-*Jules*-Auguste DES
ROTOURS DE (1781–1852), 127,
199
*Raoul*-Gabriel-Jules, 127
family, 199
CHAZAL, Jean-Pierre (1766–1840), 50,
61
CHAZELLES[-LUNAC], Augustin-Jean-
Baptiste-Louis-Marie de (1779–
1862), 111–12, 165
Cher, dept., 27, 34, 162
Cherbourg (Manche), 134
Cherrier, family, 199
Chilhaud de la Rigaudie, dept., 94
CHOISEUL-BEAUPRE, Marie-Joseph-
Gabriel-*Xavier* de (1787–?), 160
CHOISEUL-D'AILLECOURT, André-
Urbain-*Maxime* de (1782–1854),
166, 185
family, 185, 188
CHOPPIN D'ARNOUVILLE, Augustin
(1776–1857), 70, 200
family, 200
Chouan, Chouannerie, 11, 14, 15, 53,
123, 179
CINTRE, Constant-Marie HUCHET DE
(1775–1861), 159
Civray (Vienne), 112
Clauzel, Lieutenant-General, 107
Clément, Jean-Claude, 126
Clermont (Oise), 98
Clock, Jean-Baptiste-Léon de, 90
family, 7
COCHELET, Adrien-Louis (1786–
1858), 60, 144
COCHON DE LAPPARENT, Charles
(1750–1825), 60, 61

INDEX

Montluel (Ain), 7
Montmorency, Mathieu de, 41
  Luxembourg, family, 187
Montmorillon (Vienne), 84
Montpellier (Hérault), 114
Montrichard, Henri-René de, 192
Montrond, Denis-François-Edouard
  de Mouret de, and family, 189
MONTUREUX, François-*Louis*-Joseph
  de BOURCIER DE (1768–1838), 68,
  147, 201
  Gabriel-*Georges*-François de
    Bourcier de, C., 190
  family, 201
Morbihan, dept., 53, 154
Moreau, General, 17
Moreau de Bellaing, Marie-*Léopold*-
  Joseph, 175
MOREAU DE LA ROCHETTE, Armand-
  Marie-Beunard (1787–1822), 102
Morlaix (Finistère), 169
Mortagne (Orne), 109
MORTARIEU, Joseph-Pierre VIALETES
  DE (1768–1849), 38, 161
Moselle, dept., 69, 81
Murat, Joachim, 62
Murat (Cantal), 119, 121, 168
Muret (Haute-Garonne), 111

Nancy (Meurthe), 47
Nantes (Loire-Inférieure), 137
Napoleon, *see* Bonaparte
Narbonne (Aude), 172
Narbonne-Lara, François-*Jacques*-
  Joseph de, 187, 194
  family, 185
Narbonne-Pelet, Michel-Claude-
  Gaspard-Félix-Jean-Raymond de,
  121
Navarre, Parlement of, 188
Nays-Candau, Louis-Mariano de, 13,
  188
  family, 188–9
Neffiès, Joseph-Alban Bonnet de
  Maureilhan de, 189
Nerac (Lot-et-Garonne), 91
Ney, maréchal [prince de la Moskowa],
  10

NICOLAY, *Scipion*-Cyprien-Jules-
  Louis-Marin-Marie-Elisabeth de
  (1780–1843), 184, 194
  family, 184, 200–1
Nicollon des Abbayes, Pierre, 195
Nièvre, dept., 58, 121, 140
Nîmes (Gard), 141
Niort (Deux-Sèvres), 18
Noailles, Achille-Charles-Victor de,
  100
NONNEVILLE, André-Louis-Marie
  TASSIN DE (1775–?), 205
Normandy, Parlement of, 27, 190
Nord, dept., 46, 47, 94, 106, 108
Noue, Charles-Joseph-Guillaume-
  Gaucher-Valérien de, 165–6
NUGENT, François-Louis-Basile-
  Antoine-Aimé de, 28, 148
Nyons (Drôme), 153

Odru, Auguste-Hippolyte, 113
Oise, dept., 148, 154, 155, 157, 163
Ollivier, Emile, 3
Onfroy de Bréville, Jean-Baptiste, 112
Orange (Vaucluse), 197
Orfeuille-Foucaud, Arthur-Marie-
  *Edouard* d', 117, 190
Orléans (Loiret), 57
Ormescheville, Alexandre-François-
  Frédéric Bexon d', 122

Paimbœuf (Loire-Inférieure), 171
Pamiers (Ariège), 84
PANAT, Dominique-*Samuel*-Joseph-
  Philippe BRUNET DE CASTELPERS
  DE (1787–1860), 38–9, 189
  family, 189
Papal Zouaves, 205–6
Paris, 2, 10, 12, 36, 38, 40, 44, 46, 56, 58,
  62, 63, 69, 93, 116, 136, 140, 150,
  153, 163, 169, 170, 174, 184, 204
  Cour des Aides, 182, 191, 200
  Cour des Comptes, 200, 201
  Grand Council of, 200
  Parlement of, 180, 181, 182, 184,
    191, 199, 201
  (First) Treaty of, 24
  (Second) Treaty of, 25

For EU product safety concerns, contact us at Calle de José Abascal, 56–1°, 28003 Madrid, Spain or eugpsr@cambridge.org.

www.ingramcontent.com/pod-product-compliance
Ingram Content Group UK Ltd.
Pitfield, Milton Keynes, MK11 3LW, UK
UKHW010343140625
459647UK00010B/790